Child Soldiers

From Violence to Protection

Michael Wessells

Harvard University Press

Cambridge, Massachusetts

London, England

First Harvard University Press paperback edition, 2009.

Library of Congress Cataloging-in-Publication Data

Wessells, Michael G., 1948–
    Child soldiers : from violence to protection / Michael Wessells.
        p. cm.
    Includes bibliographical references and index.
    ISBN 978-0-674-02359-8 (cloth)
    ISBN 978-0-674-03255-2 (pbk.)
    1. Child soldiers.   2. World politics—21st century.   I. Title.

    UB416.W47 2006
    355.3'3083—dc22   2006049507

To my mother, Virginia Gibbs Wessells, with love

Contents

Preface

Civility has always been one of the first casualties of war. Today, a barbarous form of incivility is the widespread exploitation of children as soldiers. Worldwide, large numbers of girls and boys, some 7 years of age or younger, are soldiers in government forces, armed opposition groups, militias, and paramilitary groups. At an age better suited for education, many children carry guns and fight, while others serve as porters, security guards, laborers, decoys, medics, cooks, sex slaves, and spies.

It is time for the world to confront this problem, which has inflicted untold misery on many thousands of children, trampled children's rights, and made a mockery of peace. Addressing this problem requires a dual emphasis on helping child soldiers transition into civilian life and preventing child recruitment. To accomplish either task, however, we must first understand why children become soldiers and how their war experiences affect them.

Recent advances in the study of child soldiers provide a much more grounded, contextualized understanding of child soldiers than had been available previously. Earlier ideas of a universal child soldier have given way to a more nuanced view of the enormous diversity and fluidity within the category "child soldiers." Western concepts of childhood have been contested, yielding a richer understanding of how culture and social relations shape children's roles and the various definitions of childhood. Previous tendencies to infantilize children and to regard them as passive are giving way to a view of children as actors who have a strong sense of agency, participate in the construction of political discourses and social identities, and in some cases lead political action. Also, the distorting lenses of gender and culture biases are slowly being corrected. Not long ago the term *child soldiers* meant "boy soldiers," but recent research has brought to light the situation of girls and challenged us to construct gender-appropriate reintegration programs. Although

Western approaches to reintegration and prevention remain dominant, there is increasing attention to local cultural mechanisms for protecting children.

Current research is also correcting biases such as sensationalist images of predatory child killers or a "lost generation." Equally simplistic are psychological portrayals of child soldiers as emotionally crippled and damaged for life. This emphasis on deficits, which overlooked children's resilience, is now giving way to an understanding that most former child soldiers are functional and, with proper support, can transition to positive lives as civilians. A new generation of research is also bringing forward children's voices, which only a short time ago had been conspicuously absent in both research and applied work.

Drawing on recent learning from research and practice and offering a psychological perspective largely absent from previous works, this book analyzes from a holistic perspective the causes and impact of child soldiering and outlines practical steps for addressing the problem. To make children's voices central, I have built much of the analysis around children's narratives, which are presented without editing for errors of grammar and diction. Wanting to stimulate hope, I also present field lessons that can guide programs for reintegration and prevention. To help build the knowledge base needed to advance practice, I have throughout the book suggested areas warranting additional inquiry.

This book is also a space in which to share the children's narratives from my field research and child protection work through Christian Children's Fund (CCF). Between 1995 and 2005, it was my honor to interview more than four hundred former child soldiers, both girls and boys, ranging in age from 7 to 18 years old, in Afghanistan, Angola, Kosovo, northern Uganda, Sierra Leone, and South Africa. With local staff as translators and cultural guides, in local communities I interviewed girls and boys, community leaders, elders, traditional healers, and religious leaders. The interviews, which were conducted with both individuals and groups, were a key part of an action research strategy of working in partnership with national staff and local communities to understand and address the most urgent child protection issues.

On hearing repeated stories of children's resilience in very difficult situations, it became clear to me that former child soldiers' resilience has been seriously underestimated. It is also clear that images portraying child soldiers as having a pathology, or as unable to rebuild their lives, suffocate hope and nourish apathy. These children's narratives led me to write a different kind of book that tells both sides of the story—the hopeful and resilient side as well as the side steeped in pain and suffering. Seeing the urgency of child soldiers' needs and hearing their pleas for help moved me to write this book as part of an effort to mobilize international action on behalf of child soldiers.

This book's plan is straightforward. Chapter 1 provides a general introduction that assumes no prior knowledge about child soldiers, which knowledgeable readers may want to skim. Chapters 2 to 4 analyze children's entry into and life within armed groups, while Chapters 5 and 6 probe the impacts of this life on children. Working from the macro to the micro level, Chapters 7 to 9 examine reintegration, and Chapter 10 delves into prevention issues. This book reflects my conviction that we know much about what needs to be done. The question now is whether we have the vision, fortitude, and commitment needed to end this cruel form of child exploitation.

Acknowledgments

I wish to thank the Christian Children's Fund, particularly Michelle Poulton, for having supported my writing, believing in the value of telling the story of child soldiers, and pioneering holistic, culturally grounded assistance that is bringing hope to former child soldiers and millions of children worldwide. I am indebted to Carlinda Monteiro and Davidson Jonah, global leaders in CCF's child protection work, who taught me patiently about Angola and Sierra Leone, respectively. I also thank Randolph-Macon College for having granted me a leave of absence, providing much-needed space for humanitarian work and writing. I thank Columbia University for providing a warm and stimulating environment in which to complete this book.

In my field research, I was moved deeply by the stories and the kindness of the many children, youths, women, elders, community leaders, chiefs, and local healers who took time to talk with me. Their resilience and courage resonated in their songs and dances, not to mention their ability to thrive in very challenging circumstances. To them I owe an enormous debt of gratitude.

I am highly indebted also to the CCF national staff in different countries whose support made this work possible. Living themselves in difficult circumstances, they took time to teach me about the local culture and conflict situation and to organize everything from security to translation and food. Most important, they helped to support the community-based programs that brought relief to large numbers of children, including former child soldiers. Because each national office operates as a team, there are too many people to thank individually. In naming one person from each office, I intend to thank all the people in that office who helped me in countless ways. My thanks go to Dr. Feda Mohammed in Afghanistan; Carlinda Monteiro in Angola; Dr. Sami Rexhepi in Kosovo; Dan Kaindaneh in Sierra Leone; Dr. Sheila Zwane in South Africa; and Edward Nfulgani in Uganda. I also learned much about child soldiers from CCF staff from conflict-torn countries in which I did not conduct research for this book. I wish to thank Jorge Velasquez in Colombia; Paco Batres in Guatemala; Saturnina Hamili in the Philippines; Gamini Pinnalwatte in Sri Lanka; and Lola dos Reis in Timor Leste (formerly East Timor).

I thank the people who generously gave of their time to review all or part of the book: Jo Becker, Neil Boothby, Susan McKay, John Williamson, Michael Shipler, Jo Boyden, and Kunera Korthals Altes, among others. I wish to thank Elizabeth Knoll for her careful editorial guidance. My son, Aaron, deserves special thanks for his incisive reviews at multiple stages.

Above all, I wish to thank my loving wife, Kathleen Kostelny, for her wonderful support, her patience with my absence, and her passion for helping the world's children.

Abbreviations

AFRC	Armed Forces Revolutionary Council (Sierra Leone)
AI	Amnesty International
ANBP	Afghan New Beginnings Program
AUC	United Self-Defense Groups (Colombia)
CCF	Christian Children's Fund
CDC	Community Development Committee
CDF	Civil Defense Force (Sierra Leone)
CRC	United Nations Convention on the Rights of the Child
CSC	Coalition to Stop the Use of Child Soldiers
DDR	disarmament, demobilization, and reintegration
DRC	Democratic Republic of the Congo
FARC	Revolutionary Armed Forces of Colombia
FARC-EP	Revolutionary Armed Forces of Colombia–People's Army
FRELIMO	Mozambican Liberation Front
HRW	Human Rights Watch
ICC	Interim Care Center
IDP	internally displaced person
IRC	International Rescue Committee
LRA	Lord's Resistance Army (Uganda)
LTTE	Liberation Tigers of Tamil Eelam (Sri Lanka)
LURD	Liberians United for Reconciliation and Democracy
MILF	Moro Islamic Liberation Front
MLC	Movement for the Liberation of the Congo
RCD-ML	Congolese Rally for Democracy–Liberation Movement
RENAMO	Mozambican National Resistance
RUF	Revolutionary United Front (Sierra Leone)
SC	Save the Children
UC-ELN	Camilist Union–Army of National Liberation (Colombia)
UNAMA	United Nations Assistance Mission to Afghanistan
UNAMSIL	United Nations Mission in Sierra Leone
UNICEF	United Nations Children's Fund
UNITA	National Union for the Total Independence of Angola
UNMIL	United Nations Mission in Liberia
UPDF	Ugandan People's Defence Forces

Child Soldiers

Child Victims, Young Combatants

In August 2002 I visited northern Sierra Leone, which had recently emerged from its decade-long civil war. In the searing heat of a remote village, a 15-year-old girl named Fatmata sat with her listless baby girl on her lap in a dirt-floored hut that had never been graced with electricity or running water. Like many people from Sierra Leone, Fatmata was eager to tell her story so the world would know of the enormous needs she and her people face. Speaking in a monotone voice betraying heavy emotional burdens, she said, "The rebels—they came and attacked my village . . . They burned many homes and took girls like me as wives. I was 12 years—just a young girl . . . I was so scared." Unlike some girls, Fatmata had not been gang-raped, a tactic the rebels had used to terrorize civilian populations. But her life had been very difficult. "They made me carry supplies—really heavy things—on my head, and I thought we would be shot." When I asked about her captor, whom she referred to as her "husband" because she had lived with him and had eventually borne his child, she replied, "My husband . . . he beat me and had sex with me. He protect me some, too . . . I got pregnant and had my baby in the bush." When I asked whether she had received any medical assistance while giving birth, she shook her head to say no, and her eyes glazed over in the blank stare one sees all too often on the faces of children who have experienced war's horror firsthand. "Now," she said, "I have AIDS and my baby too . . .I'm too poor to buy medicine. . . What will happen to me and my baby?"

Fatmata's case, like the phrase *child soldiers*, offends most people's sensibilities and challenges cherished assumptions about children, humankind, and good and evil. When most people in Western societies think of children, they think not of war and horror but of images from their own childhoods of play, outings with their family, summer travels, and going to school. As parents, we would cringe at the thought of our own children being "child soldiers." Most adults assume that parents have a responsibility to protect their children from harm, and that societies also should exercise responsibility in protecting children. In fact, most states have laws to protect children and have ratified international legal standards such as the U.N. Convention on the Rights of the Child (CRC) and its Optional Protocol on Children and Armed Conflict. The latter sets 18 years as the minimum age for combat participation and outlaws all child recruitment by groups outside official governments.

The existence of child soldiers, however, punctures these assumptions and highlights the enormous gap between legal standards and the harsh realities of children's lives. Although Fatmata's story is not uncommon, it is not particularly extreme in terms of the levels of brutality, deprivation, and violence experienced by child soldiers (Brett and McCallin 1996; Cohn and Goodwin-Gill 1994). Furthermore, child soldiering is not uncommon. Worldwide, government armies, warlords, rebel groups, paramilitaries, and other militarized groups include an estimated three hundred thousand children (Machel 2001), defined under international law as people under 18 years of age. If these children stood side by side, locked their hands, and spread their arms, they would form a human chain 250 miles long. This chain only hints at the magnitude of adults' and societies' failure in their responsibilities to protect and care for children. Why does this failure occur?

Although this question warrants much additional research, the short answer is that many people and groups stand to benefit from exploiting children as soldiers. Most do not use children as a last resort or out of desperation, although occasionally some do. More often the adults who start and guide the war, or the local commanders who implement it, use children as soldiers because doing so is convenient and cheap. Children are nearly always available in abundance, and those who exploit children are often very clever and successful in hiding their actions from international view. This willingness to exploit children creates a profound need for child protection and raises difficult questions. For instance, How can children be protected before, during, and after armed conflict? What can be done to prevent children from becoming child soldiers in the first place?

In probing these and related issues, I will develop three key themes: peace, meaning, and hope. Although child soldiering is a profound human rights issue, it is an equally profound peace issue. Local tyrants such as Charles Taylor, the former president of Liberia, launched his takeover of Liberia using a scantly trained group consisting mostly of child soldiers (Singer 2005). No society can achieve peace by militarizing its young people. When children are engaged as soldiers, spend their formative years immersed in systems of violence, and construct their values and identity guided by military groups, they become vehicles of violence rather than citizens who can build peace. Denied their rights to education and protection, child soldiers often become a means of continuing protracted armed struggles and cycles of violence (Machel 2001; Wessells and Monteiro 2001).

In some conflicts, children are the main combatants and child recruitment is the chief means of enabling fighting. Even when the fighting in one country has ended, child soldiers who see no future for themselves in civilian life may cross borders and become soldiers in neighboring countries. The regional problem of soldiers for hire applies to adults, too, but most people can fight for only so many years. Children who grow up having learned fighting as their only means of livelihood and survival are likely to continue fighting for more years than adults. Child soldiering, then, damages societies, threatens regional stability, and is a high-priority issue in building peace, which is indivisible from human rights.

Second, children are makers of meaning who are influential actors in political conflicts (Boyden and de Berry 2004; Wessells 1998). Too often, children have been portrayed as passive innocents whom adults have forced and intimidated into soldiering. Although forced recruitment is pervasive in some conflicts, this one-dimensional portrayal misses an important part of the picture of child soldiering. Children who grow up in war zones might not see any positive place for themselves in society; in their situations they are oppressed, have little or no access to education, feel powerless and alienated, and have been denied positive life options. As a result, they may see violence as an acceptable way to replace the existing social order with one offering social justice and positive economic and political opportunities. Finding meaning in the struggle for liberation and social transformation, they may be drawn into armed groups without explicit coercion. Also, by joining armed groups, children may obtain respect or a sense of family, and they might gain access to some benefits that are inaccessible to them in civilian life, like protection, food, medical care, or training. Soldiering is often attractive to children because it provides meaning, identity, and options civilian life does not afford.

It is essential to understand the meaning children construct as soldiers. Only when we probe the subjective world of child soldiers do we put ourselves in a position to prevent children's exploitation as soldiers and to help former child soldiers make the transition to civilian life. For this reason, I have attempted to bring forward the voices of child soldiers from around the world. Their words and testimonies tell the story of child soldiering in the most powerful way and without the biasing lens of adult preconceptions. An important subtext of this book is adults' failure to listen carefully to children and to respect their agency and creativity.

The third theme, hope, is the most challenging because the harsh realities of child soldiers corrode even the most robust optimism. The pessimistic portrayals of child soldiers found in popular writings—where they are depicted as "damaged goods" or as bloodthirsty predators who are beyond rehabilitation—promote a cynicism, though, that is part of the problem rather than part of the solution. In fact, child soldiers exhibit considerable resilience, and much can be done to prevent child soldiering. Once citizens and policy makers become aware of the urgency and scale of the problem, it is possible to leverage both public support and governmental and intergovernmental action to end child soldiering. The study of child soldiers is in its infancy, and the subject admits no easy answers. However, a sufficient and growing body of evidence allows provisional but useful answers to questions such as these: Why do children become soldiers? How are they affected by soldiering? What can be done to enable their reintegration into civilian life? In Chapters 8 through 10, I will describe examples of effective reintegration programs and specific steps to prevent child recruitment. This book is ultimately about hope—hope for better lives for children and families living in war zones, and hope that the international community will accept its responsibility to end the scourge of child soldiering.

A Global Problem

An essential step in addressing the problem of child soldiering is to identify how widespread it is, and this in turn requires a clear definition of child soldiers. Initially this may seem to be a simple matter. Why not define child soldiers as children who carry a gun and wear a military uniform? Such a definition, however, begs all the really important questions, such as What is a child? and What is a soldier? The challenges of definition, however, should not allow us to overlook the significant risks faced by all children who associate with armed groups in any capacity.

What Is a Child Soldier?

Numerous challenges arise in defining child soldiers. For one thing, notions of childhood are culturally constructed and vary across societies. Western countries and developmental sciences generally view a person under 18 years of age as a child. This view is enshrined in the CRC, the world's most widely endorsed human rights instrument. In non-Western societies such as those of sub-Saharan Africa, however, particularly in rural areas where traditional ways remain strong, a person is regarded as an adult once he or she has completed the culturally scripted initiation ceremony or rite of passage into manhood or womanhood (Boyden 1997). Typically, such rites occur around 14 years of age. Also, many developing societies define childhood and adulthood in terms of labor and social roles, saying that people become adults when they do adult work. Owing to this definitional gap, a 15-year-old boy carrying an automatic rifle and traveling with a military group might be viewed as a child by international human rights observers, but the same individual might be viewed as a young adult by people in a rural African village.

Fortunately, even though the term *child* is contested, many elders and state officials in predominantly rural societies in the developing world either regard a person under 18 years of age as too young to join armed groups or can accept this view following a mixture of reflection and persuasion. Local elders and traditional leaders often prefer to speak of young people such as the 15-year-old boy described above as "underage soldiers" or "minor soldiers." Most important is their acceptance of the principle asserting that people under 18 years of age should not be soldiers. One can simultaneously endorse the CRC and respect local culture by speaking of "minor soldiers" or "underage soldiers" rather than "child soldiers." Humanitarians often use these terms interchangeably.

Another challenge arises from the wide range of armed groups to which children may belong. The term *soldier* may evoke images of uniformed people, mostly men, who use guns, answer to a particular commander, and travel with well-organized fighting units. Although some children in armed groups fit these images, others, including many girls, may never use guns or wear uniforms. Many children abducted by armed groups serve as laborers or porters, for example. Furthermore, analysts debate whether to count as child soldiers stone-throwing Palestinian youths who are not part of an organized command structure. Similarly, should teenagers in gangs in Los Angeles or Chicago be counted as child soldiers? Gang members have much in common with those viewed as more typical child soldiers, and children in both categories cite similar reasons for having joined violent groups. But counting young gang members as child soldiers may blur categories that have distinct features. For example, child soldiers who see themselves as participating in a liberation struggle may derive meaning from their participation in political violence in ways that gang members do not. It seems wise to adopt a relatively expansive definition of child soldiers in order to avoid narrowing the field prematurely, but the definition should focus on mistreatments of children stemming from association with armed forces in the context of political violence.

In addition, the term *child soldiers* applies to a wide range of people with enormously varying experiences and roles and who may have divergent life pathways as a result. In northern Uganda, for example, some children were taken mainly for sexual purposes, while others served mainly as porters who carried supplies. Some of these children stayed with armed groups only a short time, even just a few days or weeks, never regarded themselves fully as soldiers, and retained their civilian identities and desire to return to their communities of origin. Should these children be grouped into the same category as those who fought, killed, assumed command responsibilities, and adopted military identities? Will children who were laborers in armed groups be stigmatized and placed at risk of revenge attacks or re-recruitment if they are labeled "child soldiers"?

In view of these complexities, many analysts prefer the label *children (or minors) associated with fighting forces (CAFF)*. This label is also imperfect, however. Terms such as *CAFF* may deny children who had been laborers, scouts, couriers, guards, drill instructors, porters, or sex slaves access to privileges and supports extended to child combatants as part of disarmament, demobilization, and reintegration processes. Following a war, a high priority is to enable all children associated with armed groups, regardless of their roles, to reenter civilian society. In light of these complexities, it seems appropriate to retain the widely used term *child soldiers* and to define it broadly.

I shall follow the definition set forth in the Cape Town principles, constructed by leading scholars and practitioners convened by the United Nations Children's Fund (UNICEF 1997, 1):A child soldier is "any person under 18 years of age who is part of any kind of regular or irregular armed force in any capacity, including but not limited to cooks, porters, messengers, and those accompanying such groups, other than purely as family members. Girls recruited for sexual purposes and forced marriage are included in this definition. It does not, therefore, only refer to a child who is carrying or has carried arms." On this view, "child soldier" is a highly diverse category, and the term implies neither that the child was a combatant nor that the child participated willingly in wrongdoing. As argued throughout this book, it is adults who start wars and create the problem of child soldiering.

Age and Roles

Teenagers are frequently targets of recruitment because they have advantages over young children in regard to size, strength, and cognitive ability. Also, teenagers are regarded in many societies as adults whose role is to work and help provide for their families. In times of war, many cultures regard fighting as an appropriate form of work, an extension of the labor adults provide for their families. Worldwide, most child soldiers are 13 to 18 years of age (Brett and McCallin 1996; Coalition to Stop the Use of Child Soldiers [CSC] 2001).

There are many exceptions to this picture, however, as many armed conflicts exploit younger children. A disturbing trend globally is toward the recruitment of preteenage children. The wars in Liberia and Sierra Leone were notorious for the use of "small-boy units," which were known for their fearlessness and willingness to commit barbarous acts. Typically, the small-boy units consisted of children under 12. Also, there has been a tendency to recruit younger children. In northern Uganda, where a decade ago most child soldiers had been teenagers, the average age of child soldiers is now under 13 years (Derluyn et al. 2004). In a recent survey of six Asian countries, the average age of recruitment was 13 years, and one-third of child soldiers were under 12 years of age

(UNICEF 2003). In countries such as the Democratic Republic of the Congo, armed groups have recruited boys and girls as young as 7 years (CSC 2004). And in some conflicts where fighters travel with their families, children are literally born into armed groups.

Inside armed groups, children perform diverse and multiple roles, only one of which is fighting. Depending on the context, child soldiers may serve as sentries, bodyguards, porters, domestic laborers, medics, guards, sex slaves, spies, cooks, mine sweepers, or recruiters (CSC 2004). Roles may vary significantly by age and gender. For example, smaller, younger children often serve as spies. Girl soldiers perform the same wide variety of roles performed by boy soldiers (Save the Children UK 2005), and in African countries commanders frequently seek girls because of their impressive capacities for portaging heavy loads (McKay and Mazurana 2004). Girl soldiers also are frequently sought for purposes of sexual exploitation, as are boys in some contexts. The remarkable diversity of children's roles in armed groups cautions against the tendency to equate child soldiers with child combatants.

Prevalence

Hard data on child soldiers are difficult to obtain. Many commanders who exploit children threaten whistle blowers and cloak their actions behind lines of combat where international observers cannot enter safely. Also, the mass displacements and turmoil caused by armed conflict make it very difficult to register people and to count accurately. Even if one gained access and could count accurately, doing so might threaten children's best interests. To identify children as former or current child soldiers can place them at risk, since former commanders may re-recruit the children or local people may retaliate against them for wrongs they had presumably committed. Children themselves may wish not to be identified or labeled. Following a ceasefire and their return home, for example, former child soldiers may find it damaging to be singled out or to be called a "child soldier"—this label simultaneously awakens painful memories, risks stigmatization, and reflects only one small dimension of their life experience. A young man from Sierra Leone who had fought with the Revolutionary United Front (RUF) vented his frustration to me after repeated discussions in which he had been identified only as a former child soldier. "Everyone calls me soldier and talks child soldier this and child soldier that . . . Look at me—I'm a human being!" The same point applies to attempts to reduce children to numbers.

For these reasons, all figures regarding child soldiers must be regarded as soft or provisional. Although soft estimates are often the best one can obtain under difficult circumstances, they are useful. No one knows exactly how many people are on the planet, for example, yet experts' use of sampling and extrapolation to make informed but imperfect estimates are useful nonetheless. The same is true in regard to child soldiers.

The first global study of the prevalence of child soldiering, the 1996 U.N. study *Impact of Armed Conflict on Children* (Machel 1996), indicated that there were approximately a quarter of a million child soldiers, with the largest numbers found in Africa and Asia. Subsequent reports, such as *Child Soldiers Global Report 2001* of the international Coalition to Stop the Use of Child Soldiers (CSC 2001), have estimated that there are approximately three hundred thousand child soldiers at any point in time. Singer (2005) estimated that children serve as combatants in over two-thirds (37 of 55) of current or recently ended conflicts. Although the majority of child soldiers are boys, girls constitute a significant percentage of the child soldiers in particular countries or armed groups (McKay and Mazurana 2004). As many as 40 percent of child soldiers may be girls (Save the Children UK 2005).

Those who challenge the three-hundred-thousand figure point out the problems of obtaining accurate counts and suggest that the figure came from a "back-of-the-envelope" estimate rather than from systematic research. Fortunately, claims of the wide scale of child soldiering do not stand on any single numerical estimate. The prevalence of child soldiering has been established also by careful country studies conducted recently by groups such as UNICEF, Human Rights Watch (HRW), Amnesty International (AI), and the CSC, which collects global information on child soldiers from a wide array of sources. Additional information on the situation of child soldiers comes from practitioner organizations such as Christian Children's Fund (CCF), International Rescue Committee (IRC), Save the Children Alliance, and World Vision.

All the same, the estimate of three hundred thousand child soldiers is best taken with a grain of salt. In addition to the aforementioned problems of measurement, no estimate of how many child soldiers there are at a particular moment reflects the total number of children who have been in armed groups. Armed groups are often like revolving doors. As child soldiers die or leave military life, commanders recruit other children to fill the ranks, just as they recruit new child soldiers in recently erupted conflicts. For example, over the twenty-year period from 1985 to 2005, the total number of child soldiers would have been far more than three hundred thousand. Also, the claim that child soldiering is a prevalent, global problem does not stand or fall on any single global numerical estimate.

The prevalence of child soldiering is evident in the large number of countries where children are exploited as soldiers. The recruiters are not only governments but also a host of nonstate actors—groups that are not part of an official government. These are the countries or territories in which children were involved in armed conflict in the period 2001 to 2004:

Africa
Angola
Burundi
Central African Republic
Côte d'Ivoire
Chad
Democratic Republic of the Congo
Republic of the Congo
Guinea
Liberia
Rwanda
Sierra Leone
Somalia
Uganda

Americas
Colombia

Asia/Pacific
Afghanistan
India
Indonesia
Myanmar (Burma)
Philippines
Nepal
Sri Lanka

Europe/Eurasia
Russia

Middle East/North Africa
Israel/Occupied Palestinian Territories
Iran
Iraq
Sudan
Yemen

In some of these twenty-seven countries during this period, multiple groups recruited children. Although this list is extensive, it would be considerably longer if it included all countries for which there is evidence of child soldiering as far back as 1960. For example, the list for Africa would also reflect the conflicts in Burundi, Liberia, Mozambique, Rwanda, and South Africa, which included large numbers of child soldiers (Brett and McCallin 1996; Cohn and Goodwin-Gill 1994). Similarly, a partial list for Asia would include the conflicts in Cambodia and Vietnam. The list for Central America would reflect conflicts in El Salvador, Guatemala, and Nicaragua. Europe's would include the U.K. (Northern Ireland) and the Netherlands, the governments of which previously had legalized combat participation of people under 18 years. And the list for South America would include Paraguay. Even this brief account indicates the global scope of child soldiering.

The global scope, however, should not obscure the regional and country-specific variations in child soldiering. The variations and the profundity of the problems children face are best illustrated by contextualized descriptions of specific conflicts, by regions, in which children have been soldiers. The cases presented below are only a partial list, but they illustrate the extensive, recent use of child soldiers. The descriptions draw on my field experience and also rely extensively on information compiled by the Coalition to Stop the Use of Child Soldiers in its *Child Soldiers Global Report 2004*.

Sub-Saharan Africa

Angola. The Angolan war began in 1961 as a struggle for liberation from Portugal. After independence was achieved in 1975, the ensuing power struggle between three parties evolved into a fight between the socialist government of Angola and the opposition group, UNITA (the National Union for the Total Independence of Angola), led by Jonas Savimbi. During the 1980s the Angolan war became a proxy war in the superpower struggle, as the Soviet Union and Cuba supported the Angolan government while the United States and South Africa, fearful of a socialist regime sympathetic to communism, supported UNITA. Over time, Angola effectively became a country inside a country. UNITA controlled some parts and used its control of diamond fields to support its war efforts, while the government controlled other areas and used Angola's vast oil riches to support its war efforts. In the 1990s two ceasefires occurred: the Bicesse Accords in 1991 and the Lusaka Protocols of 1994. The latter aided demobilization of nine thousand child soldiers, mostly teenagers, who had been recruited mostly by UNITA but also by government forces. These ceasefires, however, proved to be only brief interludes in a longer stream of fighting, leading entire generations to grow up having war as a constant part of their social reality. By the end of the war in April 2002, new evidence indicated large numbers of girls— tens of thousands—had been abducted by armed groups during the war (CSC 2002). Whereas many boys had been fighters, the girls had mostly been forced into carrying heavy loads or sexual activity. Recent evidence indicates that approximately 8 percent of Angolan children participated in armed groups, mostly through force (Stavrou 2005).

Democratic Republic of the Congo (DRC).   The conflict in the DRC is the deadliest current conflict and has already killed nearly four million people (Coghlan et al. 2006). In 2003 approximately thirty thousand children were soldiers in DRC, and children constituted nearly 40 percent of some armed groups in the eastern DRC (CSC 2004). In the 1996–97 war against former president Mobutu, Laurent Kabila and his Alliance of Democratic Forces for Liberation used an estimated ten thousand child soldiers. As Kabila's new government was challenged, it urged youths between 12 and 20 years of age to enlist to fight the government's opponents. Nonstate actors—particularly the Movement for the Liberation of the Congo (MLC), the Congolese Rally for Democracy–Liberation Movement (RCD-ML), and the Ugandan People's Defence Forces (UPDF)—have also recruited large numbers of children in their ongoing war against the government. During 2002, for example, the RCD-Goma recruited children as young as 8 years old and forced children to kill relatives or cannibalize the corpses of enemies (CSC 2004). Although government recruitment of children ended by 2003, nearly half of the Mai-Mai group supporting the government consists of children. At present, there are over thirty thousand child soldiers in the DRC (Watchlist on Children and Armed Conflict 2006).

Sierra Leone.   The war in Sierra Leone began in 1991 with attacks across its eastern border by troops from neighboring Liberia. Over the next ten years, an estimated ten thousand child soldiers participated in the Sierra Leone war, the main combatants in which were the government forces and the Revolutionary United Front (RUF). The RUF, which supported its war efforts by controlling diamond fields, regularly abducted large numbers of girls and boys during attacks, forcing them to provide labor and sex and participate in combat. Children constituted nearly half of the RUF forces (Radda Barnen 2002). Initially, the RUF said it advocated social justice, but over time it became known mostly for its brutality, including mutilations, such as arm and hand amputations. Unable to count on government protection from the RUF, civilian groups, including traditional hunter societies, organized themselves into militias known as the Civil Defense Force (CDF), which supported the government. A U.N. assessment mission reported in May 2000 that children between the ages of 7 and 14 years constituted 25 percent of the CDF forces in the town of Masiaka (CSC 2002). Over time, CDF forces engaged increasingly in looting villages to obtain supplies and committed heinous rights abuses such as executions. In 1997 former Sierra Leone army officers staged a coup, formed the Armed Forces Revolutionary Council (AFRC), and fought alongside the RUF. The AFRC also forcibly recruited children, forcing them into combat and sex slavery. With the achievement of a durable ceasefire in May 2001, the government and the international community launched a major program of disarmament, demobilization, and reintegration of former soldiers, including child soldiers.

Uganda.   Over the past two decades, the Ugandan government has fought in northern Uganda against a rebel group, the Lord's Resistance Army (LRA), in a conflict embodying a surreal mixture of spiritualism and barbarity. Joseph Kony, the LRA leader, claims to have spiritual powers and an agenda of bringing the country under rule according to the Ten Commandments. Lacking popular support among local people, Kony has used abduction as his primary means of replenishing his small army, which for many years received harsh training in southern Sudan and then slipped across the border to attack villages in northern Uganda. More than thirty thousand children, some as young as 7, have been abducted over the course of the conflict, while others have been born into the LRA. Although many of these children have escaped, many others are believed to have died in captivity, and thousands remain unaccounted for. Before the turn of the millennium, the abductions of children seemed to be decreasing. But they skyrocketed after March 2002 when the government launched a military campaign, Operation Iron Fist, against the LRA. Since then, the LRA has expanded the war into the Teso region, abducted more than twelve thousand children, terrorized villages on an expanded scale, and displaced large numbers of people, forcing them to live in difficult conditions in camps for internally displaced people. In 2003 the LRA used increasingly brutal tactics, including torturing parents to give up their children and forcing children to hack their own relatives to death. Sadly, pro-government paramilitaries such as the Arrow Boys in Teso, the Amuka militia in Lango, and the Frontier Guards in Kitgum and Pader have also recruited children from northern villages as part of the ongoing war against the LRA, and the Ugandan government army has sometimes recruited former child soldiers who had escaped the LRA.

Asia and the Middle East

Afghanistan. Afghanistan has been plagued by war since 1979, when Soviet troops invaded. The Afghan resistance, the mujaheddin, created an extensive command structure down to the level of village commanders. Commanders frequently recruited children, mostly teenage boys but also girls who were treated as sex slaves, and some commanders kept "dancing boys" for their private entertainment and sexual exploitation. Afghan children learned about violence at an early age, if not through firsthand experience then through schools, where math was taught according to formulae such as "One dead Russian plus one dead Russian equals two dead Russians." Children continued to be warriors in the fighting between warlords following the defeat of Soviet forces. Torn by chaos, poverty, and war, some Afghans and international observers expressed relief when the Taliban came to power in 1995 and restored law and order. But the Taliban regime of religious extremism proved to be highly oppressive not only of women but also of different ethnic and religious groups, and fighting against the Taliban continued, particularly in northeastern provinces, the stronghold of the Northern Alliance. To maintain their fighting strength, the Taliban recruited thousands of children from madrassas, including those in Pakistan (Rashid 2000), which traditionally had provided religious instruction but under the Taliban had reoriented toward preparing students for military service in the jihad (holy war) against those who opposed the Taliban. In the fight against the Taliban following the 9/11 attacks on the United States, large numbers of 14- to 18-year-old Tajik and Uzbek boys fought in the Northern Alliance forces (Wessells and Kostelny 2002). Following the defeat of the Taliban, some child soldiers remained with their commanders in local "security forces," and ongoing Taliban activity and ethnic tensions threaten to destabilize the country, which in 2004 conducted its first national elections.

Myanmar (Burma).   At the turn of the millennium, Myanmar was believed to have the largest number of child soldiers of any country worldwide, despite its repeated claims of prohibiting child recruitment. Myanmar's military government, the State Peace and Development Council, is pitted against numerous armed ethnic opposition groups. The government forces, the Tatmadaw Kyi, and supporting militia groups are the largest recruiters of children, who are often put into forced labor and are sometimes required to burn homes and villages or to execute people without trial. A 1997 study estimated that there were more than fifty thousand child soldiers in Myanmar. According to a 2002 report by Human Rights Watch, approximately 20 percent of soldiers on active duty in 2002 were children, and children as young as 11 years were forced into combat. In 2004, homeless children were at increased risk of recruitment by government forces. Opposition forces such as the United Wa State Army recruited children extensively, and up to half the new recruits may be children (CSC 2004).

Sri Lanka.   Since 1983, Sri Lanka has been torn by a civil war in which a separatist group, the Liberation Tigers of Tamil Eelam (LTTE), famous for its use of "suicide bombers," has fought against Sri Lankan government forces and pro-government paramilitaries, mainly the Home Guard, for increased control over the north and east. The LTTE, which was initiated by youths, began extensive recruitment of women and children following 1987, when it declared war against the Indian Peacekeeping Force. The LTTE had two armed children's units, the Baby Brigade and the Leopard Brigade; the latter drew its members initially from LTTE orphanages (Machel 2001). No one knows exactly how many children the LTTE has recruited, and the group has promised repeatedly since 1998 to stop using child soldiers. However, evidence continues to indicate rather wide use of child soldiers. In October 1999, for example, at a battle in Ampakamam, government security forces killed 140 LTTE soldiers, including 49 children. Among the children were 32 girls between the ages of 11 and 15 years (CSC 2002). Despite the establishment in 2002 of a ceasefire, increasingly fragile in light of renewed fighting in 2006, the LTTE has continued to recruit children. In 2003 the LTTE pledged to UNICEF to end all child recruitment, but it has been estimated that twelve hundred children remained in the LTTE as of July 31, 2005. Experts believe this figure underestimates the actual total—many families do not report their children's recruitment to UNICEF, either because they do not know of the reporting option or because they fear reprisal by the LTTE (J. Becker, personal communication, Aug. 16, 2005).

South America

Colombia.   Nearly fifty years of armed conflict in Colombia have shattered many rural communities and displaced approximately two million people since 1985. On one side of the conflict are government forces and pro-government paramilitaries, the AUC (United Self-Defense Groups). On the other side are guerrilla groups such as the FARC-EP (Revolutionary Armed Forces of Colombia–People's Army) and the UC-ELN (Camilist Union–Army of National Liberation). Up until December 2000 the government forces regularly recruited children—a total of approximately sixteen thousand—but the Colombian government now prohibits the recruitment of people under 18 years of age (CSC 2002). Paramilitaries, however, continue to recruit children, particularly from urban militias. Urban militias consist mostly of children called "little carts" because they are used to transfer drugs and weapons, escaping local authorities' attention. In addition, paramilitaries use children called "little bells" as an early warning system, deploying them to front lines to draw fire and identify traps. Up to fourteen thousand children have been recruited by armed opposition groups and paramilitaries (CSC 2004). Women and girls are believed to make up half of guerrilla groups such as the FARC. In rural Colombian villages, families live in fear, not only of attack by paramilitaries or rebels, but also of their sons' and daughters' recruitment.

Any doubts regarding the global scope of child soldiering evaporate in light of the wider pattern discernible in these country descriptions. The country profiles, however, should not obscure the regional dimensions of child soldiering. A child soldier in Liberia at one time may subsequently become a child soldier in Sierra Leone, Côte d'Ivoire, or other neighboring countries. Porous borders, fluid population movements, and a shortage of civilian opportunities for children make child soldiering a regional problem transcending national boundaries.

The country profiles also display the diversity of child recruiters. It is tempting to see children as recruited mostly by warlords, paramilitaries, and armed opposition groups whom many people regard as rogues operating outside the law. The bankruptcy of this view is evident in governments' large-scale recruitment of children. Furthermore, governments are sometimes the worst perpetrators of abuses of children. It is not only corrupt, totalitarian governments that exploit children as soldiers—the United Kingdom and the United States have recruited children for many years. Until recently, the United Kingdom permitted 17-year-olds to enter combat, and it continues to recruit 16- and 17-year-olds with parental permission. The United States uses child recruitment to maintain a steady stream of recruits prepared for combat by age 18 and to avoid the reinstitution of a politically unpopular draft. Between January 1 and September 30, 2002, some 26,755 recruits joined U.S. armed forces at age 17 (CSC 2004). This normalization and legitimation of child soldiering by countries such as the United States and the United Kingdom, which claim to protect children and to have children's best interests at heart, creates an international climate conducive to children's exploitation as soldiers by rogue groups such as the LRA of northern Uganda.

A vexing question is why child soldiering is so widespread at this moment in history. The answer has to do with recent changes in the nature of armed conflict and the resulting patterns of children's vulnerability.

The New Face of War

The term *war* evokes images of clashing armies from different nations, using large weapons such as aircraft, tanks, and missiles. In the context of the U.S. wars against Iraq in 1991 and 2003 or the U.S. war against the Taliban in Afghanistan, the term *war* leads most people to think of high-tech fighting involving precision-guided munitions and massive air strikes against military targets. Although civilian casualties occur, the image is mainly of combatants being killed in battle. These images, bolstered by videos of smart bombs destroying military targets with "surgical" precision, are emotionally safe because they depict war as sanitary, precise, and not aimed at hurting civilians.

These images provide a stark contrast with the realities of most wars, which are more accurately reflected in images of bloody street fighting in Iraq, where Iraqi combatants blend into the civilian population. Most armed conflicts are animated partly by struggles over resources such as diamonds, oil, and timber (Klare 2001), which may be valued above human lives. Seen from civilians' perspective, contemporary wars are bloody affairs having disastrous consequences for children and families.

Light Weapons

Most wars today are fought in poor, developing countries, not with high-tech weapons or massive air strikes but with small, lightweight weapons such as the AK-47 (Kalashnikov) assault rifle, which in many parts of Africa can be purchased for the price of a chicken or goat. In the 1990s, 46 of 49 conflicts involved only light weapons (Klare 1999).

Worldwide, there are approximately 500 million assault rifles and military-style weapons (Renner 1999). This includes an estimated 125 million automatic weapons (Klare 1999), sold or traded mostly by countries such as the former Soviet Union or the United States. The profusion of light weapons such as rifles, rocket-propelled grenades, light mortars, light machine guns, and land mines has catalyzed armed conflict in developing countries. Small-weapons trafficking has contributed to the militarization of societies such as Afghanistan, which some have called a

"Kalashnikov culture." The easy availability of small, low-cost weapons enables the arming of factions, creating a context ripe for armed conflict. Children can easily learn to operate these weapons, and many take pride in their skill. A 14-year-old boy from Sierra Leone said:

> I knew everything about my rifle—how to take it down, clean it, assemble it, load it. [I could do this] really fast! I could repair it, too. I was the fastest in my company . . . The commander had me train new soldiers. I liked the training . . . they looked up to me, and I taught them how to be good with the gun.

Using such weapons, even a 10-year-old child can be an effective fighter, a fact not lost on most commanders. In previous ages, young children lacked the size and strength to wield effectively the weapons of the day, such as swords, spears, shields, and heavy muskets. Weapons like the AK-47 have changed this, opening the door to the pervasive use of child soldiers.

Targeting Civilians

Civil wars have become far more common than international wars. Nearly all contemporary wars are internal wars fought between a government and one or more nonstate actors such as a warlord-led group or an armed opposition group. During the 1990s, approximately thirty-five armed conflicts occurred each year, and over 90 percent of these conflicts occurred inside states rather than between them (Smith 2003).

Civil wars, however, defy their name; they exhibit little civility, and they target noncombatants directly. Typically the fighting occurs not on well-defined battlefields but in and around communities. In Colombia, for example, the pro-government paramilitaries and the main opposition group, the FARC-EP, often attacked or threatened to attack villages as a means of controlling them. In Guatemala's civil war, government forces gained control over suspected rebel areas by means of a "scorched earth" policy of destroying all living things within a designated area (Landau 1993).

The deliberate targeting of civilians is evident in Angola, where UNITA committed odious assaults on children. An 11-year-old Angolan girl said:

I used to live in the bush in the area of the River Kwanza with my mother and my brothers and sisters . . . My second brother had gone to the fields to get cassava with a friend when the attack started. He got shot in the foot . . . Then later he got a sickness in his chest and he died. My other sister died when we went to the river to wash our mother's blankets. We were attacked . . . I saw my sister fall dead. I went to tell my mother with my little brother on my back . . . My other sister died when she got sick and her stomach and legs got swollen. My little brother also died from sickness because my mother no longer had milk in her breasts . . . Five more people died while we retreated. One aunt and four men . . . We traveled with other people. But the other people did not want to be with us because my little brother made noise and he cried. Before, when we had been with the soldiers, when a child cried, they gave the mother a knife to stick in the child's head because the child was making noise and we could all be caught. If the mother did not want to do it, they killed her and the child . . . When I think about what I went through, my heart cries non-stop. (CCF 2002, 24–25)

This girl, whose father had been forced to be a soldier, saw her family members die either through wounds from the attacks or through lack of health care and proper nutrition. Her experience was far from unusual, as UNITA routinely attacked, terrorized, and looted villages as a means of controlling them.

Because of this direct targeting of villages and ordinary citizens, contemporary conflicts claim large numbers of civilian casualties. There have always been civilian war casualties, but previous wars such as World Wars I and II were less deadly for civilians than current wars are. In the first half of the twentieth century, over 90 percent of war-related deaths were soldiers (Garfield and Neugut 1997). By the latter part of the century this pattern reversed, with nearly 75 percent of the casualties being civilians (Smith 2003). Women and children are now the majority of the casualties in armed conflicts (UNICEF 1996).

Divided Societies

Internal armed conflicts shatter social trust and leave in their wake deeply divided societies mired in suspicion and fear. During the anti-apartheid struggle in South Africa, for example, the government often planted informants in black townships as a way to identify and target those who organized the resistance. In retaliation, liberation supporters, including children, executed suspected informants through a practice called "necklacing," in which a tire was placed over the informant's head, filled with petrol, and set afire (Straker 1992). The strong suspicions created by pitting community members against one another often persist for many years following the armed conflict.

The pattern of oppression and injustice evident in many divided societies is a recipe for armed conflict (Gurr 1993). Conflicts often erupt along ethnic or religious fault lines in divided societies that extend privileges and status to some groups while denying them to others. Feeling excluded and humiliated, people who belong to oppressed ethnic groups often decide to fight as a way to retaliate, reform the political system, or achieve independence or liberation. In Sudan, the Muslim-dominated north has fought against the predominantly non-Muslim south in a decades-long war involving many child soldiers. In 2004 this conflict assumed even deadlier proportions when Arab-dominated militias (the janjawid) launched a genocidal assault against the predominantly African population of Darfur, creating a profound crisis that was as much political as humanitarian (Prunier 2006). In Northern Ireland, Catholic and Protestant communities have clashed repeatedly, particularly at such times as the "marching season," and they remain deeply divided even following a major peace process. Politicians skillfully manipulate ethnic, religious, and regional fears to advance their own agendas. In the former Yugoslavia, leaders such as Slobodan Milosevic used ethnic tensions and grievances to mobilize Serbs for ethnic cleansing and war, which engaged children as soldiers, against Croatia and Bosnia. The manipulation of fear has long contributed to war (White 1984), but contemporary politicians who are skilled in using mass media have developed it into a high art.

In divided societies, children are at great risk of becoming soldiers because their families and leaders teach them to pursue the struggle. In Rwanda a mostly Hutu political regime orchestrated a genocide in 1994 that killed some eight hundred thousand people, mostly Tutsi. Not by accident, many teenagers belonged to paramilitary groups, such as the Interahamwe, that did much of the killing (Prunier 1995). Preceding the

Rwandan genocide, Hutu children learned to see themselves not only as Hutu but also as opposed to Tutsis, who were demonized by hate radio. In Afghanistan, the Taliban taught extremist forms of religion that provide motive and rationale for killing those who hold other beliefs.

Also, communities in divided societies teach their children the key wrongs done by the Other, stirring a desire for revenge and the fear that motivates preemptive action. This poisonous mixture of fear and hate heightens perceptions of evil and wrongdoing by the Other and strengthens children's own sense of victimhood, motivating attacks and encouraging ongoing cycles of violence.

Children who grow up in deeply divided, violent societies typically have many reasons for becoming warriors for their group (Brett and Specht 2004). Having lost people they know or having been victimized themselves, they may see violence as a means to gain revenge or free their people. Adults encourage children through both words and actions to join the struggle, emphasizing their responsibility to protect their families and end their collective oppression and dishonor. Children who have lost their parents may decide to join the struggle to avenge their loss, to protect their villages, or to seek protection and access to necessities such as food and health care. War crushes children's hope by destroying the schools, markets, health posts, and other structures children need in order to have a positive future. As the war continues, children may see life inside an armed group as their best option. Children's decisions to become warriors, whether attributable to hate, necessity, or a combination of motives, help to make war a multigenerational process that reproduces itself and visits untold suffering on following generations.

In divided, war-torn societies, ceasefires are very fragile, as civilians and combatants alike may suspect that ceasefires will become a tactic exploited by the opposing group. Even following the ceasefire, young people may continue attacks on other groups. Following the Serb attacks on Kosovar Albanians in 1999, the mass displacement of Kosovars, and their return home in the summer of 1999, Kosovar Albanians threatened and attacked Serbs who lived within Kosovar borders. As one Kosovar teenage boy said to me, "I remember what they [Serb paramilitaries] did to my family. I will make them pay for what they have done." In this situation, and more recently in the postwar situations of Afghanistan and

Iraq, the world confronts evidence that child soldiering is a stimulus for protracted violence.

Children's Vulnerability and Resilience

Two great fallacies have grown up around the topic of child soldiers. The first is that child soldiers have the worst lot among children who live in war zones. In fact, child soldiers often have better access to food and protection than do other children, who are subject to scourges such as attack, displacement, and HIV/AIDS, and who have no means of defending themselves. Child soldiers may also be better off because their groups meet their basic needs by looting and robbing villages. Although many child soldiers suffer profoundly, former child soldiers are neither uniquely vulnerable nor definable in terms of vulnerability. In fact, the vast majority of former child soldiers exhibit remarkable resilience. Also, a narrow focus on the plight of child soldiers is misleading and sets the stage for a litany of errors discussed in the following chapters.

The second fallacy is that child soldiering can be understood in singular terms by analyzing the plight of child soldiers apart from the wider suffering of all children in war zones. This fallacy is evident in discussions focused only on child soldiers with nary a mention of the masses of other war-affected children, few of whom become soldiers. The new pattern of fighting discussed above amounts to an assault on children's well-being in all its dimensions—physical, cognitive, emotional, social, and spiritual. This assault harms all children living in war zones, which are spawning grounds for children's suffering and exploitation. There are intimate connections between child soldiering and the wider suffering of war-affected children. A clear understanding of child soldiering emerges only when one learns how children's vulnerability in war zones sets the stage for them becoming soldiers. In war zones, the sources of children's vulnerability are many.

Poverty

War zones embody the truth of Mahatma Gandhi's famous dictum that poverty is the worst form of violence. Poverty, which often contributes to war, intensifies during war. Following war, poverty continues to damage well-being as societies slide into economic collapse (Collier et al. 2003). Furthermore, the destruction of infrastructure and reductions in family income take a devastating toll on children and families in war zones. Too often, these children grow up in inadequate shelters, living in families too poor to obtain adequate food or health care.

The lack of physical necessities and the inability to purchase them, however, do not capture the essence of poverty as seen through children's eyes (Boyden et al. 2003). In contrast to adults' tendency to define poverty in terms of money or household income, children frequently have different understandings of what it means to be poor. During the war in Angola, one child told me being poor meant he could not go to school. When I asked why, noting school was free and open to all children, he said, "I can't go because I have no shoes . . . The other children tease me and I feel bad." For children, poverty means not only lack of money and material items but also social exclusion, shame, humiliation, and loss of social status.

Health and Nutrition

The armed conflicts of the 1990s killed an estimated two million children (Machel 2001). Large numbers of children die from bullets, shrapnel, and wounds received during attacks. An Angolan woman described how UNITA treated babies:

> I saw a lady [with a baby], they took the baby from her back, put the baby in a mortar and they hammered the baby to death [in front of the mother] and the mother could not even cry because otherwise she would also be killed. UNITA's main order was to kill, always kill, they never pardoned anybody. (Honwana 1998, 52)

This murder of infants was part of UNITA's strategy of terrorizing local villages, but it is only one way in which war ravages children. Although large numbers of children are injured or killed by bullets, shrapnel, land mines, and unexploded ordnance, the greatest toll on children's physical well-being comes from food insecurity, inadequate nutrition, preventable diseases, and damage to infrastructure such as water supplies, sanitation systems, and health care facilities. Environmental damage also compromises children's health. Desperate for security, people often move to places that lack the resources, such as clean water and firewood, that are needed to support the displaced population. Walking long distances daily to obtain firewood, girls and young women frequently fall prey to sexual assault.

Orphaning and Separation from Parents

Of all the losses children suffer in war zones, none is greater than the death of their parents or primary caretakers, their main sources of love, care, and protection. The loss of one's parents not only creates heavy emotional burdens but can also begin a downward spiral into increased poverty and vulnerability (Petty and Jareg 1998). Like orphans, children who become separated from their parents or primary caretakers, for example, during the chaos of flight from attack, are at high risk. Although separated children may live with members of their extended family, their abject poverty frequently propels them into dangerous activities. At greatest risk are unaccompanied children who not only have become separated from their parents or caretakers but lack adult care or supervision. Unable to meet basic needs and desperate to survive, orphans, separated children, and unaccompanied children may join armed groups, perform dangerous or heavy labor, be drawn into trafficking, or become prostitutes.

Displacement

Armed conflict displaces masses of people, including children who have seen their homes, properties, and futures destroyed. Worldwide, there are an estimated forty million displaced people, approximately half of whom are children (Machel 2001). Those who cross an international border seeking political asylum may become refugees. Not infrequently, refugees lack basic materials and a cultural identity, and suffer discrimination, alienation, and difficulties earning a livelihood and negotiating the complexities of their new social system. Refugee camps, with their arduous living conditions, frequently become political hotbeds where radicalized youths fuel continued armed conflict.

In addition, armed conflicts displace large numbers of people who stay within the borders of their country. These internally displaced people (IDPs), one of the least visible at-risk groups of our time, may live in or near zones of active fighting and face daily insecurity. For example, war in northern Uganda has displaced over 1.5 million people, most of whom live in crowded camps lacking adequate sanitation, shelter, health care, food, and education. Within camps, sexual and gender-based violence pose severe threats. A Ugandan woman in Soroti said,

> The men go to town and get drunk. They drink away all the money. Then they come home and rape or curse at any women they can find. It is a really big problem because they attack all the women, girls too. Nobody feels safe here, and it is like living in hell.

In addition to sexual violence, displaced children face increased risks such as separation from parents during flight, abduction into soldiering, and exposure to land mines.

Living on the Streets

In war zones, a common sight is children rummaging through garbage heaps for food or clothing, or selling small items on the streets to meet basic needs. Typically, significant numbers of children live and sleep on the streets, where they are vulnerable to abduction by armies and to dangers such as working long hours in abusive sweatshops under conditions that ruin eyesight and limit healthy growth. Lacking adult protection and supervision and also the means to meet basic needs, many street children turn to prostitution to obtain necessities. As a 15-year-old Sierra Leonean girl, already a mother, asked me, "How else am I going to feed my baby girl?"

Family Violence

In war zones, violence spreads as if it were a cancer through family, community, and societal levels, creating a system of violence. Many families become a microcosm of the violence permeating the wider society, creating a highly toxic environment for children. Although family violence is notoriously difficult to document, extensive self-reports from women suggest that family violence rates soar during armed conflict. In addition to weakened social controls that limit violence, this may reflect the increased stresses associated with men's inability to fill their role as provider, since unemployment rates as high as 70 percent are not uncommon in war zones. One useful hypothesis is that in societies like Angola and Afghanistan, long-term unemployment has threatened masculine identity and men's sense of power and authority. As a result, men may be more likely to beat their wives and children, both to vent their frustration and to reassert their authority.

In addition, highly stressed parents might discipline their children by using corporal punishment so harsh that it breaks their children's bones. Evidence indicates that in a war zone, a child's family situation mediates the impact of armed conflict on the child (Garbarino and Kostelny 1996). Warm families buffer the effects of armed conflict by providing emotional support. Conversely, family violence increases the chances that children will suffer negative social and emotional effects from living in a war zone. This simple insight highlights the necessity of thinking of a child's well-being not only in individual terms but also in terms of family context.

Sexual Exploitation

Large numbers of children, mostly girls but also boys, are exploited sexually in war zones. Rape is perhaps the most publicized form of sexual exploitation, but more hidden forms of sexual violence are also widespread. The entry of peacekeeping forces into a conflict zone, for example, typically spawns a cottage industry of prostitution by girls or boys who need money to support their families and who have no other way to obtain basic goods. In refugee camps, girls may be forced into transactional sex, trading sex for essential items such as food rations or plastic sheeting used as housing material. Sexually exploited children are at high risk of contracting sexually transmitted infections, including HIV/AIDS.

Accumulating Risks

Any one of these sources of vulnerability, which are called risk factors because they place children at risk of harm, can damage children emotionally or physically. For example, displaced children may suffer emotional scars associated with such experiences as having seen their homes destroyed, and physically they are at risk of abduction, attack, and health problems. However, the greatest hazard arises from the combination of risks—or risk accumulation (Masten 2001; Werner and

Smith 1992). Risk accumulation greatly increases children's distress and threatens to overwhelm their capacities for coping. Children who are exposed to one or two risks tend to fare much better than they would have if they had been exposed to three or four risks. The risks do not simply add up. The addition of a third risk, for example, increases tenfold the chances of serious harm (Rutter 1979, 1985).

In war zones, risks accumulate rapidly, and children typically lack space in which to "unpack," or think through and come to terms with, the multiple adversities. A child who has seen her home destroyed may suffer feelings of loss and also disparagement as a poor person. While dealing with this situation, she might also suffer sexual exploitation or experience her mother's death. When children do not have spaces in which to recover from such experiences, these risks pile up, taking a heavy toll on them. Although international attention often focuses on children who have recently suffered acute stress from being attacked, the greatest damage to children may come from the accumulation of multiple, though less visible, risks.

Furthermore, risks such as poverty, losses, and marginalization are chronic and do not end with a ceasefire. In thinking about war and children's well-being, it is misleading to see the end of the war as having created a "postconflict" environment in which children thrive. A 15-year-old girl from Sierra Leone said: "Before the war, I was poor and always hungry. I couldn't go to school because I had to work. My brothers and sisters were always dying. The war killed them . . . Now they talk about peace. I'm still hungry . . . My family has no food. There is no school. I have no skills or [means of earning a] living. How is this better?" As her words indicate, the worries spawned by war often do not decrease in postconflict situations. A legitimate question to ask in many postconflict zones is, Where's the "post-"?

Balancing Vulnerability and Resilience

Discussions of children's vulnerability in war zones frequently fall into the trap of picturing all children in war zones as emotionally crippled and traumatized or as helpless victims. Public media have often spoken uncritically of a "lost generation," portraying entire generations of war-affected children as beyond repair and unable to assume socially constructive roles.

Contrary to such images, most children in war zones show significant resilience—the ability to withstand adversities without suffering long-term damage. In nearly every war zone, children play games and make toys, embodying the maxim of child development that "play is the work of children." Except in the most threatening environments, many children perform age-appropriate activities such as tending to animals, fetching water or wood, or watching over younger siblings in the ways expected of children in the local cultural setting. Most children remain functional and engage in the roles and activities appropriate to their culture, age, gender, and historical context.

Children's resilience has many sources, including individual temperament, emotional support from a caring adult or parent, the development of age-appropriate competencies, group support from peers, and participation in local traditions or stable routines that provide a sense of meaning and continuity. Communities support resilience by meeting children's basic needs. Also, they introduce children to safe public spaces, enabling positive relations with teachers and mentors, and expanding children's life opportunities. Quality education is one of the most important sources of resilience because it strengthens children's developing competencies, increasing their capacities for solving problems and coping with adversity.

As dangerous as war zones are, they may nonetheless contain sources of resilience and assets supportive of effective functioning. For example, a child might be under the care of a loving mother, and even refugee camps may contain former teachers who organize educational activities for children. No matter how war-stricken, local people everywhere have assets or strengths to draw upon in supporting children. These assets frequently include social networks, kinship ties, traditions, teachers and religious leaders, elders, and local women's associations and youth groups, all of which may support children. In regard to child soldiers and all war-affected children, then, a balance should be struck between competing images of vulnerability and resilience.

All images of children in war zones demand a critical perspective, because they can be manipulated in ways harmful to children. A leader who is eager to demonize the adversary and stir public sentiments for war might play up images of children's vulnerability in order to publicize the horrible things done by the other side. Images of resilience, too, are subject to political manipulation. Seeking to avoid paying for the aid to which children are entitled, a government may use inflated claims of children's resilience to argue against providing needed services. With respect to all images of child soldiers, a fundamental question to ask is, Who benefits?

As the next chapters show, leaders in war zones have too seldom had children's well-being as their top priority and have promoted instead their own political agendas and interests. We live in an age in which armed conflicts pose unprecedented risks to children. It is time to reduce these risks and prevent damage to future generations. The first half of this book discusses children's vulnerabilities and experiences as soldiers. The second half (Chapters 7 to 10) examines the steps we can and ought to take to fulfill our collective responsibility to protect children.

2

Entry into Armed Groups

Diverse narratives surround the question why children become soldiers. One narrative, attractive in its simplicity, emphasizes forced recruitment, portraying child soldiers as victims of abduction. This narrative is comforting in its depiction of wicked people as the cause of children becoming soldiers. A Sri Lankan girl recounted how she had been taken by the LTTE at age 16:

> My parents refused to give me to the LTTE so about fifteen of them came to my house—it was both men and women, in uniforms, with rifles, and guns in holsters . . . I was fast asleep when they came to get me at one in the morning . . . These people dragged me out of the house. My father shouted at them, saying, "What is going on?" but some of the LTTE soldiers took my father away towards the woods and beat him . . . They also pushed my mother onto the ground when she tried to stop them. (HRW 2004b, 2)

As her testimony illustrates, because children or their families can meet with violence if they resist, children faced with such circumstances have no choice but to go with the armed group.

A competing narrative emphasizes war as a source of opportunities for children, who willingly join armed groups to obtain things—protection, a sense of family, education and training, power, money, or a sense of purpose, among others—denied to them in civilian life. Exploding the myth of children as innocents, this narrative depicts children as actors who have a strong sense of agency and can exercise choice. By emphasizing parents' and adults' failure to create safe, meaningful lives for children, this narrative also points out the responsibility of all adults, including ordinary parents and citizens, for children becoming soldiers. A boy in rural Colombia tells of the positive reasons he joined the guerrilla group FARC-EP:

> The guerillas used to come around a lot. They came to buy milk, chickens, and bananas. I left when I was thirteen and joined the 24th front of the FARC-EP. They brought me to their camp and gave me everything. I went with them because I was really sad and unhappy. They were like my family. (HRW 2003e, 37)

Children such as this boy are not passive victims but active agents who decide that they are more likely to get a positive future by casting their fate with an armed group than by living the lives their biological families and societies have sculpted for them. This example, which contradicts infantilized views of children, also illustrates the progressive nature of child recruitment. Often children's decision to join comes not as a moment of epiphany but through a slow accretion of smaller decisions and gradually increased engagement with members of an armed group.

A third narrative, favored by particular governments, says children become soldiers to fulfill their patriotic duty to their countries. In fact, governments have made child conscription a common practice. In the U.S. Civil War, both armies conscripted children as the conflict wore on and death and disease thinned the ranks (Werner 1998). Today, government armies find it easy to conscript minors in countries that lack accurate birth records.

Each narrative discloses part of the wider picture of child recruitment. Children become soldiers through many different channels and for many different reasons, and this diversity has not always been reflected in the literature on child soldiers. Even within a single conflict zone or country, children's recruitment may vary greatly according to context, making it specious to think in terms of any single motive or pattern of entry. Whereas one child may join in hopes of earning money, another may join out of a mixture of desires for security, family, and revenge.

Voluntary recruitment and forced recruitment provide anchor points for thinking about this diversity. It is too simplistic, however, to think of these in Manichean terms, because the realities of children's lives in war zones blur the boundaries between choice and coercion. If a child witnesses his parents' murder and he joins an armed group to obtain protection and food, is this choice free or the product of desperation? The complexity of such situations defies neat categories. Even where a child does not appear desperate and chooses to join an armed group for money, this choice may reflect a lack of options available in civilian life. The child may see himself as a burden on his family and may regard his entry into soldiering as a way to support them. Although children in war zones are sometimes portrayed as having made unfettered choices, their decisions reflect a complex interplay of perceived or real necessity, obligation, hardship, and agency.

In addition, coercion and choice may impact children at different points in their journey as soldiers. Children who decide to join armed groups may enter without obvious coercion yet may subsequently be forced to stay with the armed group. I have talked with quite a number of former child soldiers who had chosen to join an armed group but subsequently regretted their decision because they had underestimated the level of hardship, danger, and isolation from their families. Once they enter an armed group, however, children typically are not free to leave.

In analyzing child recruitment, a key step is to listen to the voices of children, learning why they deliberately entered an armed group. Perhaps assuming that adults know best, the study of child soldiering has only recently begun paying close attention to children's perspectives. What children tell us—that their families have abused them, they have few life options as civilians, or their governments have failed to protect them—is deeply disturbing. Only when we discern how children themselves understand their recruitment can we position ourselves to prevent child recruitment and to support the reintegration of former child soldiers. Before probing how children are recruited, however, it is important to ask why children are recruited at all.

Why Children Are Recruited

Convenience, low cost, and impunity are significant factors in commanders' decision to recruit children. Field-level commanders often say they recruit children because they cannot replenish their troop losses by recruiting adults. In war zones there is a ready supply of children, who typically compose half or more of the population. Although their superior officers may say their group prohibits child recruitment, field commanders frequently bend the rules by recruiting children who look tall or old enough to pass as adults. Even if accurate birth registration or identification documents exist, commanders may ignore them with impunity.

Child recruits are as cheap as they are convenient. Recruiters frequently promise money, which is a powerful "pull" factor for poor children (Delap 2005). Whereas adult soldiers may demand to be paid, children lack the power to do this or may have been sufficiently intimidated that they dare not ask. The story of a 16-year-old boy from Burundi is not uncommon:

> We were told that we would get 50,000 Burundian francs (Fbu)(approximately equivalent to US$50) in Bujumbura straight away and 4 million afterwards. When we got to Bujumbura though we were told we would get the money in the cantonment site. (AI 2004b, 6–7)

Like many child recruits, he received hard physical training and frequent beatings but no pay, leading him to desert. Other pull factors include glamour and propaganda. In Colombia, guerrilla groups send out as recruiters child soldiers who are physically attractive and articulate as a means of glamorizing military life and providing peer role models that aid recruitment (HRW 2003e). In the Philippines, armed groups send out child soldiers to recruit other children by spreading propaganda and calling children to join the struggle out of solidarity with the movement (Keairns 2003b). Many recruiters, however, prefer the use of brutality and forced recruitment, as terrorized children are easily manipulated and do not have to be paid.

Convenience, low cost, and impunity, however, tell only part of the story, as more sinister motives are also at work. In fact, commanders recruit children because they have shock value. On the battlefield, child soldiers sow disarray and confusion by confronting opposing troops with the prospect of having to kill children, which most troops are reluctant to do. In West Africa, younger boys have formed small-boy units that have spearheaded assaults and in some cases have been sent forward naked as a means of confusing and terrorizing opponents (Singer 2005). Also, child soldiers are pliable, exploitable, effective, and expendable. At particular risk of recruitment are teenagers, who in most situations are the largest pool of child recruits.

At-Risk Youths

Recruiters frequently target teenagers because their larger size enables them to carry heavy loads, perform difficult labor, and fight with an efficacy that rivals that of adults. Having relatively advanced cognitive competencies, teenagers are effective problem solvers who can plan and lead attacks, develop strategies for avoiding capture, and participate fully in all aspects of military life. Far from being passive recipients, teenagers often help to construct the political discourses that guide armed groups' struggles for liberation or domination of a political rival. These discourses bind together many armed groups and attract new recruits.

Cultural norms can also place teenagers at high risk of recruitment. As one Afghan commander rationalized, "This soldier—he's 14, but he's not a child anymore. In our culture, he is expected to do the work of a man, and this work includes fighting." This type of answer is not uncommon in rural Africa, where 14-year-olds are regarded as adults and expected to work to help support their families. In this context, both children and families may regard child soldiering as a natural extension of children's obligation to their families. Of course, this situation provides no excuse for children's exploitation as soldiers. Although local cultural norms may contradict children's rights, the U.N. Convention on the Rights of the Child (CRC) takes precedence because it constitutes a binding legal obligation. Where gaps exist between local norms and the CRC, there is a need for ongoing education and dialogue to close the gap and enable children's protection.

Pliable Youths

Children are pliable in that they are flexible and easily manipulated and controlled. Young children are controllable through terror and brutality, a point not lost on older, stronger, and more cunning commanders. Through violence or threat of violence, young children can be trained to obey commands that many adults would contest or find ways around. Entering an armed group and a new world suffused with danger, and recognizing their ignorance of the group rules and lack of survival skills, young children use obedience as a survival strategy.

Children's pliability derives in part from their early level of psychological development and limited life experience. Some commanders prefer child soldiers because they accept the most dangerous assignments, including ones that adults might recognize as too hazardous. Psychologically, young people may not be able to assess fully the depth of the danger associated with a particular action, and they lack a sense of their own mortality. Teenage boys may take on dangerous assignments to demonstrate machismo at a time in their lives when they feel it is vital to impress their peers and demonstrate their manliness.

Children's cognitive and moral development also underlies their pliability and increases their openness to new ideas. Unlike adults, young children are just beginning to think about complex moral issues and to develop the self-regulation and restraint evident in later stages of moral development. Teenagers, including child soldiers, exhibit complex moral reasoning and may follow a highly developed moral code tailored to their lives in difficult, politically charged situations (Cairns 1996; Straker 1992). However, teenagers are at a stage in their lives in which they are forming their own identity, achieving autonomy, and defining their wider beliefs and world view (Erikson 1968). Teenagers are often more receptive to new ideologies and systems of thought than adults are. Also, young people tend to be more idealistic than adults. Recruiters play on this idealism and openness by promising opportunities to help overthrow an unjust regime and build a new social system founded on principles of social justice. Many a child soldier's idealism, however, has been fractured by the realities of life with the armed group.

Exploitable and Expendable

Commanders also regard children as rich resources who are exploitable in a multitude of ways. Because children are small in size and unlikely to be suspected as enemies, commanders frequently order children to act as spies. Their small size also leaves children unable to protect themselves from being sexually assaulted by commanders and soldiers. Children's enormous capacity for learning enables them to fill diverse roles such as cook, bodyguard, porter, fighter, sex slave, and spy. In Angola, UNITA commanders preferred young children as laborers because they could carry heavy loads of material more quietly than could trucks and other vehicles (Stavrou 2005).

In children, commanders see unformed raw material to be molded as they wish. In Sri Lanka, the LTTE has developed the exploitation of children into an art. The LTTE took children from orphanages at an early age, indoctrinated and trained them, and subsequently used them to make some of the most dangerous assaults on well-fortified Sri Lankan army bases (Singer 2005). Because these youngsters—with their limited sense of mortality and their susceptibility to being trained to accept the most dangerous assignments—are in such bountiful supply, commanders can easily replace children who are killed in such suicidal operations.

Children's expendability is evident in the lethal orders commanders issue. In some cases, children who have received little or no training have been issued guns and thrust into firefights (UNICEF 2003). Children have also been used as mine detectors, sent unprotected into minefields to reduce the damage to adult troops who followed. In Myanmar (Burma), children were ordered to make frontal assaults against highly fortified positions, creating a field of slaughter (HRW 2002). Ultimately, the most exploitable are also the most expendable.

Forced Recruitment

Whether children want to become soldiers is beside the point for many commanders who use violence or the threat of violence to recruit children. Children are particularly susceptible to forced recruitment due to their small size and the ease with which they can be intimidated. The most commonly used methods of forced recruitment are abduction, press ganging, and the quota method.

Abduction

Abduction is an illegal practice that perpetrators seek to hide, so it is difficult to estimate the percentage of children who have entered armed groups through abduction. Still, in various countries children have offered frequent and adult-corroborated testimonies that indicate that abduction is relatively widespread.

A 12-year-old from Colombia tells how he was forcibly recruited by the FARC-EP in what appears to have been an opportunistic act:

I was invited to go and work in another village where I wasn't known at all. I had a .38 revolver for my own protection. Some guys from the FARC spotted me with the gun and suspected that I was a paramilitary. They captured me and tied me up. They investigated me, but because I had never been with an armed group and they couldn't kill me without proof, they didn't do anything to me. I did not want to join, but I was convinced that if I did not go with them they would kill me. I felt I had no choice. (HRW 2003e, 43–44)

Abductions typically are not opportunistic, however. Armed groups often have a norm of abducting any children who happen to be in their path. In Sierra Leone, a 20-year-old man told me how he had been abducted at age 16: "My Dad and I were planting rice and the RUF came and captured us. Dad begged the soldiers to release me, but they insisted . . . Dad trailed them since he couldn't let me go . . . So they killed my Dad." Similarly, a 19-year-old girl told how the RUF had abducted her at age 16: "I was captured in Kono where I was with my aunt. Initially I escaped to the bush, but the RUF captured me and offered two options—kill or be taken." To reduce their accountability, armed groups typically cloak the systematic nature of the abductions by claiming only a few misguided commanders recruit children.

Camps for refugees and internally displaced people are favored sites for child abductions because they contain large numbers of children and little or no police presence or other means to stop abductions. A boy who lived in the Goma (Democratic Republic of the Congo) camps into which hundreds of thousands of Rwandan refugees had poured following the 1994 genocide told of his experience:

I was coming home from school at about 5 P.M. I went to school in the afternoon. I was heading home when soldiers in a vehicle stopped me and made me get in. They were Rwandans. There were lots of other young boys in the vehicle. We went to the airport in Goma and from there to Kalemie by plane. We were all ten, twelve, thirteen years old and older. Then we were sent to Camp Vert in Moba and trained there. Lots were killed in the training. Lots died of sickness. (HRW 2001, 10)

In some situations, armed groups recruit children through a mixture of organized abduction and positive inducements. In Afghanistan, forced recruitment often occurred through house-to-house abductions mixed with felt loyalties and a sense of duty. During the war against the Soviet occupiers of the country, Afghans organized around mujaheddin commanders, referred to internationally as warlords. Aside from the high-level commanders such as Masoud, Dostum, and Hekmatyar, local villages each have their own local commander who typically wields enormous power and controls access to basic resources such as health care, food, and other necessities. Local commanders had the power to recruit 14- to 18-year-old boys. During the post-9/11 fight against the Taliban in northern Afghanistan, Northern Alliance commanders frequently recruited by going house to house. Said one 15-year-old Afghan, "The commander came to my house and told me to come with him . . . If I had not gone with him, I would have been beaten or bad things could have happened to my family." Many Tajik and Uzbek youths expressed mixed motives, saying they had gone with their commander because it had been their duty to protect their village and also because they feared the consequences of not going with him.

Organized abduction has been taken to a new, even more contemptible, level in northern Uganda by the LRA. Many of this group's members are abducted children. Recently the LRA expanded its theater of operation from the northern districts of Gulu, Kitgum, and Pader into the eastern districts of Lira and Apac. To fight the government's Operation Iron Fist, the LRA has abducted more than twelve thousand children since June 2002, and it attacks villages for the purpose of abducting people. The abductions are notorious for their brutality. A 13-year-old boy told of his capture in 2002:

> Early on when my brothers and I were captured, the LRA explained to us that all five brothers couldn't serve in the LRA because we would not perform well. So they tied up my two younger brothers and invited us to watch. Then they beat them with sticks until two of them died. They told us it would give us strength to fight. My youngest brother was nine years old. (HRW 2003d)

A 12-year-old boy also told a harrowing story:

> That night, the LRA came abducting people in our village, and some neighbors led them to our house. They abducted all five of us boys at the same time. I was the fifth one . . . We were told by the LRA not to think about home, about our mother or father. If we did, then they would kill us. Better to think now that I am a soldier fighting to liberate the country. There were twenty-eight abducted from our village that night . . . We were all tied up and attached to one another in a row.

After we were tied up, they started to beat us randomly; they beat us with sticks. (HRW 2003b, 5)

The terror induced by these abductions has a profound social impact on the lives of Ugandan children and families. Nightly, swarms of "night commuters," whose numbers rise to tens of thousands when the risk of attack is high, walk long distances from their homes in unsafe areas into towns such as Gulu, where they sleep on church grounds, in hospitals, or on verandas in the hope of avoiding attack and abduction. Sadly, the plight of the night commuters and the masses of abducted and formerly abducted children has not adequately captured the attention of the international media or galvanized a concerted action by the international community. To a large extent, the child abductees remain invisible.

Although child abductions have been conducted frequently by armed opposition groups, governments also recruit by abducting children. In some situations, governments make no attempt to hide their practice of organized, systematic abduction through devices such as house-to-house searches. In Myanmar, a 21-year-old boy related how he had been taken at age 9:

A group of soldiers knocked loudly on the door. Five others, all about the same age, did not escape and were taken by the soldiers. I was crying. I was dragged out of my house and put on a boat and taken to Rangoon. I was considered an adult. (UNICEF 2003, 25)

Similarly, an Angolan boy told how he had been taken by the national army: "I was fifteen when rounded up by the FAA [Angolan Armed Forces]. I had already fled from my home area and was living with a family outside Andulao. I was taken to a training center of the military by truck. There I was trained with 180 other children. During a battle in Moxico, I was wounded, receiving a bullet on the left side of my temple" (HRW 2003a, 14). The example of states' armies abducting the children whom they are supposed to protect indicates how predatory and corrupt states can become in war zones. Little wonder, then, that many young people become alienated from their governments and societies.

Press Ganging

When mass recruitment is the goal, the method of choice for many commanders is press ganging, a form of group abduction wherein soldiers sweep through marketplaces or streets, rounding up youths like fish in nets, or raid institutions such as orphanages or schools. A notorious case was the LRA capture of 139 girls from the Aboke school in 1996 (De Temmerman 2001). In 2001, armed groups in Burundi abducted approximately three hundred children from schools and forced them to carry military equipment or help wounded soldiers (AI 2004b). It is a tragic irony that schools, which are intended to protect children and support their healthy development, frequently become sites for child recruitment.

IDP and refugee camps are also favored targets for press ganging. In Liberia, a 16-year-old boy told how the opposition group Liberians United for Reconciliation and Democracy (LURD) had taken him:

> We were all taken from here [an IDP camp], at least fifty boys on that day. The youngest boy fighter was probably fifteen, younger ones were taken but only used for labor. We were taken to Bomi and trained in how to fire, how to take positions during the fighting. How to take cover and to dodge bullets. There were probably one hundred boys who did the training, the others came from neighboring camps. The training lasted about two weeks and right afterwards, I was on the front lines. (HRW 2004a, 10)

It is not only displaced children who are at increased risk of forced recruitment. All dispossessed children—those who are poor, marginalized, or who live on the streets or in orphanages or camps—are at great risk of forced recruitment. Before war erupts, children from lower socioeconomic classes carry a heavy burden of poverty and social exclusion. When the war erupts, they may carry the added burden of being forced into the fighting. And following the war, they remain trapped in the web of poverty that war had worsened.

Recruitment by Quota

To subjugate and control local people, armed groups seek to co-opt local authorities, forcing them to act as agents of the armed group. In Angola, for example, the opposition group UNITA recruited children by telling village leaders to provide a particular number of youths, typically ten or more, or else UNITA would attack and destroy the village. Faced with the impossible choice of sacrificing children or sacrificing the entire village, most leaders turned over the required number of young soldiers, including children. Psychologically, this weakened leaders' prestige since it highlighted their inability to fulfill their obligations as leaders to protect the children. It also put the leaders in the position of supporting UNITA when the majority of the villagers had wanted not to support UNITA, either for political reasons or to avoid retaliatory attacks by the government forces.

In Sri Lanka, the LTTE has also recruited via the quota method. Said a 15-year-old girl,

> Each house had been told to hand over one child. The LTTE had already issued the order, but the parents had ignored it. First, they sent letters, then they started to visit homes. They came to my house and said, "You know about our announcement. Each house has to turn over one child. If you don't agree, we will take a child anyway." (HRW 2004b, 17)

Current evidence indicates that the LTTE has made good on this promise, despite its repeated statements that it no longer recruits children (HRW 2004b). If a family refuses to hand over a child, the LTTE threatens to force the family from its home. Faced with such threats, some Sri Lankan girls have acceded to the recruitment pressures in order to protect their families.

In Afghanistan, the Taliban regime used the quota method in the northeastern provinces, where the Northern Alliance fought against them. Taliban commanders ordered villages to hand over a number of youths, typically six to ten, for duty as soldiers for three to six months. When one group had completed their time, the commanders returned and demanded another quota of recruits. There was nothing voluntary about this recruitment; a village that failed to deliver its quota would be attacked. This system placed the young recruits in a severe psychological bind. If they did not fight as their Taliban leaders commanded, they could be killed. To obey, however, meant killing their own people, with whom they felt strong bonds, and the risk of being branded as traitors (Wessells and Kostelny 2002).

To prevent recruitment of their children, relatively wealthy families often sent their sons to Pakistan or paid poor families to send their sons to fight in their place. That not all social classes are equally at risk of recruitment illustrates the risks created by poverty, which also fuels children's decisions to enter armed groups.

Unforced Recruitment

In war zones, most children, typically over 90 percent, do not enter armed groups. Although this 90 percent includes children who have been affected by war, they may benefit from protective factors such as having caring family members who urge them to stay out of armed groups. Others have strong coping skills and competencies that enable them to construct a way to earn a living, meet basic needs, and gain respect outside of an armed group. Unfortunately, large numbers of children lack these protective factors and coping skills. Easily coaxed by recruiters, they enter armed groups without explicit force or coercion. Too often, failed social systems set the context for unforced recruitment by offering few positive alternatives for young people, who spend most of their time in idleness, and creating a multiplicity of risks. In a very real sense, the children do not go to war—the war comes home to them (Brett and Specht 2004).

The War Comes Home

For millions of children, war is not something fought "out there" in a distant land and experienced by enlisting and traveling to the front. Because war is part of daily life, it redefines the horizons of their experience and transforms the social contexts in which they develop. Affected by increased poverty, and feeling powerless and alienated over the government's failure to protect them or to provide jobs, children may find not only a sense of power but also a job and a means of livelihood through association with an armed group.

That children find soldiering attractive becomes understandable in light of the transformation of the entire social system, and of children's understanding of their social world, during war. To begin with, war creates a highly militarized environment in which power and authority are openly contested. With no rule of law, armed groups—including government forces and opposition groups or militias—openly attack and plunder local villages, eliminating all vestiges of security and protection and placing all children at risk. For children who live in such a dangerous situation, joining an armed group may be their best hope of survival and protection.

War causes profound damage to societal systems that are intended to support children and meet their basic needs for food, water, shelter, and health care. War is often the product of failed or failing governments that have poor capacity and are cobbled by crime and corruption. The eruption of war worsens this situation, plunging society into a downward spiral of increased poverty and increased inability to meet basic needs. With the destruction of schools and other vital infrastructure, children in war zones see their key supports and hope for the future shattered, and they may see armed groups as their best option for obtaining basics such as education and health care.

The declining options offered by civilian life weigh heavily on teenagers, whose joblessness and alienation combine with their political consciousness and idealism in a highly combustible mixture. Economies ravaged by war typically afford few jobs, creating high levels of unemployment and social disaffection. The result, visible in nearly all war zones, is large cadres of idling youths who engage in little purposeful activity and whose alienation fuels their desire to join armed groups to overthrow the government that has failed them. Particularly if they belong to minority groups, they may see armed struggle as a way to end oppression and create a brighter future. Under these circumstances, decisions to join armed groups can be quite rational and offer a means of adapting to a militarized environment (Peters and Richards 1998).

The transformations brought about by war are not only economic and political but also moral. At the heart of the moral transformation is a shift in the values children learn. In most societies, children learn to see fighting and killing as undesirable and peace as the preferred mode of living. But war zones reverse these views. Violence and killing are normalized because they are daily occurrences in the streets, markets, and communities. Children's values may be skewed in such contexts as they adapt to a world suffused with violence. Not only do they learn to steel themselves to deaths and losses and to regard violence as normal, they may also fail to develop a full sense of the sanctity of human life. Never having experienced peace, and watching adults deal with conflict through fighting, children learn quickly that might makes right. Although adults may express values of peace, children are quick to spot the prevalence of soldiers, military vehicles, guns, and all the power associated with armed activity. They also understand that the breakdown of law and order means there are no police to protect them and their families, who can be attacked at any moment. Seeing their families and their governments as unable to protect them, children learn to view guns and fighting as necessary and legitimate.

In war zones, children also learn from role models the behaviors, attitudes, and skills associated with militarized social roles. Influenced by the warrior imagery and the fighting they see in the media and real life, children in war zones often play war games in the streets, as if they were rehearsing for the roles that lie ahead. Many children learn to envy those who wear uniforms and carry weapons. Lacking peaceful role models and never having learned peaceful habits and values, children do not regard peace as part of their social reality. In fact, many children who grow up never having experienced peace literally do not know the meaning of the term. Living in a culture of violence, they adapt themselves to the war situation, choosing to become soldiers in order to obtain power, wealth, education, or other things they cannot obtain readily in civilian life.

Personal and Situational Influences

Although child soldiers have sometimes been disparaged as "bad seed" who are born killers, this portrayal contradicts much evidence and does injustice to the rich interplay between personal and situational influences on decisions to become soldiers. Personal factors include temperament, beliefs, values, and identity. Children who are characteristically fearful or passive are much less likely to choose to join an armed group than are children who are aggressive or excitable. Children who have internalized beliefs that war is necessary or justifiable, or who identify with warriors or a political cause, are much more likely to join an armed group than are children who believe that fighting is futile or who find a meaningful identify in civilian life.

More powerful in many cases are situational factors such as family pressures, lack of access to education and training, poverty, unemployment, and political socialization. These situational factors are part of the social ecologies that shape child development (Bronfenbrenner 1979; Dawes and Donald 2000). A simple metaphor for conceptualizing these ecologies is the Russian matrushka doll that hides one doll inside another, and another inside that one. If the child is the center, the first surrounding piece—the foundation of child protection—is the family, which in optimum circumstances provides the care, love, security, and support needed for a child's healthy development. The family is nested inside the community, which includes the civic and religious groups, schools, peers, and local government agencies that help to create a protective environment for children. Beyond the community is the societal level, at which government institutions, societal norms, macroeconomic, and ethnic factors shape children's lives. If, for example, societal gender norms limit girls' access to school, girls will lack the education they need to develop a full range of competencies and livelihood options. At the widest level are the international factors such as cross-border flows of displaced people, which are increasingly important due to forces of globalization.

Ideally, each level of children's social ecologies would provide protection and opportunity for positive development. But armed conflict destroys shielding systems and creates multiple risks at each level. Typically, at each level these risks include both "push" and "pull" factors (Brett and Specht 2004).

Push and Pull Factors

Push factors are negatives that children escape by joining an armed group. Abuse suffered in the family is a push factor—the child might join an armed group to escape the abusive situation. Children decide to join armed groups to escape a wide variety of negatives—abuse, boredom, physical insecurity, extreme poverty, and the humiliation associated with personal or family victimization and shame, among others. These push factors are causes only in a statistical sense, because most children who have difficult family situations or live in abject poverty do not become child soldiers.

Equally or more compelling are the pull factors, which are positive rewards or incentives for joining armed groups. Analysts have tended to underestimate the importance of pull factors, probably because the emphasis of much child-soldiering literature has been on protecting children from exploitation. Although most analysts, the author included, view child soldiering as a heinous form of exploitation, children who join armed groups often see soldiering in different terms. Many children view joining an armed group as entering an opportunity space in which they can obtain things they could not have obtained otherwise—including a family, power, revenge, wealth, education, and a means of achieving a cause. To understand the lure of these incentives, one has only to imagine the power felt by a child who comes from a very poor family and has always felt powerless but who now carries a gun and is feared and respected by many.

Family Matters

No situational influence has greater potency than the family (Brett and Specht 2004). The profound importance of the family in children's recruitment is most visible in regard to separated children, who are no longer under the care of their parents or primary caretakers (Delap 2005). Separation typically occurs when a village is attacked; in the chaos of people's desperate flight, young children become separated from their parents, ripped away from their primary supports. Some children's parents are killed, leaving the orphans with little means of protection and in a perilous situation. Separated children are at increased risk of nearly every form of exploitation, whether it involves trafficking, sexual violation, or child soldiering.

Not uncommonly, a separated child who encounters an armed group joins because the armed group provides the only hope of food, medical support, or protection from further attack. In Sierra Leone I interviewed a 25-year-old man who at age 15 had joined the CDF, which had resisted the RUF rebels. He said, "The RUF killed my father and also my mother. I had no way of getting anything—I joined the CDF to get food and water."

Even if children who have been separated from their parents live with members of their extended family, the separation from parents imposes a heavy psychological burden. A Philippine boy who had joined an opposition group at age 14 recounted:

> I was 14 when I joined the NPA [New People's Army]. I was out of school then. My grandfather and grandmother sent me to school but I did not take my studies seriously. I had a friend who joined the movement. I thought that my life was meaningless because I had no parents to look after me. I went along with [my friend] because I thought what the heck my life is meaningless anyway. (UNICEF 2003, 30)

The link between separation and soldiering is intimate because the vast majority of child soldiers have been separated from their families. Indeed, their separation from parents and family is among the most painful and dangerous aspects of child soldiers' situation and frequently keeps them with the armed group.

Recent research has underscored the importance of family pressures in children's choices to join armed groups (Brett 2003). Many children join armed groups to escape negative family situations. A Colombian girl described her desire to leave home to escape physical and emotional abuse by her mother:

> They (people in the group) asked me why my legs were like that and so I told them it was because my mum used to beat me a lot and that's why I was like that and so they said to me why didn't I go with them, because the guerillas didn't beat people, they didn't treat you badly, they didn't insult you, nothing. (Keairns 2003a, 41)

Fathers' abuse also drives young people to join armed groups. A girl from the Philippines described her situation with her father:

> My father seemed to be always mad at me and at all of us. My elder brother told me that our father doesn't love us. He had a big stick that he would use to beat us up; this was a branch of the guava tree. That's why we had to follow him. Just one mistake and he would hit us directly . . . Our mama was also being battered. But we would rather stay with her. We didn't want to be away from her. My father would threaten us that when those two children come, I will kill them! From grade three onwards, I stayed in my aunt's house . . . After I finished grade five, I couldn't stand it any more. I wasn't very comfortable in my aunt's house. I was wondering, "Who is my family?" (Keairns 2003b, 33–34)

Many children living in abusive situations see an armed group as providing a better "family" than the one they are living with.

Family connections also provide a "pull" factor that encourages children to join armed groups. In Afghanistan, children reported that they had joined in part to be with older brothers, uncles, or their father. An extreme example of the importance of family connections comes from Angola, where UNITA soldiers typically traveled with their families, making the entire family part of the UNITA group. Significant numbers of children were born into UNITA in this manner, and many grew up in constant association with UNITA troops and activities. Although they did not volunteer to be with UNITA, choice contributed to their decision to stay, as many feared that they could not survive outside the armed group or would be prosecuted as traitors to the Angolan government. In northern Uganda, Joseph Kony exploits the family connection by having sex with abducted girls, whose children are then reared to become members of the next generation of LRA soldiers.

Revenge

Children also join armed groups out of desire for revenge. The importance of avenging the killing of family members rings in the sentiments of a boy from the Philippines who had joined a rebel group at age 7: "I joined the movement to avenge my father's death in the hands of the military. When I was seven years old, I saw the military take away my defenseless father from our house" (UNICEF 2003, 28). Similarly, a boy from Papua New Guinea told why he had joined an armed group at age 9:

> Why do I feel angry, why did I join the BRA [Bougainville Revolutionary Army] to fight? They killed my brother and uncle (an old man) when they went [to the fields]. They all the time came around to shoot so we got angry. We want to go and make payback with them, remove them from our area. (UNICEF 2003, 28)

In other cases, the revenge motive is directed against police or armed forces that have abused children. As a Liberian boy who had joined the opposition group (LURD) explained:

> The reason I joined LURD is because of police abuse. I was selling bread at the market, trying to make some money to have something to eat and survive. A policeman came up to me, threw all my bread in the water and said I should go away. I was later beaten for that. When the fighters came to our area, I joined with them. (HRW 2004a, 12)

Victimization, whether it occurs inside a family or at the hands of a government force or an armed opposition group, compels many children to become soldiers.

Education

Although education is children's fundamental right, many societies fail to provide quality education for children. War exacerbates this situation. During war, many schools are destroyed, teachers flee, and public resources flow increasingly to the war effort rather than to services such as education. Children's lack of access to school weighs heavily on them, because most children view education as their hope for the future and a better life (Delap 2005; Williamson and Cripe 2002). Denied this, many begin searching for other venues where they can develop skills and competencies that can enable them to build their future. Military life often provides one such venue.

In Sierra Leone, teenagers who had joined the rebel group RUF said they had done so to obtain training and skills. Some said they had learned to read by studying the revolutionary literature distributed by the RUF. One 16-year-old girl who had been a commander with the RUF told me:

> I'm proud of what I learned—how to speak to groups, organize people, command, use weapons. I never got this from [the] government. How else am I supposed to have a future? If I had it to do again, I'd join again.

Her comments reveal that war and military life provide children with skills and options that are unavailable to them through civilian channels. As we will see in later chapters, such newly acquired skills have important implications for reintegration. In particular, the likelihood of soldiers' reintegration depends on the extent to which they can transfer to civilian life the useful skills they acquired in military life.

Lack of access to education also supports recruitment in other ways. For example, children who are out of school and who sleep and work on the streets are at increased risk of recruitment, either through round-ups or through falling prey to fast-talking recruiters who promise them money. In other cases, education has provided a stimulus for recruitment by perpetuating oppression that creates deep grievances and desire for liberation. In Kosovo under Serb rule, Kosovar Albanians lacked access to equal education, even though they were nearly 90 percent of the population. This created deep grievances and a desire for liberation that led the Kosovar Albanians, including children, to fight the Serbs. Education, then, can be either a tool for war or an instrument of peace.

Power, Excitement, and Glamour

Children who grow up in a war zone typically feel powerless, disaffected, and unable to obtain basic necessities and improve their life circumstances. Unable to prevent their exploitation and attacked by armed groups on various sides, they feel trapped and abused. The fact that their abusers may include troops or local authorities creates in these children a strong sense of humiliation and a desire to achieve power so that they can restore their lost dignity and regain a sense of personal efficacy. In Liberia, a 13-year-old boy joined to escape abuse by government forces:

> Last year before the war came here, government fighters forced me to work for them. I was made to carry things from the surrounding areas to the paved road, where they would be collected. I had to carry pieces of zinc (corrugated iron sheeting) that were very heavy, we were not allowed to rest. The soldiers didn't ask you to do this, they would force you, there was no pay. Sometimes if you tried to run away, they would catch you and this is when they would beat you. I was beaten on the back and shoulders with the end of their rifles. When LURD came to this area, I decided it was better to join them and escape the abuse. (HRW 2004a, 11)

In addition to protection, joining an armed group can give children a sense of physical power and respect achievable only through bearing a gun (Delap 2005). Child soldiers often talk about feeling strong when they carry a weapon. A Pakistani boy who joined the Taliban said: "I enjoyed the task of patrolling Kabul in a latest model jeep, with a Kalashnikov slung over my shoulder. It was a great adventure and made me feel big" (Laeeq and Jawadullah 2002, 7). In Angola, a 7-year-old boy who was playing war games with his friends, said, "I want to be a soldier so I can wear a uniform and carry a gun. Then people respect you." This kind of sentiment is common in war-torn countries, where children learn to see guns, uniforms, and military vehicles as symbols of power and as "cool" (HRW 2003e). For a child from a poor village, joining an armed group increases access not only to clothing, food, and health care but also to a sense of power and respect not attainable through civilian means.

The excitement associated with wielding military power can be highly seductive to children who seek escape from the tedium of rural life. Teenage boys, many of whom crave excitement and are eager to demonstrate their machismo, may seek the adventure of battle. In a discussion with teenage boys from Sierra Leone, a 15-year-old boy told me, "I come from a farmers' village and life was boring. Patrol with the CDF was exciting, and I liked the thrill of combat. It was no play—it was kill or be killed."

Poor children also see armed groups as glamorous and a means to a good life. The following testimonies, one from a Colombian boy who had joined the FARC and the other from a Myanmar boy who had joined at age 14, illustrate this clearly.

> They move all around the countryside, and you see them in good spirits these people, with their guns and their uniforms. You get infected with the same spirit. That's what happened to me. I had some friends among the guerillas who invited me to join. I didn't have a lot of contact with them, but they told me that the life was good, that there was plenty of food, clothing was provided, you wanted for nothing, so I got excited and off I went. It was my decision. (HRW 2003e, 37)

> I left home in 1992 and traveled to the border, to a school in a Karenni village, with about 10 friends. I just wanted to be a soldier. I was attracted by the Karenni soldiers when I saw them in the village. I think soldiers are very beautiful. It makes me want to join the army. (UNICEF 2003, 29)

Political Socialization

To grow up in a society is to learn a distinctive set of values and norms and to acquire a sense of identity defined along lines carved by language, culture, ethnicity, religion, and politics. The group's identity is expressed in their food and language, and is honored through the use of flags, songs, memorials, and other symbols. In this process of socialization, societies teach children to sacrifice for their group, fighting when necessary, and to honor their history and way of life. Over many years of socialization, children internalize a social identity that defines who they are and gives them a sense of meaning and place in the world. Throughout the process of political socialization, children are far from passive recipients but are actors who shape political discourse, particularly among the peer groups so important in teenagers' lives.

In war-torn societies, identity and politics are hotly contested. Living under a military occupation, children often learn to define themselves in part by opposition to the enemy. For a Palestinian youth in the West Bank of the Occupied Territories, for example, to be a Palestinian is to oppose the Israeli government. In East Timor during the Indonesian occupation, Timorese teenagers, both girls and boys, often joined the resistance and defined themselves in part by opposition to the Indonesian regime. In such contexts, youths construct meaning through participation in a liberation struggle (Garbarino, Kostelny, and Dubrow 1991; Punamaki 1996; Straker 1992). They see their choice to join armed groups and to fight as rational and purposeful, and in their struggle they may be willing to use tools such as terrorism that others regard as irrational. The armed struggle provides unwavering direction and creates solidarity with others who also engage in the struggle. In deciding to join an armed group for ideological reasons, children take on a new identity not as civilians but as warriors or soldiers who fight for a cause. Through this identity and their actions on behalf of the cause, child soldiers achieve a strong sense of agency and meaning in life.

Political identity and ideology are levers recruiters activate using tools such as propaganda. In Rwanda, as preparation for the 1994 genocide, Hutu extremists used hate radio to send messages of intolerance and encourage mistreatment of Tutsis, who were portrayed as outside attackers of Hutus and less than fully human. This propaganda helped swell the ranks of the Interahamwe, the extremist militia that killed large numbers of Tutsis and moderate Hutus during the 1994 genocide. Teenagers are susceptible to manipulation by propaganda because they lack the broad life experience needed to think issues through critically, particularly in contexts where they have had little education or education that does not favor critical thinking. At a developmental stage in which they search for meaning and direction in their lives, teenagers often find that the heroic imagery in propaganda speaks to their idealism and provides a clear sense of direction.

Through socialization, many children acquire a strong desire to serve and a willingness to sacrifice that leads them to join armed groups. A Philippine boy who joined at age 14 said, "I joined to serve the people in the mountains. We protected them from violence and harm, from the government soldiers. These soldiers, they were abusive; that's why we kept watch" (UNICEF 2003, 26). Armed groups often teach children to become martyrs, who are honored through ceremonies, posters, and legends that may be passed on to encourage future generations of warriors.

Armed groups are clever in using propaganda to aid children's recruitment. In Sri Lanka the LTTE combines family visits and appeals to family responsibility with emotionally charged street plays:

> It was a very emotional drama about the struggle, basically asking peo-
> ple to join the movement. There were all ages present in the audience,
> but it was really a drama for children. The story of the drama was that
> of a family—a father, mother, and two children. One child gets shot
> and killed by the SLA. The remaining child—in the drama, he was of
> school age, still a child—then decides to join the movement. In the
> drama, the mother resists and begs her remaining child not to join the
> movement, saying she only has one child left. The mother is hysterical.
> Then the father speaks. He is calm and rational, although also very sad.
> He talks to the mother, saying that the correct thing for them to do is to
> give their remaining child to the LTTE. (HRW 2004b, 23–24)

Through such dramas, the LTTE teaches children that it is their obligation to join the struggle and that good families will support their decisions to join.

Extremist forms of religion also play a prominent role in children's socialization. In the same way that the Crusades had attracted many Christian children into war, militant forms of Islam call many youths to jihad.
The same happened in Afghanistan under the Taliban. And during the
U.S. occupation of Iraq in 2003, youths in Baghdad who had never before been fighters felt called to join the jihad against the occupying U.S.
forces and other outsiders (Wessells 2003). Extreme religious ideologies
enable youths and adults to rationalize violence as moral, making it easier to kill. By imbuing the fighting with divine sanction, these ideologies
encourage young people to sacrifice themselves and to become martyrs
who will reap eternal rewards and become legendary figures among their
people. The fact that children find meaning and purpose in violence
challenges views that see youth violence and terrorism as senseless and
irrational (Boyden 1994).

Poverty

Children often cite poverty as one of the primary considerations in their
decision to join an armed group (Delap 2005). A Colombian boy who
had joined the paramilitaries when he was 14 explained,

> After school I was a baker's assistant. It was hard work and paid badly. I
> went to work on a farm but the work was hard too, so finally I joined
> the paras. I had friends inside. It paid 300,000 [US$100] a month. It
> seemed like an easier life. (HRW 2003e, 41)

Many children in destitute war zones are unemployed, so the promise of a paying job lures many into soldiering. Unfortunately, child soldiers seldom receive the pay they were promised.

When children are paid, they often use the money to support their families. A Cambodian boy who had enlisted at age 13 said, "I send most of the money I am paid each month back home. To this day I have never admitted to my family that I am in the army—I am too afraid that they would force me to return home. How would I provide for them?" (UNICEF 2003, 31).

Although most poor children do not join armed groups, it is understandable that poverty places children at risk of soldiering. Poverty is widely regarded as a root cause of many armed conflicts, and it interacts with and amplifies the impact of most of the factors discussed above. By increasing family stresses, poverty increases the risk of family violence, which in turn often leads children to join armed groups. Poverty also increases the sense of powerlessness, boosting the lure of the uniform and gun. Poverty keeps many poor children out of school because they have to work to meet basic needs, and children who are out of school are at increased risk of recruitment. Although poverty does not by itself cause child soldiering, it exerts a significant impact through interaction with other influences.

Multiple Causation

This interactive view highlights the fact that children's choices to join armed groups seldom reflect only one motive. Children may choose to join because they are beaten at home, tired of doing hard work at a low-paying job, and long for training they cannot attain through school. In this respect, it is inappropriate to single out any particular risk or set of risks as "the cause of soldiering." The causes of soldiering are contextual, vary across individuals, and are embedded in wider systems of exploitation and violence.

Multiple influences also affect the choices of young people in contexts that are not clearly defined war zones. For example, the United States and the United Kingdom are not war zones, as typically defined, yet in both countries large numbers of military recruits come from the ranks of the poor, the marginalized, and the powerless. Youths who have no way to obtain a university education or a job that pays a living wage may see the military as their best path to these ends and to becoming somebody. Although both countries have signed and ratified the Optional Protocol on Children and Armed Conflict, this instrument legalizes the recruitment of people who are over 16 years of age so long as they have parental consent and do not participate in combat. Many youths in both countries enlist in the military as a way to access opportunities they do not enjoy in civilian life. It is a bitter irony that teen recruitment occurs in some of the wealthiest countries and owes to the same patterns of relative deprivation and lack of positive life options visible in the world's war zones and corners of destitution.

3

Inside Armed Groups

A child's entry into an armed group marks a profound life transition. Separated from parents and the supports of family and friends, child recruits enter a new world governed by strict military rules, harsh discipline, multiple hardships, and frequent exposure to deaths. It is a world full of risks—attack, exploitation, disease—and the child's survival is very much at stake. The multitude of hardships include deprivations of freedom, grueling marches, heavy labor, shortages of food and water, and health problems. This social world is a culture of violence, because violence saturates daily activities, children face constant danger, and the armed group deliberately uses violence as a means of achieving its objectives.

Adaptation to life in an armed group entails a process of resocialization (Schafer 2004) that may reshape behavior, roles, values, and identities. In its extreme form, the process involves both taking apart and remaking the child. Although child soldiers are sometimes portrayed as having been programmed or brainwashed, this term can be misleading since child soldiers undergo self-guided, internal changes in adapting to their new situation. To survive, children often have to submit to group rules and accept their new situation. In doing so, they may commit unspeakable acts that their morals and values would have prohibited in civilian life. Cut off from their previous lives, they learn to put their past behind them and reconstruct themselves in the context of the armed group. Most children will become conditioned to violence and death, experiencing as normal what most people would regard as abnormal. Many learn to embrace military codes of honor, carve out new identities as fighters and assume names such as "Rambo," and become reluctant to leave the armed group. Those who joined an armed group willingly may experience the group as their new family and find meaning in the group's activities. However, resocialization does not invariably transform children's values. Many children, particularly abductees, actively resist full resocialization, shunning soldiers' identities and looking for opportunities to escape. Even abductees, however, may learn to view the armed group as their source of protection and survival.

The resocialization process takes different forms, depending on the context and the mode of entry into the armed group. Fearing the escape of abducted recruits, armed groups may use terror and brutality as modalities of social control. For child recruits who had joined in hopes of liberating their people, the resocialization process might rely more on political propaganda and appeals to engage in correct behavior on behalf of a higher cause. Politically engaged children who see themselves as fighting a jihad or a liberation struggle may contribute to the group's political narratives of freedom and social transformation. Resocialization is not only something done to the child but a process of reciprocal influence between the child and the group. Children are political actors, and their life inside an armed group both stirs and gives expression to their political consciousness.

However resocialization occurs, it takes place over time and across diverse contexts. Typically it begins with training and continues as children move into various roles within the armed group. For many soldiers it extends into combat, which both adult and child soldiers universally describe as one of the most transformative experiences of their lives. For all, it includes some measure of adaptation to a system of violence in which extreme violence is normalized and the specter of one's own death is a constant companion.

Subjugation and Obedience

When children enter armed groups, they frequently receive "training," a euphemism often obscuring a regime of brutality and psychological manipulation. Typically the training agenda is not to develop military or survival skills but to break children's will and to achieve high levels of dominance and control. Not uncommonly, forced participation in atrocities provides the rite of initiation into an armed group.

Baptism by Fire

Killing is the method many armed groups use to cut child recruits off from their former lives, rupturing their bonds with family and community. In Sierra Leone, the RUF abducted children and forced them to kill neighbors or family members in full sight of other villagers. A boy who had been 16 at the time told me:

> The rebels attacked my village—all the huts were burned and many people were killed. The RUF rounded up those who lived. Then they took some young boys to go with them. They said they would kill us if we did not go. They gave me a rifle and told me to kill this woman . . . She was my relative [aunt] and I didn't want to hurt her. They told me to shoot her or I would be shot. So I shot her . . . I did it to survive.

This tactic of forcing children to kill relatives or other people they know while family and community members watch has enormous psychological potency. Such children realize that their communities, and possibly their own families, now view them as killers and may attack them if they attempt to return home. Some armed groups use this as a strategy to reduce the chances that child soldiers will attempt to escape.

Forced participation in killing is also a way to harden new child recruits to violence and make the horrific seem normal. A boy who had been taken by the LRA in northern Uganda told how escapees were dealt with:

> One boy tried to escape and was caught, tied up, and marched back to camp. All the recruits from the various companies were told that we were never going home, that we were fighting now with the LRA so as a symbol of our pledge to fight on, this boy would be killed and we would help. Soldiers then laid the boy on the ground and stabbed him three times with a bayonet until the blood began seeping from the wounds. Then the new recruits approached the boy and beat him on the chest. Each one had a turn and could only stop once the blood from the body splashed up on to you. This boy was sixteen years old. We were beating him with sticks, each recruit was given a stick. (HRW 2003b, 8)

This savage practice makes use of well-established psychological principles that through progressive exposure to violence and removal of personal responsibility for killing, even normal people can become effective killers (Staub 1989; Waller 2002). No child was forced to deliver an extreme, decisive blow, so each child was enabled to believe that he or she only hit the boy. Because it was uncertain who had dealt the death blow, no child had to deal with the thought he or she had been the killer. The children also could absolve themselves of responsibility by reminding themselves that they were following orders and that if they disobeyed, they would be next.

Subjugation and Control

Training is very much about transforming children who had previously been relatively autonomous civilians into soldiers who subjugate themselves to the group rules. All armed groups demand compliance, since breaking the rules (for instance, by making noise while moving through enemy territory) can jeopardize the entire group. More to the point, breaking the rules challenges the group's hierarchical command structure. Universally, armed groups subjugate recruits through a process designed to break their sense of autonomy and the sanctity of life, tear them away from their previous lives, and establish high degrees of control.

Subjugation typically occurs through a process of teaching rules that are enforced through increasing levels of punishment and brutality. In Angola, a 14-year-old girl, whom UNITA had recruited, described the punishment for speaking against UNITA.

> You couldn't say anything. They would immediately say that if you spoke against them you spoke against the party. So whenever a party meeting was held you might hear that some woman had spoken against the party and had been summoned to the meeting to be tried. If it were necessary to beat her at the place, she was beaten. And if they said there would be 10 for 10 then there were 20. That is, two men beating her. Each one with a stick . . . Even if you are pregnant they'll beat you around here—they'll dig a hole. They put you in the hole. They put your belly in the hole, and will beat you about the thighs and legs. (CCF/Angola, 2005)

UNITA's strict prohibition against questioning them, enforced by harsh punishments, successfully squashed dissenting views, giving the party full control over child soldiers.

A common practice is to administer stiffer punishments for more severe infractions, though the penalties and the rules vary by context and armed group. Some armed groups allow sexual relations between group members; others regard this as a severely punishable offense. Commanders might see their graded system of punishment as rational, but child recruits may feel overwhelmed by the frequency of punishment. Said a 14-year-old boy in the Burmese army,

> Sometimes they beat people, and sometimes they punished them with very hard work. I was beaten many times, about twenty times in five months of training. Because I didn't understand their instructions, punch, kick, hit with sticks, they beat us in many ways. (HRW 2002, 60)

How children experience the punishment depends on the conditions of their entry into the armed group. Children taken by force typically view the punishments as being as unjustified as their abduction had been. A boy abducted by the LRA described the senseless violence meted out by commanders.

> As we continued on the endless marches, I got bad blisters on my bare feet. Thorns embedded in the bottom of my feet became infected. Eventually, I could no longer keep up and the commander who had initially abducted me told me I was useless as I could not walk. He turned away and then two soldiers, in full uniform, approached and started beating me with the heavy ends of their RPG's (rocket propelled grenades). I was repeatedly beaten on the head and body and left for dead. Two days later, a local farmer found me. (HRW 2003b, 9)

In contrast, children who joined the armed group by choice might accept its ideology and rules, viewing punishment for bad decisions as justified. A boy from Papua New Guinea who had been part of the liberation group BRA told of his punishment at age 16:

> I was beaten only once. They told us not to go home and drink alcohol. I went home and got drunk and fired my gun. We were told not to use our weapons in the villages. Some BRAs heard it and reported me . . . The commander, in his 30s, threatened to kill me if I ever did it again. The whole section beat me up. I broke a rib. I accept it. I know it was my mistake. (UNICEF 2003, 42)

Commanders understand the desire of many children to run away and return home to their parents. Typically armed groups inflict the most severe punishments on escapees, both to deter escape and to prevent leaks of information about the group's location or vulnerabilities. Although many escapees received the death penalty, commanders may use other forms of punishment, such as the torture one boy witnessed in the Burmese army:

> If they [escapees] were caught, they tortured them, they put them in the leg stocks and then poked them in the legs with knives and they bled. They poked each leg about five times . . . The youngest one they did that to was twelve years old. He was afraid and cried very loudly, and he called out "I'll never do it again." They beat him as well. After they caught him they tortured him like that, and then left him in the leg stocks for fifteen days. (HRW 2002, 71)

Similarly, an Angolan boy described how commanders dealt harshly with escapees:

> Escapees who were found were generally killed. They were tied to a post and all the troops would be called to watch. They were killed, and the killer had sometimes to drink the victim's blood. The blood was said to be good for the person not to feel remorse. (Honwana 1998, 40)

Forcing recruits to drink blood is a potent way to blunt the emotions children might feel at the sight of blood and to harden recruits to bloodshed and killing.

Severe punishment also applies to infractions, such as falling asleep on watch, that could jeopardize the group. Of the Colombian paramilitaries, which have notoriously harsh discipline, a boy said:

> The organization has tough discipline. There are great commanders, but there are others who love to kill. Those guys are real assassins. If one of them catches you asleep on guard duty, he'll cut your throat there and then so that you never wake up. (HRW 2003e, 75)

Isolation

To control new child recruits, armed groups isolate children from their familiar surroundings and supports, shrinking their world and sealing them off from public view. Most armed groups disallow family visits, which could lead homesick children to seek protection through the family and its networks. For forcibly recruited children, family separation is one of the most painful experiences, as attested to by this 13-year-old Burmese boy:

> When I arrived there the other trainees said, "You can't contact your family." I just wanted to go home and study. I missed my family. I cried twice each night. I thought my parents must be thinking "Where is our son? Maybe he's dead." The other children also cried and said, "I want to go home to my family." (HRW 2002, 66)

In many armed groups, crying itself is a punishable offense. Cut off from their family and feeling overwhelmed by their painful situation, some child soldiers commit suicide (HRW 2002).

Armed groups do not deny permission for home visits only to abductees. They also frequently deny such permission to children who had joined by choice. Armed groups fear that these children will regret their decision and use home visits as escape opportunities. Furthermore, children who continue to see family and friends will remember their former lives and be less willing to see themselves as soldiers whose future lies with the armed group. For similar reasons, armed groups often isolate child soldiers from civilians in nearby communities. In Mozambique, leaders of the Mozambican National Resistance (RENAMO) prohibited soldiers from mingling with local populations, both to maintain tight control over the soldiers and to shroud the armed group in a powerful mystique (Wilson 1992).

To increase child soldiers' isolation, groups such as the LRA regularly lie, saying the Ugandan army will capture escapees and mistreat or execute them. This message persuades many children that their greatest chances of survival lie in staying with the LRA. Lacking contact with the outside world, the children have no way of testing the veracity of the LRA messages. Isolation increases both the child's dependency on the armed group and its control over them. Isolation also seals the children off from public view, reducing the armed groups' accountability.

Isolation tactics also apply within armed groups. Within the LRA, for example, talking with other new recruits is a punishable offense. Youths in Sierra Leone who had been with the RUF have told me that they were not permitted to discuss their former lives as civilians but were encouraged to discuss only the movement and the RUF strategies and tactics. In Angola, a girl whom UNITA had abducted told how talk about the past was monitored and controlled:

> When you are speaking, sometimes they hear what you are saying
> about your past, how you lived, then they say that you are preparing to
> escape and they control you all the time. We knew because when you
> talk about the past they stay alert listening: these girls have a program
> to escape. We saw that they don't like when we talk about the past.
> (Stavrou 2005, 29)

For UNITA, constant listening and discouragement of talking about
one's past were means of ensuring the group's control over recruits and
preventing their escape.

Obedience

In armed groups, commanders often take extreme steps to ensure high
levels of obedience, the central mechanism of resocialization. The Colombian opposition group FARC-EP prohibited sexual relations among
recruits except by a commander's approval. A 12-year-old Colombian
girl who had joined the FARC-EP recounted how she was forced to administer the group's punishment for a friend's sexual activity:

> I had a friend, Juanita, who got into trouble for sleeping around. We
> had been friends in civilian life and we shared a tent together. The
> commander said that it didn't matter that she was my best friend. She
> had committed an error and had to be killed. I closed my eyes and fired
> the gun, but I didn't hit her. So I shot again. The grave was right nearby.
> I had to bury her and put dirt on top of her. The commander said "You
> did very well. Even though you started to cry, you did well. You'll have
> to do this again many more times, and you'll have to learn not to cry."
> (HRW 2003e, 73)

Children forced to commit such acts may react in a variety of ways, depending on their temperament, resilience, and dominant coping strategies. Initially most children experience a mixture of disgust, guilt, and
self-contempt. These normal reactions reflect the strength of children's
deeply held civilian morals and social commitments not to murder or to
hurt friends. Faced with the magnitude of their actions, children may
also rationalize their actions by telling themselves, "I didn't want to do
it. I had to follow orders or I would be killed." Such rationalizations,
which in this case are accurate, reassure children they have not become

bad people and assuage their potentially overwhelming guilt. Still other children may see such acts as surreal, as if they occurred in a dream world, and they may feel quite split off or dissociated from them. This splitting process is a normal self-protective reaction to the strain induced by the enormous gap between children's previous morals and the atrocity they have been forced to commit.

Commanders, however, seek to break these humane reactions by hardening children to killing and achieving unquestioning obedience. The agenda behind forced killings such as this is to test the child's obedience, forcing her into a "kill or be killed" mentality that breeds complete obedience and also prepares her psychologically for more killing. In this manner, child soldiers learn to devalue human life and to dehumanize themselves, relinquishing their independence and accepting their violations of previously embraced moral sanctions against killing a friend. Forced into a new moral space, children put aside previously learned moral codes and sanctions against killing. Inside the armed group, killing is normal and the core values are self-preservation and following orders. Over time, most child soldiers adapt to these new values, learning to live in a revised moral space that stands their former morals on their head. The children's former values might not be lost so much as suspended, a point we will revisit in Chapter 6. In light of these inner changes, one sees obedience not only as adherence to external authority but also as an internal process of accepting one's subjugation and adapting one's morals and values to fit the new context.

A desire to survive is one of the main reasons child soldiers obey commanders. However, their obedience is also rooted in socialization and cultural processes antedating entry into the armed group. In Mozambique, the armed group RENAMO gave child soldiers who had reached the final stages of training a ceremony similar to traditional rites of passage (Boothby, Crawford, and Halperin 2006). Psychologically, this tactic forges strong allegiance to the armed group, equating his role and identity as a man with belonging to the armed group.

Highly patriarchal societies prize obedience to the father, bestow on him considerable power and authority, and treat his word as unquestionable. Living in a dangerous environment, vulnerable children may tend to follow the patriarchal norm, seeing obedience to a powerful, domineering adult as offering protection (Bhabha 2005). Armed groups exploit this cultural tendency by promoting themselves as a surrogate family and invoking father imagery. In Liberia, child soldiers who fought on the side of the government regarded Charles Taylor as their "pappy" (Ellis 1999). In Mozambique, the competing armed groups RENAMO and FRELIMO (the Mozambican Liberation Front) both cultivated father images portraying them as father of the nation and, by implication, of the soldiers in their units (Schafer 2004). A former FRELIMO combatant explained, "People think of the government as a father because he does everything. He protects, gives orders, forbids certain things, and many other things" (Schafer 2004, 93).

Obedience may also reflect a psychological process called Stockholm syndrome, wherein captives identify with their captors. The process is named for a 1973 bank robbery in which four hostages who had initially been fearful of their captors developed a strong association with their robbers, even fearing rescuers who had come to help them. This process occurs in situations in which the captives experience a strong fear of death and have no way of escaping. That their captors, who could kill them, spare their lives, creates a strong sense of gratitude in the captives. Isolated from the outside world, they come to see their captors as good people or even as saviors, forging bonds of identification with them. A similar process may affect child soldiers, who recognize that the armed group could kill them at any moment but who see particular commanders as having saved them. The resulting gratitude can create a strong sense of loyalty and obedience to the commander.

Identification with the captor may occur through means other than Stockholm syndrome. By identifying with the commander, children gain a sense of power that they are otherwise denied. Identification can also have instrumental aspects, since children come to believe that if they do what the commander wants, they might get additional rewards. Commanders can further amplify this loyalty by providing rewards that previously were unavailable to the child. These processes, backed by survival fears, typically instill high levels of obedience.

Training and Preparation

Armed groups give child and adult soldiers the same kind of training, using a mixture of physical and psychological means. Often children learn to drill collectively, assemble and disassemble automatic weapons, and shoot weapons. Some armed groups train children specifically for combat, exposing them to conditions of live ammunition. A Liberian boy who had fought with the LURD received two months of training: "There we learned to fire, to take cover and how to kill. We were made to crawl under barbed wire while they were shooting at us, we were forced to advance towards the gun fire. This was to make us brave" (HRW 2004a, 19). Harsh physical training is often part of the regimen and may involve long marches and carrying heavy loads. For abducted children, this training occurs not in safe camps but on contested ground, with fear as a constant companion.

In many situations, training is cursory and does not prepare children either to protect themselves or to achieve significant combat objectives. In northern Uganda, the LRA has since 2002 followed a pattern of abducting younger children, who receive little training. According to one formerly abducted boy:

> The training lasted about one week, we were shown how to load, shoot, and fire. Following the training I was given my own submachine gun and a pair of military trousers. I fought twice with the LRA. The first time we attacked a military detachment in Moyo district. We suffered heavy losses, and many of the LRA soldiers were killed. In the second battle, we laid a successful ambush on a passing UPDF convoy. (HRW 2003b, 13)

Inadequate training is often the norm. Said a Philippine boy who had joined an armed group at age 14: "There was no formal training. If we were needed in combat, we were just told to shoot" (UNICEF 2003, 38). A boy from Papua New Guinea who had joined when he was 10 said, "I was given one week of [advice]—they taught me to shoot, to make a gun, to use a grenade, to make ambush. They had to share guns in the section" (UNICEF 2003, 38). This pattern of inadequate training places children at severe risk of injury and death. Unable to protect themselves properly and knowing little about how to deal with land mines and other hazards, child soldiers are often treated as expendable.

The training itself often is deadly. In Burma, boys were forced to participate in live-fire exercises, sometimes with deadly results:

> We called it "Chay Mone Yay," fighting the enemy. We had to cross obstacles and crawl on the ground. We had to lay down because someone

was shooting over our heads. Three trainees were killed by the shooting because they stood up. (HRW 2002, 62)

Conveniently, the training overlooks many young people's inability to appreciate fully the risks they face and to comprehend their own mortality.

In some situations, however, children liked their training and valued their newly acquired skills. A Colombian boy who had joined the FARC-EP at age 15 spoke of his training with pride:

My training was four-and-a-half months. I learned how to use a compass, how to attack a police post, how to carry out an ambush, and the handling of weapons. By the end I was using an AK-47, a Galil, an R-15, mortars, pineapple grenades, M-26 grenades, and tatucos (multiple grenade launchers). (HRW 2003e, 62)

A boy from East Timor who had joined the liberation struggle at age 17 said:

The good thing that I learned from Falantil was about discipline. For example, the discipline of how to live under military command and how to respect each other. The commander always treated us well, for example, he taught me the right way and wrong way for soldiers to behave toward the people. (UNICEF 2003, 39)

Positive views of training are probably enhanced by ideological preparation, which armed groups use frequently to justify the armed group's struggle and present romantic images of revolutionary heroes and martyrs. As a 17-year-old Colombian girl described her training:

They teach us history: the history of Che Guevara or Jacobo Arenas or Marxism-Leninism every day from 3:00 to 4:00 p.m. We read. There isn't any math or science taught, only politics, weaponry, and the FARC's rules. Before we go out to fight, there is a talk: "We are going out to defend Colombia, so that equality can come—to help the poor—so that the rich don't take from the poor." (HRW 2003e, 62)

Political Education

Political reeducation might also be used to convert recruits taken by force. Talking in a group of ex-combatants in Sierra Leone, a 25-year-old who had been abducted at age 17 told me, "They [the RUF] attacked the mines and captured us. They said they wanted to liberate the country from poor education and poverty. I got convinced because I knew these things were lacking . . . I played by their rules." His report evoked enthusiastic head nods from other former combatants, one of whom added, "I didn't believe in fighting the government at first, but they convinced me. It sounds stupid now, but I really believed them and felt motivated by what they said." For some recruits, the training creates a political awakening that repositions young people with regard to the conflict and instills a sense of commitment to a higher cause. The propaganda and brainwashing methods used by armed groups is particularly likely to have an impact in a context of isolation. Robbed of competing sources of information and shown models of revolutionary fervor on a daily basis, young recruits tend to believe what they hear inside the group.

Political education and combat training may also occur through the use of media showing macho war images and demonstrating basic tactics. For example, armed groups in Sierra Leone and Liberia used Rambo films such as *First Blood* to pump up young recruits for combat and to illustrate basic jungle warfare tactics. Many RUF recruits, who fought in part because they believed the government had failed to provide basic education, found meaning in the film's messages of righteous indignation over social exclusion and violence as a means of correcting an unjust social order. Mirroring the Rambo image, RUF youths often donned Rambo-like headbands or adopted Rambo-based nicknames such as "bad Rambo" (Richards 1996).

Training is not only a set of activities imposed on recruits but also a process of internal restructuring of recruits' beliefs, attitudes, and motives. This internal process entails resocialization through interactions with others and through recruits' own decisions made in context. Children are active participants who help shape each other's beliefs and discourses as the training proceeds. Discussing the purpose and meaning of the struggle, they debate strategies and analyze how to treat civilian populations, among other things. This amounts to nonformal peer education that produces change through both internal and external means. Internally, changes in attitudes and behavior can occur as children develop new understanding of what the conflict is about and whether it is justified. This understanding guides their decisions about what their own role should be. Externally, strong pressures for compliance are brought to bear on child recruits. Children and teenagers everywhere are susceptible to peer pressure, but this pressure becomes even more potent in the narrow confines of the armed group, whose members children depend upon for their survival.

Behavior Modification

Commanders frequently use behavior modification methods of reward and punishment to change children's behavior and sculpt new attitudes and values. Typically, children who show exceptional motivation and obedience receive command posts with privileges such as increased access to food or health care. As children engage increasingly in behavior the armed group deems desirable, they undergo attitudinal changes that "justify" or are consistent with the behavior. In some cases, the nature of the rewards has greater influence than ideological instruction. In Sierra Leone, for example, one teenager told me, "When I was trained, I had a shirt and a gun—where else could I get these things?" For this boy, the rewards of shirt and gun reduced deprivation and bestowed a sense of power and respect unattainable in civilian life.

Behind these "pull" aspects of training, however, lie an omnipresent fear and threat of death that pervade life in an armed group. These "push" factors simultaneously induce behavior change and serve the armed group's agenda of steeling young recruits to killing and death. In Colombian paramilitaries, a standard training tactic is to force recruits to watch the killing of captives and even to participate in the killing. One boy described this:

> They bring the people they catch, guerrillas and robbers, to the training course. My squad had to kill three people. After the first one was killed, the commander told me that the next day I'd have to do the killing. I was stunned and appalled. I had to do it publicly, in front of the whole company, fifty people. I had to shoot him in the head. I was trembling. Afterwards, I couldn't eat. I'd see the person's blood. For weeks, I had a hard time sleeping . . . Some of the victims cried and screamed. The commanders told us we had to learn how to kill. (HRW 2003e, 64)

Gruesome atrocities committed against captives may also be part of what new recruits witness. A 16-year-old Liberian boy told of the horrendous mistreatment of one captive:

One boy from the government side was caught near the Broadville Bridge; he had been wounded in the leg and unable to retreat. LURD caught him and tied him up attached to a stick. They then cut off his toes, fingers, nose and ears. Then they cut off his private parts and left him to bleed to death. They later threw his body in the river. (HRW 2004a, 22)

In addition to numbing recruits to violence, the practice of torturing and executing captives awakens children's fears of what will happen if they are captured and boost motivation to stay with the armed group.

To summarize, training awakens a process of internal evolution and adaptation complementary to the external processes of subjugation and terror. Over time, many children, though not all, break with their former lives and redefine themselves in a social context that prizes values, attitudes, and behaviors antithetical to those of civilian life. Significant individual differences exist in how rapidly children are resocialized or which experiences are most impactful in the process. Children who have a strong capacity to compartmentalize may successfully maintain their civilian identity and sense of right and wrong despite the training. For many children, however, the longer they stay with an armed group, the more likely they are to internalize the values and behaviors of the armed group (Boothby and Knudsen 2000). In this respect, a high priority should be to demobilize child soldiers at the earliest possible stage.

Children's Roles

During and following training, child soldiers perform diverse roles, such as porter, laborer, spy, cook, medic, bodyguard, and combatant. Contrary to popular conceptions, many child soldiers never fight, and many neither carry their own weapon nor know how to use one. Children's roles vary according to the context and the children's characteristics, such as their gender, age, size, and skill levels. For example, young children are often used as spies because they are small and able to move freely without arousing suspicions.

The diversity of child soldiers' roles is best shown through their own words.

[My jobs were] cooking, staying in the camp to guard, patrolling for three to four hours in the morning. Sometimes they sent me to go checking tracks, impressions in dust or look for food. [Papua New Guinea—joined when he was about 9, now 19] (UNICEF 2003, 44)

I never fought, I was a bodyguard for a general. Armed with an AK-47, I protected the general and his house to prevent other soldiers from looting him. I also had to sweep and clean, cut the brush and carry goods. [Liberia—boy who served LURD] (HRW 2004a, 24)

They could see that I was able, that I was active and alert in doing things. I started to like guns and I was good at taking them apart and putting them together and even repairing them . . . What they trained me to do was to shoot at 500, 600, or 700 meters with a rifle with a telescopic sight. Not everyone had access to a weapon like that. It impressed me and I began to like it. But it stopped being fun when I had to kill people. [Colombia—boy trained to be a sniper] (HRW 2003e, 63)

I never directly fought, I would work behind the lines. There were many people killed, so I had to do what I could to survive. I would just move with the forces, helping them carry looted items. As we advanced, civilians would flee their homes. We would go into the houses and steal whatever we could, bikes, money, radios, mattresses, and many other things. I would have to tote the goods after a raid. [Liberian boy who had been a looter and porter with LURD] (HRW 2004a, 24)

Children's roles within armed groups are highly fluid and contextual, as children may perform multiple roles in the same day. Children also juggle multiple roles simultaneously, as girls may carry their babies on their backs, performing the tasks of mothering while cooking or gathering firewood.

Role Evolution

Children's roles are far from static and may evolve alongside changes in the situation and the children's skill levels. For example, food scarcity may require nearly everyone in an armed group, including children, to spend significant amounts of time searching for food or looting. Similarly, the deaths of many soldiers may lead the armed group to use as combatants children who had formerly been porters or security guards. During such rapid role transitions, children are at heightened risk because they lack the skills needed to defend themselves. In some situations, role change and skills development go hand in hand. It is not uncommon for child soldiers to serve initially as porters and to practice military drill and tactics using wooden weapons or unloaded rifles to save ammunition. Subsequently, having learned how to clean and fire weapons, they may assume new roles as combatants or security guards.

Role evolution, however, is not invariably forced by outside pressures. Even in highly coercive and difficult circumstances, children continue to be actors and to make choices. In some cases they manage to say no to lower-level commanders. One young man from Sierra Leone, whom the RUF had abducted at age 16, told me:

> They [the RUF] captured me on my father's farm and took me away. I was forced to leave this area. They gave me a gun and forced me to go and loot. Also I was forced to carry all the loot, and if I refused [I] would be flogged or shot. We had food only sometimes . . . The leader told us to beat women and saw it [watched us] with his eyes. Also the leader told us to have sex with women older than your mother. I told him "no" and was flogged and made to do hard work. (Wessells and Jonah 2006, 35)

This example serves as a poignant reminder that not all child soldiers, even following their subjugation, robotically obey all orders. In saying no, the soldier suffered loss of stature in the eyes of his commanders, who subsequently would be less likely to assign him to preferred tasks. Although resisting orders is dangerous, children often develop keen sensitivities regarding which orders can be broken without invoking the death penalty. Furthermore, they may retain a sense of limits grounded in moral sensitivities they had developed previously as civilians. The armed groups' processes of subjugation and control, although highly influential, are not perfect, as highly resilient children often find ways of retaining elements of individuality and dignity.

Groups such as the LRA in northern Uganda afford no latitude for negotiating one's role. Nevertheless, children's agency often expresses itself, as even children who are trusted fighters may quietly watch for escape opportunities. Much remains to be learned about how children negotiate their roles within armed groups and how their decisions affect their ability to survive and make meaning in very difficult circumstances. Children's agency is a double-edged sword, though, as some children deliberately seek combat and find meaning through wielding the power of the gun.

Child Combatants

The lives of child combatants exhibit significant diversity, cautioning against stereotypes of child combatants as bloodthirsty predators or innocents herded onto the killing fields. Some child combatants fight reluctantly, kill only when necessary, and constantly look for escape opportunities, whereas others learn to enjoy combat and redefine their identities as soldiers. A small minority become hardened perpetrators who relish the sight and smell of blood and initiate or participate willingly in atrocities that no one ordered them to commit. Also, child combatants are exposed to different "doses" of fighting, which can range from participation in one or two skirmishes to repeated, high-intensity firefights. Reintegration efforts need to take this diversity into account and to accommodate the significant individual differences within the category "child combatants."

One commonality, however, is that all child combatants have been forged by exposure to combat. In some contexts, children have been the first soldiers sent to the front. For example, in Liberia the government's small-boy units were the first to enter the fighting. One member of such a unit said, "We were many, plenty small boys, from ten, eleven and twelve. You would be sent to the front first. You go and get killed and then the next one takes your place, it never ended" (HRW 2004a, 21).

Combat

Intense fear is an instinctive reaction to the danger, fury, and chaos of combat. Even adult soldiers in well-trained armies are gripped by fear in their initial combat experience. Few child soldiers have either the training or the readiness of adult soldiers in the armies of developed countries. Lacking adults' relatively advanced capacities for self-regulation and emotional control, most children exposed to combat initially feel a combination of terror and paralysis. A Colombian boy described his first combat exposure, a FARC-EP attack on a police station, at age 13:

> Lots of guerrillas were killed. I was terrified. I cried during the attack. There were helicopters flying over us. I hid in a ditch. I fired a few

shots without aiming. There was another attack on a police post when I had to go out in front shooting. I was scared. All fourteen of the police were killed. Seven of them died in the fight and seven gave themselves up and were executed. I saw it all. (HRW 2003e, 79)

A Burmese boy also reported feeling terror in his initial combat experience at age 12:

I was afraid that first time. The section leader ordered us to take cover and open fire. There were seven of us, and seven or ten of the enemy. I was too afraid to look, so I put my face in the ground and shot my gun up at the sky. I was afraid their bullets would hit my head. I fired two magazines, about forty rounds. I was afraid that if I didn't fire the section leader would punish me. (HRW 2002, 83)

In initial combat exposure, a desire to survive and fear of punishment from the commander motivate most children to fire their weapons, even if they do not take aim.

Children's fear, however, rapidly gives way to adaptation. One Burmese boy said of his first combat episode, "I was very afraid and didn't shoot," but of his second fight he said, "I wasn't afraid this time. I fired about forty rounds, and I was happy to shoot" (HRW 2002, 84). Rapid adaptation owes in part to intimidation by the commanders, who often punish fearful soldiers. Cognitive factors can also promote rapid adaptation. Following the first fight, children might realize fully that they had been in a kill-or-be-killed situation and plan to protect themselves next time. An Indonesian boy who had joined an armed group at age 16 said, "The first time I was also scared and thought that it was inhumane. But I wanted to be able to continue. Better that way than to be killed" (UNICEF 2003, 54). Children may also reflect on why they are fighting, awakening motives such as revenge that can help them manage their fear and subsequently fight more effectively.

To reduce children's fears and harden them to killing, commanders use cannibalistic practices such as forcing children to drink the blood of those who had been killed. Said a Colombian girl who had entered combat for the first time at age 12 while with the FARC-EP:

Seven weeks after I arrived there was combat. I was very scared. It was an attack on the paramilitaries. We killed about seven of them. They killed one of us. We had to drink their blood to conquer our fear. Only the scared ones had to do it. I was the most scared of all, because I was the newest and youngest. (HRW 2003e, 80)

Such barbaric practices force children to quiet their emotional reactions to seeing people killed and demolish their sense of the sanctity of life and their tendency to show respect for the dead. If barbarism fails, commanders may use drugs to steel children for combat.

Drug Use

Not all armed groups permit drug use, but many do allow, encourage, or even require it. In Sierra Leone, a boy who had joined the RUF at age 17 told me, "We smoked weed [marijuana] and took so many pills [amphetamines]. When we went into combat, we felt no fear—I mean no fear!" Similarly, an Angolan boy said, "To be fearless we often smoked traditional tobacco (liamba) . . . we also ate polvora (gun powder)" (Honwana 1998, 44). Commanders' frequent encouragement of drug use rings in this testimony from a Liberian boy:

> We smoke grass, cigarettes, *dugee* (tablets), cokis (mashed tablets in a powder). It all makes you brave to go on the front. The commanders give it out. When you take the tablets you can't sleep, it makes you hot in your body. Anytime you go on the frontline, they give it to you. Just got to do something to be strong because you don't want the feeling of killing someone. You need the drugs to give you the strength to kill. (HRW 2004a, 29)

To ensure that troops are high on drugs, some commanders have forced children to use drugs. In Sierra Leone a male former RUF member told me, "Before we fight, the commander cuts us here [pointing to his and others' temples] and pack in brown brown [amphetamines]." Other former RUF members said that their leaders sometimes made incisions in children's pectoral muscles, packed drugs in, and covered the wound.

Drugs such as amphetamines, which may be mixed with alcohol and other substances, can induce recklessness and suspend normal inhibitions by impairing judgment and other cognitive functions. An East Timorese boy reported:

> I was in my house and [the militia] came to get me when they needed me—everyday—and they were drunk. I had to drink Tuak [palm wine]. They also drank blood. The older ones took capsules [angin gila, or "crazy dog" pills, which are amphetamines]. After they took

the pills they didn't remember anything they did and they went crazy. (UNICEF 2003, 42)

In some armed groups, taking drugs and then engaging in "crazy" behavior becomes a combat ritual through which young people demonstrate their machismo in a deadly mixture of fearlessness and uncontrolled violence. Villagers in Sierra Leone have told me that although they had always feared RUF attacks, they particularly dreaded the arrival of youths who were pumped up on drugs and had "that crazy look" in their eyes, which signaled they would kill everything in sight or commit mutilations such as cutting off people's arms or hands.

Spiritual "Protection"

In many war-torn countries, the belief in unseen spirits is part of local spirituality. Throughout sub-Saharan Africa, local people believe events in the visible world are caused by events in the invisible world of the ancestors. In later chapters we will see that local spiritual practices such as cleansing rituals and burial rites can aid former child soldiers' recovery and reintegration. Commanders, however, often use these practices for cruel purposes.

To increase their control, commanders often co-opt spiritual practices, using local spiritualists and their presumed magic to manipulate child soldiers (Delap 2005). In Liberia, LURD fighters displayed scars and charms believed to make them bulletproof. One boy explained, "These marks on my chest, they were put there to make me safe from bullets. This way, bullets would bounce off me. Once they were put there, I felt fine" (HRW 2004a, 28). Another Liberian boy said, "During the fighting, I was given a charm to wear around my neck, this was from a healer. In my dialect it is called a *bang*, this would protect me from bullets. It really worked, not against the shells but against the bullets" (HRW 2004a, 28).

In other countries, too, commanders exploit spiritual means of silencing children's fears. A boy from Papua New Guinea reported, "Before going on an operation, we said prayers. There were traditional rituals of cleansing with water and bush leaves by special men from a village. We would split banana trees and walk through them to give us protection" (UNICEF 2003, 52). In northern Uganda, where many people regard Joseph Kony as having spiritual powers inherited from his predecessor, Alice Lakwena, the LRA often used spiritual means to protect child combatants. For example, abducted girls were forced to participate in an egg ritual in which a leader dipped a raw egg in ashes and water and then drew a heart on recruits' chests and backs as well as a cross on the hands, shoulders, and foreheads. Presumably, the camouflage would protect them from bullets. However, breakage of the egg during the ritual would signify possession by evil spirits, leading the LRA to kill the person being marked (De Temmerman 2001).

Regardless of how people from outside such societies view these spiritual practices, local people frequently believe in them, and strong beliefs can influence behavior. Under the commander's control, spiritual practices such as bulletproofing offer a potent means of quieting children's fears and enabling them to enter the jaws of combat. One wonders how many commanders would be willing to undergo spiritual bulletproofing and then to step into a barrage of bullets.

Child Perpetrators

In many armed groups, children become perpetrators whom local people fear and loathe. For example, the Burmese army uses villagers as forced porters who must carry heavy loads, and child soldiers are expected to push them along, using brutality if necessary. One boy soldier reported: "I just said 'Go faster, go faster.' I didn't beat or kick them, but some did. If they couldn't go, they beat and kicked them down the mountainside" (HRW 2002, 88). In other cases, Burmese soldiers destroy villages as part of a scorched earth policy intended to terrorize people and squash resistance. Child soldiers in the Burmese army have participated regularly in the burning of homes and destruction of property. Child soldiers may also engage in looting, which for many armed groups is the primary means of obtaining food and other necessities. In Sierra Leone, both the RUF and the CDF looted villages, taking food, animals, money, and belongings. These practices create deep wounds in the community. After the fighting stops, a significant barrier to children's reintegration is the searing memory of the children's attacks, destruction of homes, and theft of villagers' food and property, which can include precious livestock as well as inanimate objects.

Child combatants also learn to be repeat killers who show scant mercy or remorse. In contrast to popular claims that only psychopathic children become killers, most evidence suggests that ordinary children, faced with the extraordinary circumstances of combat, are capable of learning to kill and to kill repeatedly. This raises important questions: How do ordinary children become killers? Having killed once, how do they deal with the enormous weight of what they have done and go on to kill again?

Although much remains to be learned in regard to these questions, five psychological processes are relevant. First is the will to survive. Being in a situation of kill or be killed, child soldiers' will to live usually trumps all other concerns. Second is obedience. Many children say they killed because they had to follow orders or suffer brutal punishment or death. Obedience contributed to the My Lai massacre, in which ordinary U.S. soldiers gunned down 120 unarmed villagers, including women and children, during the Vietnam War (Kelman and Hamilton 1989). Obedience enables killing by shifting responsibility to the person who issued the orders. Obedience enables the killer to say, "It is not my fault—I was only following orders," removing the burden of guilt that killing another person typically evokes. For children, obedience to an adult authority figure, who may be regarded as a surrogate father, can be a fundamental obligation and part of their social role.

Third is the normalization of violence. The more children see people being killed, the more they become desensitized and numbed to it. Repeated and progressive participation in violence enables participation in additional acts of violence (Staub 1989). Having killed once, it becomes easier to kill again. A Philippine girl who had joined an armed group at age 13 said, "I saw a 17-year-old girl cry and pray to God to forgive her for what she did. There were those who found it easier to kill after the first one. They got used to it" (UNICEF 2003, 53). Killing produces a host of emotional and cognitive changes that enable additional killing and blunt potentially inhibiting reactions such as disgust and guilt. The first act of killing may mark a turning point, as the child realizes he or she is no longer a person who has never killed and may now be viewed by others as a killer. Furthermore, the upside-down logic and morals of the armed group makes the abnormal seem normal, as killing and worse acts may occur on a daily basis. Having killed, and having seen others kill on a regular basis, children become less responsive to killing and may rationalize their own acts of killing by telling themselves, "I'm only doing what everyone else is doing" or "It's not such a big deal." Over time, children learn to regard killing—a capital offense in civilian life—as quite normal.

Some children's sense of the sanctity of life can be diminished or suspended by the normalization of violence. For example, members of small-boy units in Sierra Leone sometimes committed devastating atrocities, such as mutilations (HRW 1998), with no apparent feelings of guilt. In response to the question of how children deal with the enormity of what they have done, the answer might be that they don't, or at least that they don't while they remain inside the armed group. The armed group constitutes an alternate moral space in which the rules of war apply, killing is deemed acceptable, and children might not experience the same moral burden that they might experience in a civilian context. When they have left the armed group, entered a civilian moral space, and think back, however, they might be overwhelmed with guilt over what they have done.

The fourth psychological factor is the satisfaction derived from killing. Killing provides satisfaction for children who seek revenge for what the enemy did to them or their families. Inside the armed group, killing the enemy is the currency through which one demonstrates one's mettle. Commanders often reward children who have killed by giving them promotions or improved access to health care, food, women, and protection. Rewards may also flow to children's families. In Sri Lanka, for example, the families of young suicide bombers receive better homes and access to better jobs (Bloom 2005).

Killing may also be instrumental in earning child soldiers the respect of their peers, which matters enormously to teenagers everywhere. In some cases, killing is a means of establishing among peers that one is "bad" and therefore worthy of respect. In others, killing the enemy establishes that one is an effective combatant, providing an entry ticket into the inner circle of the armed group.

Fifth is ideology. As we have seen, many children join armed groups to participate in a liberation struggle or other political struggle, and most armed groups seek to make new recruits supportive of their cause. Child soldiers find meaning in violence and killing by viewing fighting as a legitimate instrument for achieving liberation, social justice, or religious redemption. Although they might not support acts of random violence, they might see killing the enemy as necessary and appropriate.

A Philippine boy who had joined the Moro Islamic Liberation Front (MILF) at age 13 said:

> It feels great to kill your enemy. The MILF does not initiate attacks. If the military didn't attack us, there will be no trouble. They are the ones who are really at fault. They deserve to be killed. The other children, they are happy too. They are not sad. I really do not regret killing. If they are your enemies, you can kill them. But if they are not your enemies, you shouldn't kill them. (UNICEF 2003, 52)

Seeing their fighting as just, child soldiers take pride in their ability to kill enemies, and they may be willing to martyr themselves for the higher purpose they support. Palestinian suicide bombers have included teenagers who not only were frustrated and angry over their domination by Israelis but also believed that their martyrdom would bring them spiritual rewards (Pape 2005; Rosen 2005). In Afghanistan and Iraq, too, many teenagers have been willing to martyr themselves to kill foreigners whom they perceive as occupying forces seeking to dominate Muslims.

Ideology also provides a moral buffer against feelings of guilt. Ideologies typically dehumanize the enemy and portray the conflict as a heroic contest between the good Us versus the evil Them. This division of the social world into good versus evil denies one's adversaries any moral standing or rights, excluding them from the moral universe (Opotow 1990). If one views the Other as less than human and as evil, and sees the conflict in black-and-white terms, killing becomes easier and seems justified. After all, what better way to improve the world and help protect one's group than by destroying evil? Children, particularly teenagers, have the capacity to reason and ponder moral issues in ways that transcend such Manichean dichotomies. However, their limited life experience and limited exposure to members of other groups, coupled with political or religious indoctrination and, in many cases, limited education, can make them more susceptible to leaders' ideological manipulation.

Although not all of these factors operate in every situation, numerous interacting factors enable normal children to kill repeatedly and without being overwhelmed by guilt and self-loathing. Acts of killing move children still farther into a new moral and social space where the old rules do not apply. In this space, many children construct new identities as soldiers, internalizing their transition from civilians to combatants.

Identity

Discussions of child soldiers' identities have tended to treat identity as static and monolithic, as if carved in stone. In fact, identity is fluid and constructed through dynamic interaction between the individual and members of society. Having observed role models such as peers, siblings, and teachers, children tell themselves who they are and then act in accord with what they have told themselves (Holland et al. 1998). Although their identities are self-understandings, they are shaped by and constructed with key people in the children's environment. If a girl who defines herself as being a "good student" has received a teacher's affirmation as a good student, both the girl and her peers tend to view her in that light. If, on the other hand, the same girl had regularly received feedback from teachers and peers that she is an average student, then she might redefine her identity. In this sense, people's identities are not individual things but are socially constructed through transactions with others. Over time, people's identities are defined by how they relate to others, how others regard them, and the meanings people assign to their roles and experiences. The fluid nature of identity is prominent in teenagers, who in many societies "try on" different identities as a means of constructing and understanding their place in the world.

Also, identity is not singular. Most people learn to have multiple, hopefully complementary, identities. One can be a mother and a physician, or an athlete and a community leader, for example. As people create different self-narratives and assume new roles, they construct new identities, negotiating them with the groups with whom they interact. Which identity is most salient depends on the context. At home, the mother identity is likely to be most salient, whereas in a clinic, the physician identity is likely to be most salient.

Many child soldiers, particularly abductees, never embrace fully soldiers' identities. Still, armed groups deliberately set out to change child soldiers' identities as a means of cutting them off from their previous lives and reducing attempts to escape. Often they do this by saying, "Now you are soldiers," requiring them to wear uniforms and other symbols of their identity, and subjugating them through brutality and control processes. Through political education, they also shape children's beliefs and values, enabling them to view the armed group's struggle as legitimate and to invest personally in it. Armed groups often succeed in remaking children's identities because of their skillful use of isolation, indoctrination, and systems of behavior modification.

Children also play an active role in constructing new identities as soldiers. This process is visible as children, particularly boys, assume a "combat name" based on the qualities they exhibit in combat. A 12-year-old Liberian boy who had fought with a small-boys unit in the government forces said:

> As a commander, I was in charge of nine others, four girls and five boys. We were used mostly for guarding checkpoints but also fighting. I shot my gun many times, I was wounded during World War I [a bloody battle in the recent Liberian war], shot in the leg. I was not afraid, when I killed LURD soldiers, I would laugh at them, this is how I got my nickname, "Laughing and Killing." (HRW 2004a, 20)

Liberian children also acquired nicknames such as "Ball Crusher," "Castrator," or Nut Bag Machine," based ominously on what they did to captured civilians and opponents. They also carved out their identities by means of distinctive dress or hairstyles. Often, children wore T-shirts emblazoned with the name of their unit, such as "Jungle Fire" or "Jungle Lion." In one unit, the "Buck Naked Unit," child soldiers went naked into combat as a way to scare opponents and civilians (HRW 2004a).

In Sierra Leone, too, boys took on combat names, like "Cock and Fire" and "Rambo." These names, many of which derived from Western war films, frequently embodied the machismo prized by teenage boys as proof of their manhood. In both Sierra Leone and Liberia, teenage boys deliberately cultivated an identity of being "bad" by wearing Rambo-style bandanas, flaunting rows of bullets slung over each shoulder, and dancing wildly following a killing spree to celebrate their toughness. Although not all child combatants do such things, depictions of child soldiers as innocents contrast sharply with the reality that some children, like some adults, learn to enjoy killing.

The development of a soldier's identity can influence behavior, self-image, and social relations in myriad ways. The bestowal of a name such as "Cock and Fire" on a child soldier is both a reward for fearless behavior and also a signal that the group expects similar behavior in the future. In groups that prize valor or cultivate an image of being "bad," the conferral of a nickname may signal acceptance into the inner sanctum of the armed group. Nicknames are also an expression of solidarity, which holds enormous significance for combatants. Combat is among the most intense human experiences, and it forges social bonds among combatants that are often more powerful than the bonds created in civilian relationships. In this context, the nickname is a ticket into the elite brotherhood whose identities have been forged in the crucible of combat. Faced with strong role expectations associated with their nicknames, child soldiers may change their behavior to conform to the expectations, continuing a cycle of self-fulfilling prophecy.

Combat-related identities move children ever farther from the world of civilian children in their society, where norms against killing apply. As they "wear" their new identities, children change their self-image in ways that redefine their future possibilities and sense of hope. Children who take on images as fearless fighters gain a sense of meaning and place in the world through their fighting. To abandon the fighting and the associated identity is to lose a sense of meaning and the power and respect accompanying a nickname such as "Beast." Having seen oneself as a commander, a jihadi, or a warrior can make it difficult to reacclimate in the postconflict environment to identities such as son, daughter, student, or village teenager. Nicknames and soldiers' identities may raise doubts as well in the minds of civilians who fear living next door to someone formerly known as "Rambo." Following the conflict, such nicknames often become sources of stigma and even retaliation.

Children's identities as soldiers or warriors, however, should not be essentialized and viewed as immutable. Children's identities, even more than those of adults, are multiple, fluid, and contextual. Pessimists have portrayed former child soldiers as damaged goods or relentless killers who can never transition either externally or internally to life as civilians. Such portrayals, however, have been overstated. The best evidence available indicates that a surprising majority can make the transition if given appropriate support, as outlined in Chapters 7–9. Also, it is a mistake to imply that all children in armed groups develop identities as soldiers or combatants. In both combat and noncombat roles, many children manage to resist soldiers' identities and look for ways out of the armed group, even the risky route of escape. Whether child soldiers stay with armed groups out of fear or necessity, or become combatants who kill, they are for the most part resilient children who are adapting and making the best of perilous circumstances. Because adults created these circumstances, adults must shoulder the responsibility for the enormous physical, psychological, social, and spiritual damage done to child soldiers.

4

Girl Soldiers

In 1995 I worked in Angola, which had been ravaged by decades of war. In visits and discussions with local child protection workers about child soldiers, I asked whether many girls had been soldiers. Invariably, the answer was no, which seemed odd on a continent that has seen pervasive girl soldiering. On the other hand, who was I to question the reports of people who were so close to the local situation of war-affected children? By the year 2000, when the war was winding down, it became apparent that thousands of girls had been soldiers in the Angolan war. In fact, many UNITA soldiers had two or more girls who had been abducted to serve as workers and sex slaves (Stavrou 2005). The girls had been invisible to analysts in part because the recruiters had wanted to hide their exploitation of girls. Also, the girls themselves had kept secret their lives as soldiers in order to avoid being stigmatized.

This story is a microcosm of the study of girl soldiers globally, which has evolved through multiple stages. Initially girl soldiers had been mostly invisible. Although analysts recognized that girl combatants existed and were a significant percentage of fighting forces in a handful of countries, the prevailing view had been that girl soldiers were present in only a minority of conflicts. In the next stage, girls were recognized as being part of many armed groups, but they were often described as "camp followers" who provided labor and support but who were not child soldiers per se. The term *child soldiers* meant boy soldiers, marginalizing girl soldiers.

In the current stage, a new generation of research has sketched a richer portrait of girl soldiers and revealed the complexities and variations of this phenomenon. What has emerged is a pattern of widespread use of girl soldiers and of girls' participation in roles that are every bit as diverse as those of boys. In the period from 1990 to 2003, girls were part of fighting forces in thirty-eight countries, serving in conflict zones as part of government forces, paramilitaries or militias, or armed opposition groups (McKay and Mazurana 2004). Although some recruitment is opportunistic, armed groups typically recruit girls systematically. In fact, in numerous armed groups a significant percentage of recruits are girls (Machel 2001; Save the Children UK 2005). In Colombia, 25 to 50 percent of FARC-EP recruits are females, including girls as young as 8 or 9 years (Human Rights Watch [HRW] 2003e). In Sri Lanka, 42 percent of LTTE members are girls (HRW 2004b). The armed groups in Sierra Leone are nearly 35 percent child soldiers and nearly 9 percent girl soldiers; girl soldiers made up over 16 percent of the RUF forces (McKay and Mazurana 2004). In Ethiopia during its war against Eritrea, 35 to 40 percent of the opposition group consisted of women and girls (Brett and McCallin 1996).

It is not just the number of girl soldiers that warrants attention, however. Girl soldiers are exploited in all the ways that boys are and carry the added burden of gender-based violence. In many armed groups, rape and sexual violence are normal features of daily life. Rape, which has long been used as an instrument of war (Allen 1996; Brownmiller 1975), is a means of terrorizing, subjugating, and humiliating the enemy. For example, when the Japanese army invaded China before World War II, it raped tens of thousands of women partly as a means of humiliating their Chinese enemies. In the 1990s, rampaging armed groups used rape as an instrument of terror, as in conflict in Bosnia and Rwanda (Reis and Vann 2006). Many women survivors of rape in those conflicts reported that the physical damage caused by the rapes was less than the psychological damage resulting from personal degradation, loss of social status, humiliation, and family dishonor.

The sexual and gender-based violence directed toward girl soldiers is part of the wider pattern of violence against girls in war zones. For example, many societies' gender roles prescribe that females collect household necessities such as water or firewood, which are frequently in very short supply in war zones. On their long daily walks to collect firewood or water, girls and women are often raped and attacked. Inside camps for refugees or internally displaced people, where men drink excessively, girls and women are in as much danger from rape, sexual harassment, and family violence as they are from armed conflict. Desperate to support their families and facing abject poverty, girls and women may resort to selling their bodies, and many fall prey to international sex traffickers. Sadly, the violence does not end with the signing of a ceasefire agreement. For example, in post-Taliban Afghanistan, impoverished families betroth their daughters at progressively younger ages in order to obtain the bride price, which improves the family's economic situation. Girls are betrothed at ages as young as 6 years, and some girls marry at age 11. Sexual consummation of such marriages and the resulting childbirths often have catastrophic results for the child.

Even soldiers who are presumably in an area to keep the peace abuse their power by raping local women. In Burundi, an increasingly conflict-torn country, one soldier forced a 16-year-old girl to fetch water, raped her, and then kept her water container (AI 2004b). Rape is such a large problem in Burundi that one woman, when asked whether rape is increasing, replied cynically, "Is rape increasing? I was raped in 1993, and again in 1995. I haven't been raped this year. How do I know if it is increasing?" (AI 2004b, 1). The normalization of rape places all females, including girls, at significant risk of sexual violence.

A common error is to define women's experiences in terms of sexual violence, which is a small part of girls' experiences in war zones. Recently, the media have overemphasized the problem by showing monolithic, sensationalized images of girl soldiers as victims of mass rape and other forms of sexual assault. In fact, girl soldiers exhibit a diversity of roles and experiences as great as those of boy soldiers. Whereas some girls are victims of rape, others belong to armed groups that prohibit sexual violence. Even among groups that make girls sex slaves, girls may also be mothers, laborers, spies, and trainers, and they may perform multiple roles simultaneously. Girl soldiers' roles as laborers often reflect the patterns of work that women are expected to do in their wider, mostly patriarchal societies (McKay 2006). These complexities must be reckoned with if girl soldiering is to be understood.

The emphasis on sexual violence can also obscure other forms of violence that damages girls. Family violence skyrockets in most war zones as increased stress and poverty, coupled with gender scripts that depict women as men's property, engender wife-beating on a wide scale. Much of the violence, however, is silent because it is structural, that is, a product of institutionalized patterns of social inequality and gender discrimination. For example, rural Afghan girls lack equal access to education, in part because girls are not permitted to walk to neighboring villages to attend schools. In Rwanda, many girls and women refugees who returned home after fleeing the 1994 genocide are prohibited by law from owning land, which worsens their poverty and threatens their and their children's survival. Girl soldiering and its effects can be understood only against this larger background of gender-based violence, sexism, and misogyny (Reardon 1985).

Entry into Soldiering

Girls' entry into armed groups marks a new epoch in their lives as they leave their families and enter a culture of violence that demands total obedience, presents great physical and psychological hardships, and normalizes violence. Although girls enter armed groups through a mixture of forced and nonforced recruitment, those who enter via abduction face the greatest immediate danger.

Abduction

In the period 1990 to 2003, armed groups abducted girls into soldiering in twenty-eight countries (McKay and Mazurana 2004). In some contexts, girls' abduction occurs as part of a wider child recruitment sweep, which is replete with bloodshed and brutality. In northern Uganda, a girl said that at age 12, the LRA had abducted her from home while she was sleeping and then went to neighboring houses to abduct others, including adults, who were tied one to another in a chain and forced to transport loot. Adults who were not selected to be porters were killed on the spot:

> Thirty-two were abducted from the village, both children and adults. I was the youngest, at age twelve. The next day they divided up the captives, and told the old people, including my father, to lie down on the ground. They started beating them with a machete. They cut him badly and left him there. (HRW 2003b, 7)

The LRA abducts children not only from within Uganda but also from Sudan, where it takes children for training and also abducts Sudanese children. One young woman who had been in the LRA from 1996 to 2002 said:

> There were abducted Sudanese within the LRA the entire time I was
> with the LRA in Sudan . . . We would abduct the Dinkas and Lukoya
> children, make them carry heavy loads, sometimes kill them. We'd
> take young girls . . . as young as eight . . . they were used for fighting,
> most were killed in battle, they would be put in front. (McKay and
> Mazurana 2004, 74)

The abduction and transport of girls across international borders to
serve in armed groups occurred in eleven countries during the years
1990 to 2003 (McKay and Mazurana 2004). This practice of trafficking
children internationally for purposes of soldiering occurs for boys as
well, although at what prevalence is unknown.

Rape frequently accompanies girls' abduction into armed groups. In
Liberia a 16-year-old girl recounted her abduction: "In 2001, I was captured in Lofa County by government forces. The forces beat me, they
held me and kept me in the bush. I was tied with my arms kept still and
was raped there. I was fourteen years old" (HRW 2004a, 31).

In Sierra Leone, too, the RUF often raped abductees. A 16-year-old
girl from near the capital city, Freetown, told Amnesty International that
rebel forces had attacked her village, killed her parents, and gang-raped
her repeatedly. Gang rapes cause profound injuries, both physically and
psychologically. Refusals to have sex with one's abductors are often punished by atrocities. One 14-year-old girl had been stabbed in the vagina
with a knife for having denied sex to her abductor (AI, 2000). The rapes
of abductees in Sierra Leone occurred on too vast a scale to write them
off as the crimes of a handful of psychopaths. They were part of accepted
practice, a de facto policy, within the RUF. One rape survivor quoted her
abductor as having said, "You don't understand. This is the reason we go
and capture you people. If you don't sleep with me today, I'll kill you"
(AI 2000, 2).

A recent example of rape following abduction comes from the Darfur
region of northern Sudan, where predominantly Arab Janjawid militias
have killed and raped people of African descent on a mass scale. A
woman who was five months pregnant at the time described her abduction together with girls as young as 8 years:

> After six days some of the girls were released. But the others, as young
> as eight years old were kept there. Five to six men would rape us in
> rounds, one after the other for hours during six days, every night.

My husband could not forgive me after this, he disowned me. (AI 2004a, 11)

In light of the genocidal nature of the attacks, the Janjawid may have been using rape also as a means of ethnic cleansing, impregnating African women to increase the percentage of people who have lighter skin.

Not all armed groups, however, rape the girls they abduct. In Sri Lanka the LTTE abducts girls, yet prohibits rape and sexual exploitation (Keairns 2003a). The highly contextual, varied nature of girl soldiering makes universalized statements regarding girl soldiers of dubious value.

Nonforced Recruitment

Girls decide to join armed groups for diverse reasons, such as family problems, poverty, a desire for education and training, a hope to acquire skills and a brighter future, and a desire to obtain the prestige associated with uniforms and guns. Some girls are born into armed groups such as UNITA in Angola or the LRA in northern Uganda. Fearing government forces will kill escapees, they decide to stay with the armed group for protection. Children's narratives illustrate this diversity. A Sri Lankan girl who had joined the LTTE said:

> I was older when I made that sudden decision to run away. It was not because I wanted to join the movement to fight, I wanted to get away from the marriage my parents were planning to force me into. I really got disturbed, they were forcing me. (Keairns 2003a, 38)

A Philippine girl who joined the opposition group explained:

> My sister told me that they [the family] wouldn't allow me to go to school or go to work . . . I was also getting fed up, I had run out of money and my family even borrowed money from me . . . I felt sorry to leave my mother, but my mother was so poor. I couldn't bear it anymore, just suffering there. For me, I was looking for a way to let off steam and have a chance to be happy. But I enjoyed it so much in the mountains, because the comrades were very good to us. (Keairns 2003b, 38)

And a Colombian girl who joined the FARC-EP said: "I joined the guerrillas to escape . . . I thought I'd get some money and could be independent" (HRW 2003e, 55).

Girls' testimonies ring with the pain of living in difficult family situations. Although many boys also come from such difficult situations, girls face specific risks in families. The first quote above shows how local gender norms, in this case forced marriage, lead to negative family practices that oppress girls, evoke great sadness and anger, and encourage girls to join armed groups. Gendered risks for child soldiering are most visible in cases of family sexual violence. A Colombian girl soldier reported:

> One of my mother's men tried to abuse me when I was younger. He tried to abuse me and because I didn't let him he got angry. He used to fight with my mum and he used to fight with me . . . so I didn't want to live with my mum anymore. (Keairns 2002, 17)

In some cases, sexual abuse produces a generalized rage. Another Colombian girl who had been a guerrilla said, "When I was twelve, a cousin raped me. I was so mad, I wanted vengeance. I wanted to hurt everyone who had hurt me" (HRW 2003e, 55). To vent this anger, she had decided to join the FARC-EP.

These testimonies reveal that girls' decisions to join are made in a context of gender injustice, deprivation, hardship, and mistreatment. It would be tenuous to call them "free" choices in the sense in which most people use that term. In addition, some girls subsequently regret their decisions. A Sri Lankan girl said:

> When I think back . . . Yes after I spoke to you and was thinking and thinking. Why did I get into to all that I did? All those actions were hardhearted actions, now makes me sad. Maybe I could have stayed at home. Everything was wrong from the beginning. Maybe I could have put up with my relatives' cruelty; after all one of them was good to me. (Keairns 2003a, 51)

Similarly, a Philippine girl regretted her decision:

> And now that I'm not with her (mother) anymore, I feel guilty and think that what I did was wrong. For example, while I was in the movement, my mother is having a hard time. My cousin sent me a letter requesting me to come home because my younger sibling is sick. Of course we're far from each other. (Keairns 2003b, 61)

Like boys, girls are not always in the best position to make informed decisions on such weighty matters as whether to join an armed group.

Being psychologically immature, idealistic, and impatient, they can make hasty decisions grounded in romanticized images of the struggle or how life will be away from home. Having limited life experience, they may also be less likely to look ahead clearly and foresee how a relative's illness or their own wounding might make them want to return home.

Not all girls who decide to become soldiers, however, are unhappy with their decisions. In some circumstances, being a soldier offers girls access to competencies, options, respect, and support that they had been unable to obtain in civilian life. Many former girl soldiers say they are happy with the skills and education they received inside an armed group, liked the feeling of family, and were happy to have escaped an unbearable situation at home. This satisfaction is found mostly in girl soldiers who were in an armed group that espouses revolutionary ideology, has a strong sense of solidarity, and harbors norms of equality and treating each other well. This combination often leads girl soldiers to view the armed group as a surrogate family and a source of social meaning and identity.

Life as a Girl Soldier

Girl soldiers' lives are steeped in hardship, danger, and exposure to violence, including gender-based violence. For abducted girls, the hardships often begin with long, forced marches as the armed group seeks to escape enemy attack and take their captives to a training base. A girl from Uganda described the severity of the post-abduction marches with the LRA:

> You were not allowed to rest because the moment you tried they would kill you. Three children with swollen legs had difficulty walking and tried to stop. The LRA tied the children's hands behind their backs and ordered the others to beat them to death with sticks as big as my arm. Later they removed the clothing from the children and threw their bodies into a swamp. (HRW 2003b, 9–10)

Having marched abducted girls and boys to Sudan, the LRA subjects them to severe training. Early in the morning, the children are forced to sing and dance at a frenzied pace. Hours later, in the midday heat, they are forced to run hills or in wide circles until midafternoon, and anyone who drops due to thirst or exhaustion is left to die (McKay and

Mazurana 2004). This wanton brutality is less a process of training than of selecting the hardiest children.

Girls who survive this ordeal enter life within the LRA, which is an endless stream of heavy work coupled with beatings and threats of violence. Younger girls are typically assigned to commanders as *ting ting* (servants). Said one of these girls, "You must work all of the time. The moment you refuse to work, they will kill you or beat you to death" (HRW 2003b, 13). Another girl in the LRA told of the senseless beatings *ting ting* received:

> The commander would call to us to come and lie down. He would say, "Do you know why I am beating you?" We didn't know, so the soldiers caned us, fifty strokes. This happened every day. They beat us on the buttocks, but if you cry, they will beat every part of your body and not count the strokes. (HRW 2003b, 13–14)

The hardships of life as a soldier are extreme for girls who had been abducted, but hardship is no stranger to girls who had decided to join an armed group. Grueling physical conditioning and an omnipresent threat of punishment are typically part of physical training, which may be coupled with teaching skills such as using weapons. For example, the LTTE in Sri Lanka initially issued girl recruits wooden guns to carry during basic training, which lasts three to five months and requires rigorous physical conditioning and development of militarily useful skills. Those who failed to obey orders or keep up with the required activities were forced to do additional exercises or to conduct the exercises holding a heavy rifle overhead. During the exercises, the girls were often hit or kicked at random. When the girls had "become one" with their wooden guns, they subsequently received real weapons and participated in combat training (Keairns 2003a).

Girl soldiers in the LTTE also face psychological hardships, such as the threat of death from attacks by the government army and the obligation to commit suicide if they are captured. Both girl and boy soldiers are required to wear cyanide capsules around their necks, with which they are supposed to commit suicide if they are captured so that they will not divulge sensitive information. The LTTE threatens to kill anyone who has been captured by government forces but did not take the cyanide. Still, girl trainees reported that they liked having the cyanide capsules because they knew that they could kill themselves to avoid being abused if captured (Keairns 2003a).

Sexual Violence

Sexual violence, although not universal, is daily fare inside many armed groups, even if the girls joined without obvious coercion. A girl from the Democratic Republic of the Congo who had joined an armed group at age 12 told of her experience.

> One day, rebels attacked the village where I lived. I hid and watched as they killed my relatives and raped my mother and sisters. I thought if I joined their army, I would be safe. In the army I was trained to use a gun and I performed guard duty. I was often beaten and raped by the other soldiers. One day, a commander wanted me to become his wife, so I tried to escape. They caught me, whipped me, and raped me every night for many days. When I was just 14, I had a baby. I don't even know who his father is. I ran away again but I have nowhere to go and no food for the baby. I am afraid to go home. (U.S. State Department 2004, 5)

Rape is also used to punish disobedient girls. In Colombia a girl who had entered the UC-ELN at age 16, and who clung to her doll while telling her story, related that a 30-year-old commander had raped her fifteen days after she had joined.

> I was very disobedient . . . He entered my tent one night. He grabbed my hair and started touching me. I cried and screamed and begged him to leave me alone. I was a virgin. It was painful. After he raped me, he left. I didn't say anything to anyone because he was part of the command . . . Four days later he came back. He did it by force again. And he did it again nearly two months later. Another commander told me they were going to kill me because I didn't obey them. (HRW 2003e, 57–58)

More than a source of punishment, rape is a powerful means of subjugation since it profoundly violates girls' sense of safety and bodily integrity and can lead girls to see themselves as impure and damaged. Rape also casts a large stigma on the survivors, who may be shunned or otherwise treated badly by others, including people from whom they need support. Strong stigma also attaches to any children conceived by rape (Carpenter in press). Having a tarnished self-image and damaged social status, girls may decide that their only alternative is to be totally obedient and cast their fate with the armed group.

The risks of sexual violence are particularly high for abducted girls, who remain at high risk throughout their captivity. In Sierra Leone, RUF male soldiers typically took the girls whom they had captured as their "wives." The term *soldiers' wives* is really a euphemism for sex slavery, because many girls who refuse to have sex are severely punished or killed. Not all girls, however, comply with demands for sex. A courageous Sierra Leonean woman whom the RUF had abducted at age 14 told me that she had said to her captors, "I am too young for sex, and we are not married. In Sierra Leone, people don't take such young girls." Facing repeated demands for sex, she tried to shame her captors, telling them, "I'm too young" and "You know better and should be ashamed of yourselves." Eventually the RUF took her to Freetown and cut off her left arm above the elbow, leaving her deeply troubled by her physical appearance and disability.

The use of girls as sex slaves, although contemptible, turns out to be more complex than it may appear initially. In some circumstances girl soldiers decide to be the "wife" of a soldier because they need protection, as their captors do in some cases protect them. Girls may also become emotionally attached to their "husbands" and see themselves in a de facto marital relationship (Verhey 2004), which outsiders would regard as illegitimate and grounded in the abuse of power. The birth of a baby adds to the perception that the relationship is more like that of husband and wife than of captor and captive. Girls may also feel bound by cultural norms stipulating that the father of one's baby is de facto one's husband. A girl who had lived for years in the bush with her RUF captor told me, "I was afraid of him at first . . . But he protected me—kept others away and got us food. He's the father of my baby and we should be properly married."

The strategy of having a "husband" for protection can backfire, however, if the man turns out to be cruel, transmits a sexual infection, or dies, leaving the woman unprotected. A Ugandan girl who had been captured by the LRA at age 16 and given to a commander told how her "husband" had protected her and was very happy when she became pregnant and gave birth. But following his death in combat, "They start to treat you like a girl again and beat you. I was beaten severely and given less food. Sometimes I didn't have food for my baby . . . Unless you get another man, you suffer" (HRW 2003b, 14).

Not all soldiers' "wives" are captives whose sex is obtained through threat of violence. In armed groups that ban sexual violence, girls may use a strategy of becoming a commander's "wife" as a way to obtain privileges and access to goods they could not have obtained otherwise. A Colombian girl who had joined the FARC-EP when she was 13 said:

> When girls join the FARC, the commanders choose among them. There's pressure. The women have the final say, but they want to be with a commander to be protected. The commanders buy them. They give a girl money and presents. When you're with a commander, you don't have to do the hard work. So most of the prettiest girls are with commanders. (HRW 2003e, 57)

Although this situation falls short of rape and physical violence, it amounts to sexual abuse and harassment since male commanders used their power to lure and exploit girls.

Girls may also use pregnancy and motherhood to avoid the worst, most dangerous, forms of labor. In Angola, girls inside UNITA sometimes entered liaisons with a soldier as a means of avoiding the long marches, which caused intense suffering and many deaths:

> Now those who have children do not go because they have children. And those who are pregnant do not go far; they stay in that place or do work close by . . . But those who have nothing, when the elders think that someone has to go and collect something then it is they who are ordered to go. They choose the older ones who have houses but do not have children or are not pregnant, and join them up with the girls and boys and send them to bring the food. You have to go collect that material if you are not pregnant or do not have a child. So I accepted the father of my child because of that suffering. (Stavrou 2005, 38)

This case, like that of the Colombian girl described above, shows how girl soldiers actively shape their own place and role in the group through the only means available to them—sex and relationships. Far from being passive victims, they actively find a way to make the best of their difficult situation.

Despite the pervasiveness of sexual violence against girls, a minority of armed groups prohibit sexual exploitation of "voluntary" girl recruits. Both the LTTE in Sri Lanka and armed opposition groups in the Philippines, which recruit without explicit coercion, disallow the sexual violation of women (Keairns 2002). Sexual violence is banned most commonly in groups that have a revolutionary agenda opposing women's oppression.

Although sexual violence has caused inestimable damage to girls, it has damaged boys as well, though on a smaller scale. In Afghanistan, where the overwhelming majority of child soldiers have been 14- to 18-year-old males, boys are at great risk of sexual exploitation. The practice of older Afghan men taking younger boys as sexual partners antedated the arrival of Islam and now exists alongside it. It is not uncommon for stronger, older soldiers or powerful commanders in the Northern Alliance forces to exploit smaller, younger recruits (Wessells and Kostelny 2002). Although the boys often regard themselves as being in a relationship with the older soldier, the enormous power difference casts doubt on the idea that the relationship could be consensual. The sexual exploitation of boy soldiers is even more invisible and taboo than that of girl soldiers and warrants the international community's concerted attention.

Girls' Roles

Within armed groups, girls may perform a wide variety of roles that do not conform to simplistic gender stereotypes. Within a particular armed group, some girl solders are fighters, whereas others serve support roles such as cook, porter, and domestic laborer. In Mozambique, girl recruits for FRELIMO and RENAMO were not only fighters but also spies and intelligence officers, recruiters, trainers, laborers, medics, and weapons experts. In Angola, where UNITA soldiers moved with their entire families, girls and boys were born into the armed group. Girls not only were exploited as sex slaves and laborers but also were forced to dance all night to get the troops pumped up and keep their thoughts off of home and civilian life. In northern Sierra Leone, the RUF preferred girls as spies because, following local gender norms, they could move as "vendors" into local markets, which are rife not only with goods but also with gossip and information. Also in Sierra Leone, girls who were wives of RUF commanders often cared for younger, vulnerable women associated with the group (McKay and Mazurana 2004).

Girls' roles within armed groups are fluid, multiple, and overlapping. On awakening, a girl soldier may initially perform her maternal duty of feeding her baby, but while doing this she might also collect the water and wood needed to prepare breakfast. Later in the morning, she might work as a camp laborer, carrying her baby all the while. Still later, under threat of enemy movements in the area, she may carry heavy loads, enabling her armed group to move quickly. In Africa, where women typically carry heavy loads, female soldiers are highly valued as workers and porters. If attacked, the girl might use her own weapon to engage in fighting. In view of this multiplicity of roles, it is inappropriate to label girl soldiers as fighters, mothers, laborers, or by any other single role. Girls frequently perform multiple roles during a single day, and they also perform multiple roles simultaneously, just as girls do in civilian life.

Girl soldiers also negotiate or construct their roles. A young woman from northern Sierra Leone told me this story:

> The RUF attacked my village and took 28 women. Twenty-four of them were killed outright—they just killed them! I myself was shot. The bullet hit my leg but bounced off—I was protected [by magic]. The soldiers came to kill me with the bayonet, and I was very scared. But a soldier named Rambo saved me. He saved me and I became his wife. I didn't want to fight . . . After training, I looked after the orphans and other girls and boys our group picked up after attacking villages. I was the "Mommy Queen" and cared for them. Nobody else wanted to do this so they all brought children to me. By the end [of the war], I had 130 children with me. I helped some of them find their families again.

The considerable pride she felt about her role as the children's protector clashes with the idea that life inside an armed group crushes all humanitarian impulses. Her story indicates that girl soldiers can in some situations carve out relatively positive roles for themselves and maintain their sense of agency and the sanctity of life.

How girls perceive their roles and themselves depends in no small part on the level of respect they receive. Although it may seem odd to think of armed groups as providing respect, the reality is that girls are treated with more respect in some armed groups than they would otherwise be accorded in a patriarchal society. Numerous guerrilla and armed opposition groups have a revolutionary agenda and view women's equality as an integral part of their struggle. In Ethiopia, a woman member of an armed opposition group said:

> It was a co-operative life. The male does not behave like the others do in the civil society. They respect us. Even they advise those males who

do not respect females. There was no forced sexual relationship with males. The male fighters did not force us to do anything without our interest. The male had no feeling of superiority over the female. (Veale 2003, 32)

Living in a context of equality, girl members of such groups experience a new sense of respect that crosses lines of gender and age. A Philippine girl described this feeling:

It was there in the movement that I experienced being respected, no matter what your age was. They were very helpful. Sometimes, I would request an older comrade to make me a knot for my hammock, and he would do it. Even they, the older ones, whatever tasks they ask others to do, they are also ready to do. (Keairns 2003b, 64)

In liberation struggles, ideology and political education shape girls' perceptions of their roles, suffusing them with meaning and a sense of higher purpose. In Mozambique the opposition group FRELIMO had a revolutionary ideology that taught girls to liberate themselves from all forms of oppression, whether by class, gender, or imperialism (West 2004). In the Philippines, girls in armed opposition groups received political education that helped them understand and appreciate their roles and find meaning in tasks of political mobilization. One Philippine girl said:

In the movement I took this course on the three main problems. It's about the country, the government. So that you understand why we are combating the government, the roots of the hardship of the people, the history of the country. Then afterwards, when you know all of this, how to contact, how to organize the people/masses. (Keairns 2003b, 48)

That many girls in armed groups embrace revolutionary ideology and seek to spread it to others shatters the popular myth of girl soldiers as passive victims. As part of their resocialization, they acquire new roles and new ways of viewing the world that transform their identity and sense of place. Their new roles reposition them, creating a new understanding and a new sense of meaning. Like boy soldiers, girl soldiers are best understood neither as passive nor as brainwashed but as active seekers and makers of meaning in difficult circumstances.

Pregnancy, Mothering, and Birth Control

Armed groups are typically rife with sexual activity. Whether sex is imposed through force, chosen by the girls and their partners, or used strategically as a means of obtaining privileges, pregnancy frequently results. Pregnancy and maternity are significant life events that lead girl soldiers into new roles as mothers and caretakers. Pregnancy and maternity also present a mixture of increased dangers and increased protections, depending on the context.

For girls who are moving with an armed group, pregnancy brings significant risks associated with lack of food and proper nutrition, exposure to attack, and difficult living conditions. Still, some girl soldiers may continue fighting up to the later stages of pregnancy. During and following pregnancy, girls face high risk of maternal mortality owing to the difficult conditions and lack of proper prenatal and maternal care (Mazurana et al. 2002; McKay and Mazurana 2004).

Commanders, however, often want to end pregnancies. A birth means another mouth to feed, and the presence of pregnant or birthing girls might slow them down or signal their position to the enemy. The methods used to terminate pregnancy or to control when birth occurs are as unsafe as they are barbarous. Some armed groups have ordered soldiers to jump on the pregnant girls' stomachs to induce birth (Mazurana et al. 2002). Stomach pounding is also used to terminate pregnancies, as indicated by this report of a Liberian girl who had been abducted by LURD fighters:

> My Ma and Pa are dead, I have no one to help. When the rebels came, I was small, they forced me to go with them. I got pregnant from the fighters. When the time came for birth, the baby died. Four or five of the boys pushed on my stomach to force me to get rid of the baby, my stomach is now broken. (HRW 2004a, 32)

To prevent pregnancies, some armed groups order girl soldiers to use contraceptives. The Colombian guerrilla group FARC-EP requires girls to have an intrauterine device and to have an abortion if they become pregnant. A girl who had joined the group at age 12 said:

> They put in an IUD the day after I arrived. That was the only birth control I ever used. If you get pregnant, you have to have an abortion. Lots

of women get pregnant. I had two friends who got pregnant and had to have abortions. They cried and cried. They didn't want to lose the baby. (HRW 2003e, 58)

Not all groups, however, demand that pregnant girls abort. Colombian girls in the UC-ELN said that when women become pregnant, they may be sent home to give birth. Groups such as the LRA in northern Uganda actually welcome births and protect mothers because they want the children as new recruits. The LRA sometimes places mothers in breeder camps in Sudan in hopes of incubating future LRA recruits (McKay and Mazurana 2004).

A profound problem that the world has failed to come to grips with is the fate of babies that are born as a result of rape or sexual activity within an armed group. If child mothers are ostracized and isolated for having given birth out of wedlock, and they are carrying the shame of rape and sexual violence, the stigma is even greater for the children. Local people may regard a child who had been conceived through rape by a rebel as both illegitimate and a reminder of the horrible things the rebels had done. Viewed as "rebel children" or "tomorrow's rebels" (McKay and Mazurana 2004), these children carry the dual burden of illegitimacy and association with rebels. The few field reports that exist regarding these children suggest they are among the most vulnerable of all war-affected children (Verhey 2004).

Girl Combatants

History is replete with legendary tales of women and girl warriors. The best known is Joan of Arc, who at the age of 16 led a French army of four thousand that broke the English siege of Orleans in 1429 (Mazurana et al. 2002). The practice of girls serving as combatants fits with timeless myths that have glorified mythical female warriors such as Kali, the Hindu goddess of war, death, and destruction. The ancient roots of women's engagement in fighting is visible also in the actions of queens and other female leaders. Queen Aahhotep I (c. 1570–1546 BCE) of Egypt was involved in quelling an uprising in Thebes, helping to unite Egypt under one rule.

Although girl soldiering echoes these ancient themes, it also embodies the new face of armed conflict, for girls now serve as combatants on a much wider scale than ever before. This owes in part to their ability to effectively wield weapons of the day such as the AK-47 assault rifle, and it also reflects leaders' will to exploit even young girls.

Fighters and Leaders

In West Africa, large numbers of girls have served as both fighters and commanders. In Liberia, armed groups segregated girls by age, with the younger ones assigned to perform domestic services for commanders while the older girls were assigned to fight. A Liberian girl who had been a LURD commander described this arrangement and also told how girls wore the distinctive colors of their group and engaged in looting and killing.

> When LURD came here, we were caught, lots of girls, and were carried back to Bomi. After training, I became a commander. There were thirty "wives" in my group; only two died, we were strong fighters. These "wives" were big girls, the youngest ones perhaps fifteen years old. The young girls, they don't get guns, they were behind us. They tote loads and are security for us.
>
>   We would wear t-shirts that were either yellow or brown and said LURD forces. My gun was a "60" that was an automatic weapon and I wore the ammunition around my chest. We would get no payment for fighting, when we attacked somewhere, we busted people's places and would eat. When we captured an enemy, if my heart was there, I would bring them to the base for training. But if my heart was bad lucky, then I would kill them right there. (HRW 2004a, 30)

Liberian girl fighters took pride in their strength and skill as combatants. A 16-year-old Liberian girl reported:

> For girls in our unit, there were many. Only ten of us would go to the front, the others stayed behind and did chores, collected food and fetched water. These nine others were strong fighters and all had "husbands" among the male fighters, other fighters would take the girls at the base for loving. (HRW 2004a, 32)

Boy soldiers, too, often admired girls' fighting ability and believed they had magical powers. One boy soldier from Liberia said:

Those girls who fight, they are big, sixteen and older, and they fight just like men. They are strong. When the fighting is rough, they move right in because they are juju (magic). They are special. They don't move in on the frontline, but they go ahead when there's a problem, we would retreat and the "wives" would go forward. (HRW 2004a, 30–31)

Whether the wives go forward because they feel protected by magic or compelled by orders, expectations, and fear of punishment, their movement puts them directly in harm's way.

In light of the high risks involved, it is worth reflecting on why many girls become eager fighters. Obedience certainly plays a significant role in some situations, particularly those in which commanders give girls who have been trained to fight direct orders to fight and are willing to administer dire punishment for refusals to fight. But obedience, although part of the story, does not explain girl fighters' sense of pride as fighters. For some girls, fighting provides a means of obtaining revenge against those who had hurt their family and village. For others, fighting brings peer approval and gains advantages through promotion. Victims of discrimination, girls have grown up hearing a steady stream of messages that boys are better than girls, particularly in regard to physical prowess. Against this sense of disparagement and inequality, proving one's mettle as a fighter affords a path to equality and respect.

Being a good fighter has strategic value because it can help prevent sexual assault in some contexts. A young woman from Sierra Leone who had become an RUF commander at age 16 told me, "No one would mess with me because I was tough and killed as many as the men fighters . . . They just stay away from me." After they leave the armed group, girls who pride themselves on their toughness or view themselves as military leaders face a set of reintegration challenges that are different from those for girls who had not been fighters or adopted military identities.

Assassins and Terrorists

Girls' roles as perpetrators contradict romanticized images of girls as inherently more peaceful than boys. Brought through a school of murder, girls can learn to be steely assassins. In Colombia, a girl who had joined the paramilitaries at age 14 was the sole child in a special assassina-

tion unit that paid its members a bonus of 200,000 to 300,000 pesos
(US$67–100) to kill someone:

> I killed a policeman a year after I joined. He was the chief of police in
> my town. He didn't allow his men to be bought by the paras. They
> showed me who he was and gave me three days. I called him as if to se-
> duce him. I was with another paramilitary girl of fourteen. We took a
> paramilitary taxi; many taxi-drivers support us. The man said: why are
> you going to kill me? I told him that he had problems with us. I shot
> him in the head with a .38 revolver. It wasn't hard for me because I
> had already been in combat and had already killed guerrillas. (HRW
> 2003e, 97)

That girls are perpetrators is particularly conspicuous in regard to girl
suicide bombings, which are regarded as terrorism because they seek to
induce public terror and fear as a way to obtain political objectives. Sri
Lanka, the site of the largest number of suicide bombings worldwide
(Bloom 2005), is an instructive case. Female suicide bombers associated
with the LTTE killed Indian Prime Minister Rajiv Gandhi in 1991 and
had also attempted unsuccessfully to assassinate Sri Lankan president
Chandrika Bandaranaike Kumaratunga in 1999. The LTTE recruits girls
as well as women into the Black Tigers, the suicide cadres of the LTTE.
Prepared to execute death missions, they wear around their necks the lethal cyanide capsules that all LTTE soldiers have sworn to take if captured. How many girls have actually participated in terror missions is
unknown, but the sacrifices of girl terrorists are prominent parts of the
Tamil people's communal memories and collective struggle.

Numerous misconceptions surround the topic of suicide bombers and
terrorism in general. Since 9/11, the media have sensationalized the
topic of girl terrorists, possibly creating the idea that large numbers of
girl soldiers are terrorists or that child terrorism is a recent phenomenon. In fact, very few girl soldiers are terrorists, a point applying equally
to boy soldiers. Another misconception equates terrorism and suicide
bombing, although terrorism includes a wide array of tools and activities, only one of which is suicide bombing. Furthermore, terrorism is
not new and has long been one of the main instruments that weaker
groups use to oppose a much more powerful adversary. Minors' engagement in terrorism has been part of many political conflicts, including the
sectarian strife in Northern Ireland and the anti-apartheid struggle in
South Africa. Although it is not a new phenomenon, it has become in-

creasingly frequent and visible in the Israeli–Palestinian conflict and many others as well.

A frequent misconception is that terrorists are irrational, even insane. Advocates of this view assert that suicide bombers receive no reward because they die in the process, and achieve nothing because the world knows better than to accede to terrorists' demands. In fact, most studies of terrorists have shown that people who commit terrorist acts are psychologically normal (Pape 2005). Beneath the presumed mask of irrationality, one finds instead a relatively coherent set of values, beliefs, and practices that support terrorist activity and suffuse it with meaning. For example, girls in the LTTE are taught that the highest thing they can do for their people is martyr themselves, which they are taught brings eternal rewards and enormous prestige for them and their families. LTTE girls who accept suicide missions dine with the LTTE leader (Bloom 2005), and following their death they receive the ultimate award, a "hero's welcome," for having sacrificed themselves and having inflicted great harm on the enemy (Keairns 2003c).

Other perceived rewards of terrorism may include inflicting pain on the enemy and achieving revenge and justice. To recognize these rewards is not to condone them but to understand terrorists' motives, moving into a better position to prevent terrorism. In a context of oppression and mistreatment of one's people, the idea of hurting the enemy, even at the cost of one's own life, can be highly seductive. For young Sri Lankans or Palestinians who carry the searing wounds of daily humiliation and who see the situation as unlikely to improve, terrorist activity offers the promise of delivering a measure of justice and even of escaping a situation not worth living in. It also provides a venue for revenge, which many girls identify as having led them to become soldiers. By achieving revenge against injustice and by fighting oppression, girl soldiers may find meaning in terrorist activities, regarding them as the highest expression of their social identity and commitment to the group struggle.

This analysis suggests the folly of writing off girl terrorists, or boys for that matter, as bad seed or as mentally ill. Terrorists are people whose life conditions have led them into the path of mass violence and who find meaning in extreme acts that they regard as thoroughly justified even though most of the world condemns both the acts and the terrorists. Children are susceptible to engagement in terrorism because of their idealism, manipulability, and limited life experience; because families and leaders have taught them to use violence as a means of obtaining the group's political objectives; and because children themselves carry the wounds of humiliation and oppression. The challenge is to enable young people to achieve meaning in life through nonviolent venues and actions, and to create conditions of social justice, thereby preventing war and healing the wounds that, left unattended, fuel the fires of revenge.

A boy fights as part of the Karen National Liberation Army in Myanmar. Photo by Robert Semeniuk, originally published in *Refugee Transitions,* no. 13.

A girl soldier in El Salvador. Photo by Martin Adler/Panos Pictures.

A boy soldier engages in militia training in the Democratic Republic of the Congo. Credit: Reuters.

"Night Commuters," these northern Ugandan children pour into cities at night to escape LRA attacks on their homes. Credit: Bruno Stevens.

A boy soldier from the U.S. Civil War era, Nashville, Tennessee. Source: Library of Congress, Prints & Photographs Division, LC-B8184–10573 (27).

An Afghan boy, survivor of a land-mine explosion, learns to use a prosthetic leg.
Photo by Robert Semeniuk, originally published in *Refugee Transitions*, no. 13.

A boy in Gaza poses with gun and uniform. Photo by Robert Semeniuk, originally published in *Refugee Transitions*, no. 13.

A local healer in Sierra Leone bathes and cleanses a girl whom the RUF had abducted. Copyright 2005, Lindsay Stark. Used with permission.

Former boy soldiers in Sierra Leone learn carpentry skills as part of a reintegration program. Photo courtesy of Christian Children's Fund.

5

Health and HIV/AIDS

The sensational media images and mind-numbing statistics through which war is depicted provide only a faint outline of the monumental damage war causes to civilians' health. To understand what war means for ordinary people, there is little substitute for seeing their situation firsthand and learning from their narratives, which convey a humbling mixture of struggle and resilience.

In 2002 I visited a village in northern Afghanistan, where the mountainous serenity belied the fury and suffering wreaked by decades of poverty and a chain of devastating wars. The village offered a hopeful, if bizarre, juxtaposition of charred ruins and newly constructed homes built of freshly hewn wood. The Taliban had attacked and destroyed the village completely in October 2001, forcing displaced villagers during the coldest days of winter into an IDP camp with minimal shelter and too little food. The elders told how some people had died in their homes during the attack, whereas others had perished during flight. Living in very difficult, cold conditions, many young children had perished from disease and lack of food and clean water. Death had also claimed many teenage boys, large numbers of whom had fought for the Northern Alliance.

Asked about the availability of health care, the elders explained patiently that their village had never had a health post. Kunduz city, which was over two hours away by car, had the closest hospital, but no one had a vehicle to transport ill or wounded people. The combination of extended drought and land mines had crippled their agriculture and threatened to kill more children. With classic Afghan stoicism, they said life had been this difficult for many years, first through the Soviet occupation and then through the fighting of the mujaheddin, the Taliban takeover, and the war of liberation. Later that day, I visited the Kunduz hospital and walked its dark, unsanitary corridors, where even the doctors spat on the floors. There I talked with a 14-year-old boy soldier who, having recently lost his leg to a land mine, discussed his worries about the future. The hospital's administrators said they could not hope to save many lives, though they did the best they could without regular electricity and appropriate facilities.

My experience in the village and the hospital show a side of war very different from that depicted in television images of deaths due to bombs and firefights. Most fatalities result not from fighting but from the chronic burdens of war, most notably the combination of disease, malnutrition, food insecurity, infrastructure destruction, and poor access to health care. In fact, nearly 90 percent of war-related deaths now occur through these indirect effects of violence (Human Security Centre 2005). The chronic burdens of war have disproportionate impact on children, whose developing bodies lack adult immunities and vigor. During the 1990s alone, worldwide, over two million children died as a result of armed conflict (Machel 2001).

The chronic health burdens of war are starkly apparent in the HIV/AIDS pandemic, which amplifies the threats armed conflict pose to children (Machel 2001). The scope of the pandemic staggers the imagination. Approximately 12.3 million African children have become orphans due to HIV/AIDS (UNICEF, USAID, and UNAIDS 2004). Globally, 143 million children have lost one or both parents to this disease. In some circumstances, orphans are at risk of child soldiering, child labor, and other potentially lethal activities. Because most armed groups are rife in sexual activity and also sexual violence and operate in HIV-infested areas, armed groups are ideal carriers of HIV/AIDS and other sexually transmitted diseases. Unprotected sex tends to be the norm in armed groups, which roam across wide spaces, cross borders, and regard sex as a reward of power.

The toll of war on health reaches the cruelest proportions in regard to child soldiers, whose lives are shattered not only by bullets, bombs, and shrapnel but also by the chronic destroyers of health such as HIV/AIDS. The same combination of health risks that damage child soldiers' bodies also damage prospects for peace by destabilizing society, corroding basic support systems and means of protection, and undermining the capacities of governments and communities to meet basic needs. Awash in unmet survival needs, these societies are at high risk of armed conflict, even if they have recently achieved a ceasefire and hostilities have ended formally.

Health

The risks to child soldiers' health owes to a dizzying array of interacting risks, any one of which is potentially lethal. The most visible risks are those associated with attack and physical wounding, which are omnipresent threats inside an armed group. A boy from Sierra Leone who had fought for the CDF against the rebels showed me multiple scars from gunshot wounds on his chest and shoulders. He said:

> We knew the land—every tree and path, and we ambushed them as they sneaked up to attack our village. We were good fighters but we only had shotguns and pangas [machetes] to fight with. They had automatic weapons . . . Many people died, but I was lucky.

With pride, he displayed his wounds, which symbolized his toughness and commitment to protect his village.

Enemy attack, however, is not the primary source of physical injuries to child soldiers. A former child soldier in the DRC said: "We were all ten, twelve, thirteen years old and older. Then we were sent to Camp Vert in Moba and trained there. Lots were killed in the training. Lots died of sickness. The food was poorly prepared and many got dysentery" (HRW 2001, 10). Often the injuries received inside an armed group from deadly training, punishments or random beatings, contaminated food, and harsh living conditions are as painful and life-threatening as injuries received in combat. Even minor injuries can become life threatening, because in many armed groups there is little health care.

Civilian children, too, suffer such hardships. Said a 16-year-old Angolan girl who had fled military attacks and had walked for days with her sisters:

> We walked and walked . . . all day walking, hungry and thirsty . . . I felt sorry for my little sisters and my grandmother who had to carry the younger one on her back . . . I was also afraid that we might be caught

by "them" (the soldiers). In the evening, we arrived in Lola, but that wasn't our final destination. My legs were swollen . . . we walked during the night until we got to Bibala. In the morning, my legs were very sore, I couldn't take the pain any more and my grandmother took me to the hospital. There they gave me an injection and I fell asleep. When I woke up my legs had been amputated. I cried a lot. (Honwana 1998, 53)

The threats to civilian children's health are related to child soldiering. In areas where armed groups are thought to have better access to health care, children may join armed groups in hopes of increasing their chances of survival. But some children's gain may be other children's loss, since armed groups frequently raid health posts to obtain medical supplies for their troops.

Infrastructure Destruction

Infrastructure damage is no incidental by-product of fighting. Many armed groups deliberately destroy homes, schools, crops, health posts, and electrical and water infrastructure as a way to terrorize and subjugate local people. The destruction of infrastructure removes the legs on which the government stands. If the civil war attests to the government's inability to fulfill its highest obligation, the protection of civilians, the damage to infrastructure cripples its ability to provide basic services and to meet fundamental needs. Continued fighting forces the government to devote an increased proportion of its wealth to the war effort, leaving fewer resources available for services such as health and education (Collier et al. 2003). These factors undermine confidence in the government, contributing further to the weak governance that is partly responsible for civil wars.

Inevitably, this strategy of devastating the infrastructure damages the health care system. Whether or not the damage is intentional, many health staff die in attacks, and others flee the country, siphoning away precious human capital. The damage to health posts and hospitals is compounded by problems of limited access, as roads leading to health facilities are destroyed or rendered inaccessible by land mines. This situation spells the death of many injured or ill child soldiers, and it wreaks untold misery on civilian children as well. The collapse of the health system and the resulting breakdown of immunization programs allows preventable diseases such as polio to spread, causing disability, illness, and deaths.

Even the health facilities that remain in areas that haven't been at- tacked become inaccessible, because they are overwhelmed by swarms of displaced people. In Angola, where the fighting in the 1990s displaced nearly one-third of the people, war swelled the population of the capital city, Luanda, by millions of people, many of whom lived in squalor and had no access to health care. Most child soldiers in Angola lacked access to those facilities because they were in the ranks of UNITA, which stayed mostly in the bush. The plight of Angolan children was shown by the fact that near the millennium, approximately one child out of three died in Angola before having reached the age of 5 years (Machel 2001).

The damage of infrastructure indirectly impacts child soldiers' health by reinforcing their tendency to stay with the armed group. After all, if war has damaged schools, training centers, and other structures vital for developing a positive future, what better options do children have than soldiering?

Food Insecurity

Armed conflict damages food security through destruction of crops and of the animals that farmers typically rely on for work and for food. A woman from Sierra Leone said:

> The rebels came every day for months and months on end. We used to have many animals here but now we have not even a single one. They took it all away from us. Even if they came and found you eating meat they would take the meat from you and beat you up. This carried on for almost one year. (Boyden et al. 2003, 73)

Many armed groups destroy agriculture and stores of food entirely through vicious "scorched earth" campaigns, killing and burning every- thing and everyone in the targeted area. In the 1980s the Guatemalan government used this ruthless tool repeatedly against Mayan villages be- lieved to harbor rebel fighters and supporters (Landau 1993).

Armed conflict also ravages systems of agriculture and the transport systems used to distribute food and farming items. The destruction of water and irrigation systems, the loss of farming equipment and sup- plies, and the displacement of entire villages either halt farming completely or reduce it to a small scale unable to feed the local population. The damage to roads and the threat that travelers will be attacked makes it difficult to transport food to markets, which are also disrupted by war, or to obtain the materials needed to rebuild local agriculture. The prevalence of land mines and unexploded ordnance thwarts efforts to rebuild roads and markets.

Villages that have been repeatedly attacked cannot sustain farming. This creates chronic food shortages, both for villagers and for the armed groups that obtain food primarily by looting villages. Said a former boy soldier in Uganda, whose gauntness hinted at the pain associated with the chronic hunger: "We never had enough food. We were always hungry . . . so hungry. But they [the LRA] made us march sometimes all night. I thought of food all the time. Feeling hungry all the time is worse than the fighting." Even when child soldiers have access to food, it often lacks the caloric value needed to sustain growth and health. Also, their food frequently lacks adequate micronutrients. A deficiency of iodine or vitamin A can cause, respectively, mental retardation or blindness.

Due to omnipresent food insecurity, malnutrition and death stalk many children. More than 20 percent of children suffered from wasting (low weight relative to height) in cities under siege in the Angolan war at its peak (Machel 2001). Particularly for children under 5 years of age, malnutrition creates severe vulnerability. Children who suffer moderate degrees of malnutrition are four times more likely to die than children who enjoy adequate nutrition, and the risk doubles again for severely malnourished children. Malnutrition boosts vulnerability to disease, since malnourished children are less resistant to infections and diseases and more likely to be severely affected when they become ill (Machel 2001).

Disease

Worldwide, disease reaps an enormous harvest of death, annually killing ten million children. War zones are spawning grounds for communicable diseases, many of which are preventable. In war zones, the primary killers are typically diarrheal diseases, acute respiratory infections, malaria, and measles (Machel 2001). Diarrheal diseases are spread by consumption of contaminated water, which in turn results from the destruction of water and sanitation systems. Tuberculosis has made a comeback in many parts of the world and spreads easily in crowded refugee camps and cities. These and other diseases, including sexually transmitted diseases, have great impact because people in war zones already live in a weakened condition. Lacking access to proper food and health care, they often face a multiplicity of health risks, any one of which is damaging.

Although diseases pose constant threats to child soldiers, the risks increase significantly when enemy troops are nearby. Limits on the movements of one's own group frequently lead to shortages of food and medicines. Also, the enemy's proximity requires constant vigilance, limits opportunities for rest and recovery, and may necessitate fast marches to aviod attack. For children who are already ill, this combination of conditions can increase vulnerability and suffering. For example, a Sri Lankan girl soldier said:

> But the worst is when you are sick and there are enemy troops around. It's likely that your condition will worsen into a very severe disease. That's the life in the group. Perhaps the hardest for me was about getting sick. Sometimes I get sick for a week. That's my most difficult crisis. I can go on without food but I really cannot bear getting sick. What I really want to avoid is the situation wherein I'm so sick, of course I'm not a civilian but in the group, but still had to walk far and fast but what if I cannot do it, what are they going to do with me? (Keairns 2003c, 59)

The prevalence of disease in armed groups is unknown. Many armed groups keep no written health records, and group norms prohibit discussion of health difficulties. Also, child soldiers often hide their illnesses out of fear of punishment or death. In Angola, girl soldiers reported that anyone who complained or was unable to continue was killed on the spot (Stavrou 2005). The prevalence of disease and other health problems is evident to anyone who has witnessed child soldiers coming out of the bush.

Inside armed groups, child soldiers may have little or no access to health care and medications. Many armed opposition groups have no physicians, nurses, or other trained medical personnel to attend to sick people, although some child soldiers may receive on-the-job training in patching people up. Armed groups often exploit this situation by using access to health care as an incentive. By giving commanders first access to health care, they fuel child soldiers' desire to become commanders.

The catch is that being a commander is hardly a ticket to good health, since children who have earned a command post are expected to lead the charge into dangerous situations.

Disability, Land Mines, Unexploded Ordnance

War cripples and maims large numbers of child soldiers, creating disabilities and suffering that last a lifetime. In the DRC, a former boy soldier recounted:

> In January, 2001, while I was staying with my older brother, the Local-Defense militia came and took all of the men, adults and youth, to Mushaki. I was 15 years old and my parents did not know I was taken. At Mushaki, we were submitted to unbearable agonies. When children were unable to keep up, they were whipped. This is why I am deformed and condemned to be handicapped the rest of my life. (Verhey 2003, 44)

Whether through brutal training or attack, some child soldiers become disabled owing to head traumas, blindness, or deafness. Their physical pain and suffering is matched by their psychological and social suffering associated with stigma and isolation from normal social activities. For many young men, the greatest suffering arises from their inability to work and provide for a family, which in many societies are necessary for social integration, marriage, and functionality.

Major sources of disability are the uncleared land mines and unexploded ordnance such as bombs, shells, or grenades that are prevalent in eighty countries worldwide. Afghanistan, which has an estimated ten million land mines, provides a stark portrait of the damage done to children. During the decade-long fight against Soviet invaders, Soviet forces dropped from the air toylike "butterfly" land mines designed to invite curious children to pick them up, with disastrous consequences.

In February 2002, I interviewed a group of nine Afghan children, each of whom had stepped on a land mine and lost a leg in the previous week. One 17-year-old boy who had been a soldier in the Northern Alliance forces said, "I had walked on that trail a hundred times before with no problem." Yet on the day he hit the mine, he lost his left leg. Usually the soldiers walked only on very narrow trails, following the exact footsteps of the soldiers ahead. That strategy, however, was far from foolproof, as numerous boys in the group said they had seen fellow soldiers, including children, wounded in mine explosions.

Child soldiers also face risks because they serve as mine layers and mine sweepers. A Sri Lankan girl who had worked in a land-mines unit said:

> Sometimes a landmine would explode and children would be injured. Their fingers, hands, face. One time we were working in a line and the last girl made a mistake when removing a landmine. It exploded and she lost a finger. She was seventeen. I was scared to handle them. (HRW 2004b, 27)

Mine sweepers' work can be even more dangerous because children frequently have little protection or training. Also, some groups force child soldiers to explore suspected minefields, clearing paths for subsequent attack forces. This is believed to be one reason why children were recruited on a massive scale by Iran in the Iran-Iraq war of the 1980s (Brown 1990).

Risks also arise from unexploded ordnance, which conspicuously litters many fields and urban areas in war zones. In northern Afghanistan, children's curiosity can be a liability, as children who pick up unexploded shells frequently trigger explosions, causing death or the loss of eyes, hands, or legs. Economic motives and disaster tourism also contribute to children's risk of handling unexploded ordnance. Many children collect bombs and grenades to supply a market created by unthinking foreigners seeking war souvenirs.

Land mines threaten large numbers of children, including girls and women who do much of the carrying, long after the end of the war. In Angola, one of the most heavily mined countries in the world, a 17-year-old girl said:

> I woke up in the morning and went out of our yard, taking a footpath that goes up to our neighbour Maria. I wanted to get fire to prepare breakfast, then I just heard it explode and found myself lying on the floor. My leg was cut off and my arm and chest injured. I cried and then people came to rescue me and take me to the hospital. (Honwana 1998, 47–48)

The disfigurement and movement disability this girl suffered as a result of the mine explosion are socially crippling and damage her prospects for marriage and earning a living. In many countries, amputees are stigmatized and isolated socially, which child survivors sometimes describe as being as painful as the physical injury. Prosthetics and physical rehabilitation are prohibitively costly for many people who live in war zones, and prosthetic support for children costs more than for adults. Young children's bones are still growing, so a 5-year-old who has lost one leg will require a new prosthetic device every six months to match the growth in the remaining leg.

Land mines are notoriously expensive to clear, as, on average, mines cost $3 to manufacture but $1,000 to remove (Machel 2001). The costs imposed by land mines, however, cannot be measured in dollar terms alone. The social costs include damaged health due to the disruption of agriculture and poor food security, and disruption of the transportation children need to reach schools, hospitals, and other social services.

Reproductive Health

Girl soldiers face significant risks associated with rape and sexual violence, which frequently causes internal bleeding, cervical tearing, uterine deformation, abdominal pain, infection, premature births, stillbirths, and even death (Mazurana and McKay 2001). The injuries inflicted by sexual violence can be lethal in the bush, where no health care and few medications are available, and they are particularly damaging to younger girls' smaller, less developed bodies. Short of death, the injuries can cause lifelong problems of reproductive health. Many girls who survive repeated rapes suffer menstrual complications and are unable to conceive (ISIS 1998). Rape and sexual violence also produce high rates of sexually transmitted diseases such as HIV, syphilis, and gonorrhea. The maladies produced by these diseases include pelvic inflammatory disease, a product of sexually transmitted infections that causes long-term damage to girls' reproductive health (Mazurana et al. 2002).

Girl soldiers frequently identify the social burdens of reproductive health problems as having the greatest impact on their lives (McKay 2006). A 17-year-old girl from Sierra Leone who had been raped repeatedly told me, "I can never have a baby. No one wants a woman who cannot have a baby." Many African women regard barrenness as a source of shame, as women pride themselves on their ability to have children and to be good mothers. To be unmarried in Sierra Leone is a condition that many young women describe as a form of social death.

Girl soldiers also experience increased health risks associated with problems during pregnancy, childbirth, and abortion. In armed groups, pregnant girls seldom receive prenatal care, and the risks of miscarriage are high due to the difficult living conditions and heavy labor they engage in. Those who reach childbirth may be at risk from poor nutrition, lack of access to clean water and quality shelter, and poor sanitation. Also, childbirth typically occurs in an unsanitary context in which there are no midwives or means of helping mothers if birth complications arise. A Mozambican girl whom RENAMO had abducted said: "I was pregnant when I was caught. I had to manage alone; no one helped me. It was not my first baby, so I had seen how to use the blade. I used the blade to cut the cord and then I just tied it" (McKay and Mazurana 2004, 70). Also, armed opposition groups in Sierra Leone and Liberia have tried to induce labor or to speed up the birthing process by pushing hard on girls' stomachs, which risks abdominal rupture and long-term damage. The rates of maternal mortality among girl soldiers are unknown but are believed to be very high owing to the combination of weakened mothers, unsafe birthing practices, unsanitary conditions, and poor access to health clinics and competent health staff to help handle complications.

Girl soldiers who abort either by choice or by order are endangered by unsafe methods of abortion. Although some armed groups include physicians, girls who plan to abort are frequently in the hands of people who use dangerous methods. A Ugandan nurse and midwife told how girls in northern Uganda used roots that stimulated uterine contractions, often with catastrophic results: "Local herbs every little girl knows; because they are young, it is logical when they get that abortion in the jungle, most of them die. But a few lucky ones go through it" (McKay and Mazurana 2004, 70–71).

The dizzying assortment of health risks to child soldiers amounts to a systematic assault on child soldiers' health. Its scale and lethality become visible in light of the HIV/AIDS pandemic.

The Silent Killer

As a killer of children, the global HIV/AIDS pandemic has far surpassed armed conflict (Foster, Levine, and Williamson 2005; UNICEF, USAID, and UNAIDS 2004). UNAIDS estimates that by the end of 2003, 37.8 million people lived with HIV, the precursor of AIDS, which kills slowly but on a staggering scale. In 2003 alone, AIDS caused an estimated 2.9 million deaths worldwide. The scale of death is expected to increase sharply, because HIV spreads rapidly by such means as unprotected sex and the sharing of needles by drug users. An estimated 4.8 million new HIV infections occurred in 2003 alone (UNAIDS 2004). Access to antiretroviral drugs remained severely limited in most developing countries, where poor people cannot afford to purchase drugs such as nevirapine, even if offered at rates wealthy nations would regard as bargains.

Children shoulder a large portion of the burdens imposed by HIV/AIDS. More than two million children under age 15 live with HIV, and each day approximately seventeen hundred additional children contract HIV (UNICEF, USAID, and UNAIDS, 2004). Infants become HIV-positive through maternal transmission of the virus during pregnancy, labor, childbirth, or breast-feeding. Teenagers acquire HIV infection primarily through unprotected sex, which is rampant in many armed groups.

The burdens on children, however, arise not only from direct infection by HIV but also from parents' illness and death. Loss of the parents' income can worsen children's poverty. Watching parents die and dealing with their deaths create large emotional wounds and alter children's role, social status, and prospects for the future. These wounds are conspicuous in HIV/AIDS orphans.

The Plight of Orphans

Throughout sub-Saharan Africa, one of the most severely affected regions, many children lose both parents to HIV/AIDS, becoming part of what has grimly become known as the "orphan generation." Having lost their parents, children lose their childhood and of necessity become heads of household. In Uganda, a 13-year-old boy named Joseph, a straight-A student who was not HIV-positive, told me how HIV/AIDS had impacted him and his family:

> First my father became very ill [with HIV/AIDS] when I was 10 years. Since I am the oldest son, I dropped out of school to work in the fields and bring our food. It was very hard watching him die . . . You know, an African father is the son's guide and head of the family. I really miss him. We did not have money for a proper funeral so we dug a grave and buried him.

Joseph's burdens worsened when his mother, also HIV-positive, began to suffer a variety of AIDS-related afflictions. His mother's illness plunged the family even deeper into the poverty it had known for many years. Joseph found himself in the position of caretaker not only for his mother but also for his five younger brothers and sisters. His youngest brother, who had been 3 years old at the time, became very sad and cried a lot when his mother had become too weak to play with him. As the family exhausted its meager savings, Joseph's oldest sister dropped out of school in order to sell things in the market. Said Joseph, "I was very worried about her, because you know in our situation, many girls sell their bodies so they can feed their families."

When Joseph's mother died, the children dutifully dug another grave and buried her unceremoniously. They had all become orphans who were on their own. Joseph recalled, "My youngest brother, then four years old, cried and looked very weak. He was constantly sick, and we thought he would die. But a doctor helped him for free and he lived." Trapped in a downward economic spiral, Joseph and his family decided that all the school-age children had to withdraw from school. No longer students, they worked on the streets, selling and trading small items to obtain food. Remarkably, Joseph stepped into his role as head of household in full stride and expressed confidence in his family's ability to survive.

> You know, it has been hard on all of us, and we are very poor, but we pull together and get by. My uncle helps us when he can, but he has eight children and cannot take us in. My brothers and sisters, we care for each other . . . I still dream of going to school again.

Not all child heads of household have Joseph's resilience, and not all orphans fare as well as Joseph's brothers and sisters. In many countries affected by HIV/AIDS and armed conflict, well-intentioned governments and organizations put large numbers of orphans into orphanages or centers. Here the children get a place to live and food to eat, but the orphanages are too overcrowded and understaffed to enable children's healthy development (Tolfree 2003). In Luanda, Angola, just after the 1992–1994 fighting, I visited an orphanage in which hundreds of children, including children under 5 years of age, sat listlessly in a very crowded space, day after day. Their gaunt bodies showed obvious signs of skin diseases, infections, respiratory illnesses, and other maladies. The two staff members who worked there wanted to attend to each child and to organize games, songs, and dances, but they lacked the time to do so. The chronic lack of attention also deprived babies of the social interaction with their caretakers that they need to form effective social attachments. These attachments are an important part of the foundation for healthy relationships later in life (Bowlby 1969; Cole and Cole 1993; Grossman, Grossman, and Waters 2005; Kagitcibasi 1996).

Orphanages can have a magnet effect that separates children from their parents. In Rwanda following the 1994 genocide, which had left in its wake tens of thousands of orphans, international agencies opened significant numbers of homes to care for the children. Wanting their babies to have a better chance of obtaining food and health care, many mothers abandoned their babies on the homes' doorsteps. In many impoverished countries, plummeting household incomes force children out of their homes and into institutions. Research on child development, however, has shown that in poor, understaffed institutions, children do not thrive and do not receive the quality of stimulation, emotional support, and care that families typically provide (Cole and Cole 1993; Frank et al. 1996; Tolfree 2003). Also, for the cost of supporting one child in an institution, one can enable several children to live with families. Orphanages are best seen as a last resort.

Children orphaned by HIV/AIDS sometimes end up living on the streets, where they might become involved in drugs and crime. In African countries, home to nearly one-third of the world's HIV-positive people, young girls are at great risk due to the widespread myth that an HIV-positive man can cure his affliction by having sex with a virgin. This belief has opened a thriving sex market in some locations for young girls. Older girls are at risk of sexual exploitation through engagement in transactional sex, which may be their only way to meet their basic needs and those of their children.

Orphans are frequently at risk even if they do not live in orphanages or on the streets. Many live in foster families or with members of their extended families. Although these living arrangements can be positive (Doná 2001), they are far from perfect and require careful scrutiny (Tolfree 2003). Children who have been taken in by another family might be exploited for their labor and might be discriminated against in regard to food, clothing, and other essential items. Feeling unloved, or lacking hope, such children frequently decide to leave their caretakers. When they do leave, their risk of becoming soldiers rises sharply.

HIV/AIDS and Child Soldiers

HIV/AIDS and child soldiering are thoroughly intertwined problems that exert reciprocal influences on each other. The narratives of two children from East Timor reflect the link between orphaning and child soldiering.

> My father was shot dead by the Indonesian military when I was 12 years old and that is when I went to join Falintil. They accepted me to join because there was no other place for me to run [his mother had died earlier] and the only choice was to join Falintil and fight. (UNICEF 2003, 30)

> Many of the other children in the militia were orphans, from broken homes. Those who didn't attend school and those who were involved in gambling rings. (UNICEF 2003, 30)

The period in which East Timor struggled for its independence from Indonesia was not one in which HIV/AIDS produced large numbers of orphans in East Timor. However, it is sobering to reflect on how much greater the problem of child recruitment would be in countries having large numbers of HIV/AIDS orphans. Sub-Saharan Africa includes countries such as the Democratic Republic of the Congo, Burundi, Rwanda, and Uganda, in which the twin ravages of HIV/AIDS and armed conflict have swelled the ranks of orphans, many of whom are recruited into armed groups.

At the household level, armed conflict, HIV/AIDS, and chronic poverty interact to propel children who are not orphans into lives as soldiers. Armed conflict in or near one's village frequently causes destruction of homes, animals, and property, adding greatly to the already severe burden of chronic poverty. Very poor children may be able to live with their families only because they earn money by working in the streets or engaging in heavy labor. If one or both parents contract HIV/AIDS, decreasing the parent's ability to work and plunging the household into deeper poverty, the children may decide to leave their homes to reduce the strain on their family's resources. On the streets, they become easy targets for recruitment by armed groups.

Inside many armed groups, HIV/AIDS is spread rapidly by rape, sexual coercion, and consensual sexual activity. Military personnel tend to have rates of sexually transmitted diseases, including HIV/AIDS, that are two to five times higher than for civilian populations (Collier et al. 2003; Smith 2002). In countries such as Angola and the Democratic Republic of the Congo, which have or have recently had armed conflicts, 40 to 60 percent of military personnel are believed to be HIV-positive (Elbe 2002). Such high prevalence rates boost the chances that child soldiers in these countries will become HIV-positive.

Nor does the problem stay confined to armed groups. As soldiers attack villages and rape women and girls, they spread the deadly virus through the civilian population. In Rwanda at the time of the 1994 genocide, some Hutu men told the women they were raping that they were giving them something that was worse than death because they would die slowly (Elbe 2002). Also, near any group of soldiers, including peacekeepers, there grows up a cottage industry of commercial sex workers who help to spread HIV. As HIV/AIDS tears through the local population, disabling and killing breadwinners, it deepens poverty, creates more orphans and street children, and plunges many children into the hands of armed groups. This cycle is self-perpetuating because child recruitment enables more fighting, increases destruction and poverty, and continues the spread of HIV/AIDS.

HIV/AIDS and Destabilization

Although HIV/AIDS exacts an enormous toll on health and well-being at the family and household level, the larger threat that the pandemic poses becomes visible only at the societal and regional levels (Foster, Levine, and Williamson 2005). In many countries, HIV/AIDS is not only a health crisis but also a development crisis conducive to political instability. Many skilled workers and professionals flee HIV/AIDS-infected regions, and this brain drain makes it more difficult to prevent the spread of the pandemic (Rosenberg 2005). Also, HIV/AIDS kills large numbers of people, stripping communities of essential human resources and capital and eroding their foundation for economic development. The deaths of large numbers of teachers, physicians, and intellectuals diminishes the societal base for education, which is essential for economic development and as a means of preparing young people to become productive members of society. Large numbers of jobless people, many of whom have already suffered the ravages of poverty and HIV/AIDS on their households, may turn to violence to meet their daily needs. As death thins the ranks of community leaders, police, armies, and agencies that support civilian society, the society risks sliding into social chaos. Engulfed in spreading turmoil, the state may lose its ability to meet basic needs and control political unrest, fueled in part by large numbers of disaffected, jobless youths.

The ability of HIV/AIDS to destabilize societies in ways that promote children's involvement in political violence is evident in countries such as Zimbabwe (Price-Smith and Daly 2004), where 34 percent of adults are HIV-positive and AIDS has orphaned 980,000 children. The Zimbabwean life expectancy plummeted from 52 years in 1970 to 40 years in 1999 and will probably decline even further in the next decade. Large numbers of deaths have sharply reduced the labor supply, crippling agriculture and industry. The fact that many workers are sick or care for family members living with AIDS contributes to Zimbabwe's problematic pattern of high levels of worker attrition and low levels of productivity. Education has been damaged severely; large numbers of teachers have died, and many children have dropped out of school to work to support their families. The economic decline, coupled with an already devastating unemployment rate of 45 percent, increases the sense of hopelessness and invites political unrest. Under President Mugabe, the Zimbabwean government has ruled with an iron fist and regularly uses torture to silence political opposition. The net result is a potentially explosive combination of tyranny, political opposition, and societal instability in which thousands of children have joined militias that allegedly train youths in torture and killing (CSC 2004).

Zimbabwe's plight has regional as well as national implications. A sudden conflict-induced collapse of Mugabe's government could unleash a civil war that, like the HIV/ADS pandemic, would spill across Zimbabwe's borders. Such an eruption of political violence could require the withdrawal of Zimbabwean troops from the Democratic Republic of the Congo, shifting the balance of power in that protracted conflict. Even more ominously, Zimbabwe's economic collapse could trigger increased regional economic instability and heighten the vulnerability of other southern African states, whose governments are at risk owing partly to HIV/AIDS. If the HIV/AIDS pandemic alone is devastating, its full impact lies in its deadly interactions with political, social, and economic factors.

Destructive Synergies

The synergistic effects of HIV/AIDS and armed conflict threaten children's well-being on a large scale and simultaneously undermine peace. Before armed conflict has erupted, the ravages of HIV/AIDS promote a sense of hopelessness and despair that fuel political unrest. Although HIV/AIDS does not cause armed conflict, it interacts with factors such as chronic poverty, youth unrest, and government frailty, increasing the vulnerability to armed conflict. For a government already cobbled by poverty and facing a crisis of legitimacy due to failure to meet basic needs, the eruption of an HIV epidemic adds to the burdens and can help to stir up political unrest, particularly among young people who most often fall prey to HIV/AIDS. In many societies, youths are at the center of the quest for political change, and youth radicalism frequently increases when there is a widespread sense of youth hopelessness. As discussed in Chapter 10, youths tend to engage in political violence in situations that combine chronic poverty, lack of opportunities, and a "youth bulge"—a large cohort of teenagers who may become disaffected due to widespread unemployment and lack of a positive future (Urdal 2004). High HIV prevalence among youths adds to the crisis of hope, leading many young people to join armed groups and to use fighting as their main strategy for achieving political and social change.

During armed conflict, too, HIV/AIDS catalyzes morbidity and fighting. Attacks on a village, for example, send many HIV/AIDS-infected people into camps for displaced persons, where the HIV virus tends to spread. Over time, the combination of HIV/AIDS and armed conflict will orphan large numbers of children, who are at increased risk of being recruited as soldiers and continuing cycles of violence. Also, as conflict-affected people sink deeper into poverty, desperate women and girls may engage in commercial sex, which thrives in war zones and also spreads HIV/AIDS. In camps or in villages, the spread of HIV/AIDS erodes human capital, weakening local people's capacities to cope and protect themselves and their children. Deaths of elders, healers, religious leaders, educators, and men of fighting age weaken villages, making them easy prey for armed groups and warlords, who exploit the village in pursuit of their own political goals.

Although armed conflict can and often does enable the spread of HIV/AIDS, there is no necessary connection between the eruption of armed conflict and the increased spread of HIV/AIDS. Armed conflict can drive HIV/AIDS rates up or down, depending on the prewar prevalence rates of HIV/AIDS and the mobility of armed groups across and within state boundaries. For example, Sierra Leone and Sudan have low HIV prevalence rates relative to surrounding countries, in part because they had low HIV prevalence before their wars, and the wars insulated them from neighboring countries (Spiegel 2004). Soldiers and armed conflict become particularly deadly platforms for the spread of HIV/AIDS when the prewar HIV prevalence rates are high. Unfortunately, the spread of the HIV/AIDS pandemic increases the chances that this condition will be met.

Following the signing of a ceasefire, the twin ravages of HIV/AIDS and armed conflict do not end. The effects are frequently visible among refugees and youths, including many HIV-positive people who return home following war. Coming home is always a challenging process, due to shortages of infrastructure, food, and income, but it is even more challenging in an AIDS-saturated context. The acute poverty and lack of jobs may make it very difficult for youths to find hope or for former child soldiers to successfully transition from lives as soldiers to lives as civilians. The paucity of government services in the face of overwhelming needs may create a loss of confidence and a crisis of legitimacy that could spark new rounds of fighting.

These powerful synergies between HIV/AIDS and armed conflict have the capacity to plunge societies into a downward spiral of misery, instability, and war that is vexingly difficult to break. The tendency of the synergies to impede prevention efforts rings through in the words of an 18-year-old from Burundi: "Without war, we could fight AIDS properly" (Save the Children UK 2002, 18). Children are at the heart of the synergies because HIV and armed conflict prey equally on child soldiers and rob civilian children of the hope and life options needed to create peace and stability. If the world is to create hope for children, it must establish alternate, life-affirming synergies that break cycles of violence by enabling children to leave armed groups and find meaningful roles as civilians.

6

The Invisible Wounds of War

War creates long-lasting wounds, both visible and invisible. Most conspicuous are the physical wounds. Less visible are the hidden wounds of the mind, heart, and soul. For many children, these wounds include the pain of multiple losses and their difficulties coming to terms with searing memories of past horrors. However, the hidden wounds often relate as much to children's current living situation as to memories of the past. Many former child soldiers experience shame and guilt or are stigmatized and isolated. Many others experience enormous stress due to poor health and joblessness, or have difficulties regulating their behavior in ways required by civilian life. The stresses of war and postwar life arise through the dynamic interaction between psychological, physical, social, and spiritual processes. Collectively, these stresses are called "psychosocial" (Williamson and Robinson 2006).

When psychologists look at former child soldiers, they often focus on trauma, which Arroyo and Eth (1996, 54) defined as "a sense of profound helplessness in the face of overwhelming danger, anxiety, and arousal" associated with life-threatening experiences. In many conflict zones, child soldiers do show signs of trauma (Mocellin 2006), and psychologists provide trauma counseling and community supports to the survivors. However, numerous analysts question the validity and utility of both the trauma concept and the Westernized practices it encourages (e.g., Bracken 1998; Summerfield 1999). To appreciate the limits of any one model or approach, one must recognize the diversity of child soldiers' experiences and situations.*

*. Though subsequent quotations from child soldiers are direct reports from individual interviews, the following three narratives are composites created from interviews with a large

Robert, a Ugandan boy whom the LRA abducted at age 13, spent two years in the LRA, seeing LRA soldiers kill children who could not keep up. Having received training in Sudan, he became a fighter, had killed villagers and abducted children, and became a commander. During a battle with the Ugandan army, he had been captured and had feared for his life, but the army released him. Having been home for six months, he expressed a mixture of relief and worry about his situation: "I am very happy to be here and to be out of the LRA. But I cannot sleep as my dreams carry me back and scare me. I see the faces of people being killed and the LRA comes after me again . . ." Avoiding situations that trigger painful memories, he spends most of his time at home with his supportive family.

Agnes is a 17-year-old Angolan girl whom UNITA had abducted at age 13. Although she never fought, she saw many people die. UNITA forced her to dance all night long, presumably as a way to keep troops alert in case of attacks. In the shadows of the dance area, men selected girls for sex, pulling them outside the dancing circle and violating them forcibly. The fact that even the elders had forced sex with girls had shattered her trust for men, preventing her from marrying in a culture in which normal girls marry. Feeling isolated and separated from her family, she doubts she will ever fit into society again.

Mirwais, a 17-year-old boy from northern Afghanistan, spent only a short time with the Northern Alliance forces fighting the Taliban. He said he had been fearless as a fighter and had stepped on a landmine while ascending a mountain trail. Having lost his right leg, he is unable to do heavy work and to support a family, creating a crisis of hope for the future. "What is left for me? Now I will be only a burden." Having lost most of his family, he wonders how he will feed himself.

Two points are noteworthy about these children. First, not all child soldiers are affected by war in the same way. They differ significantly in regard to the nature, duration, and severity of their war experiences, and equally important, in their postwar situations, which differ along lines carved by gender, disability, and their access to social support. Whereas Robert fits a relatively typical profile of a traumatic reaction, Agnes does not. Her issues of mistrust and separation are probably bigger psychosocial issues than trauma. For Mirwais, issues about how he will feed

number of child soldiers in the respective countries and situations. The composite method, common in war-zone fieldwork, protects interviewees from being identified, as they might be if very many details about a single individual were presented.

himself exceed those associated with trauma. His situation shows clearly that former child soldiers frequently regard as their biggest problem not the impact of past violence but the formidable stresses of the postwar living situation. The supports he needs are not so much counseling as access to prosthetics, occupational training, and opportunities to earn a living, enabling him to become hopeful and able to participate in major life activities. It is an oversimplification to lump all former child soldiers together in the single category "traumatized children," implying that they have all been affected similarly or require similar supports.

Second, these cases also illustrate that children's suffering does not end with the fighting but haunts them over a longer term. The lingering effects have led to portrayals of former child soldiers as people crippled by mental health issues or as hardened killers who have no moral compass. This view of child soldiers as scarred for life, however, is overplayed and out of touch with most former child soldiers' resilience and ability to function. Recent research has challenged predominantly Western understandings of how child soldiers have been affected. Although children do experience war trauma, trauma is only one element of a much larger and more complex mosaic of psychosocial impacts (Dawes and Donald 1994; McCallin 1998; Wessells and Monteiro 2000). To understand how child soldiers have been affected by war, it is useful to examine trauma, on which many psychologists have focused, but also to look beyond the trauma idiom. This approach leads us on a journey from Western psychology into a less well documented terrain that highlights the importance of local cultural understandings and the resilience of former child soldiers. This journey, which resonates with my own experience, reflects the evolution in thinking that many practitioners undergo as they gain experience in different war zones.

War Trauma

People who have had traumatic experiences can feel shattered, overwhelmed, debilitated, and alone in a very dangerous world. Following the Serb attacks in 1999, a young Kosovar woman living in a refugee camp in Albania said:

> I heard them cut the men's throats . . . and the screams . . . I saw them
> kill innocent babies. I can't sleep after what I've seen. I'm too edgy and

my dreams take me back to the killing. Being awake is no better. I hear things and suddenly it's like the horrible things are happening all over again . . . I can't think, and many things remind me. My mind is out of control. I must be losing my mind.

This woman's traumatic experiences have damaged her ordinary belief that other people are basically good and left her feeling unsafe and highly vulnerable (Janoff-Bulman 1992). Her feelings of being overwhelmed and out of her mind are normal psychological responses to life-threatening experiences. Her reaction is characteristic of a specific form of trauma called post-traumatic stress disorder (PTSD), which features symptoms such as flashbacks, heightened arousal, and avoidance. Although PTSD ought not to be the primary concern of psychologists in war zones, it warrants analysis because it affects children and people in many different cultures (Arroyo and Eth 1996; Marsella et al. 1994, 1996) and has been the dominant concern of many humanitarian workers.

War Trauma and Children

In both children and adults, trauma typically causes nightmares that disrupt sleep and flashbacks in which the mind replays painful experiences, evoking intense fear and anxiety (Herman 1997). Trauma also produces neurological changes, leaving children in a heightened state of fear and arousal (van der Kolk 1996). Unable to self-regulate and relax, people who suffer trauma frequently cannot sleep and feel edgy and irritable. In many children, traumatic reactions are often expressed somatically, in headaches and stomachaches or in other physical maladies having no organic basis.

Traumatic reactions also depend on children's age and stage of development (de Jong 2002; Pynoos, Steinberg, and Goenjian 1996; Terr 1991). For children under 6 years of age, typical reactions may include crying, bedwetting, clinging, and nightmares. Young children may be even more vulnerable than older children (Pynoos and Eth 1985), in part because they have active imaginations and are less capable of distinguishing fantasy from reality. For children of ages 7 to 12, trauma may manifest itself in social isolation and repetitive enactment of traumatic events in play. There may also be psychosomatic complaints such as dizziness, headaches, or stomach pain. For adolescents, trauma frequently leads to acting-out behavior such as skipping school or abusing substances. Fighting and rebellious behavior are typical forms of acting out (Eth and Pynoos 1985).

Collectively, these reactions can impair children's functionality, limiting their ability to do the things children in a particular culture usually do. For example, in Uganda, children commonly go to school and are expected by parents and villagers to be good students. A 12-year-old boy whom the LRA had abducted and kept for over a year said, "I go to school but my mind is not steady . . . my thoughts are back to the war and the marches, the attacks. I used to be a good student but now learning in school is difficult for me." Problems in learning are not unusual for a child who has difficulty sleeping and cannot concentrate. Nor are the difficulties restricted to school. War-affected children may be unable to solve problems they encounter in work or to interact with peers in the usual manner. The resulting cascade of problems poses additional risks to children. For example, a war-affected child who has difficulty concentrating and drops out of school could be at risk of engaging in dangerous labor to earn a living. Also, the effects of trauma can persist for many years. In Mozambique, nearly a third of former child soldiers have nightmares and show other signs of trauma nearly fifteen years after the war (Boothby, Crawford, and Halperin 2006).

Traumatic reactions also contribute to cycles of violence and war. People who suffer trauma tend to pass on their horrible memories by telling stories of their experiences to their children and friends, who in turn repeat the stories to others (Cairns and Roe 2003). This process of telling and retelling weaves communal memories, or "chosen traumas" (Volkan 1997), and can make events from several hundred years ago seem alive today. In turn, people who hear about traumatic events may show signs of traumatic reactions, a phenomenon called vicarious or secondary traumatization (McCann and Pearlman, 1990). These stories, which become part of an intergenerational narrative of trauma, encourage fighting and children's participation in armed groups. For one thing, the stories demonize the Other and provide warrants for revenge, one of the main motives underlying children's recruitment. Also, children who suffer trauma tend to see the world as a much more dangerous place than it really is. Following armed conflict, traumatized people on both sides may harbor strong, irrational fears that fuel suspicions, encourage arms races, and promote fighting (Rubin, Pruitt, and Kim 1994).

Prevalence

The prevalence of trauma among child soldiers depends on the nature and chronicity of their war experiences. One study conducted in Angola in the period 1996 to 1998 indicated the prevalence of extreme experiences among boy soldiers, whose median age of recruitment was 13 to 14 years and average length of stay with an armed group was 3.8 years (Christian Children's Fund/Angola 1998):

- 77.5 percent had shot someone.
- 67 percent had lost family members or close friends due to the war.
- 76 percent had witnessed people being killed.
- 61 percent said they had been in life-or-death situations.
- 29 percent reported that they had been wounded.

Similar rates of profound experiences have been found in child soldiers in Mozambique (Boothby, Crawford, and Halperin 2006), Uganda (Derluyn et al. 2004), and Somalia (Mocellin 2006).

Although any one of these kinds of experiences could have severe effects, even greater effects arise from the accumulation of stresses. Many children had not only feared for their lives but had also lost family members, shot someone, or witnessed people being killed. Psychological reactions were evident in the sample of Angolan children (CCF/Angola 1998):

- 50 percent said that when thinking of the past, they try to forget and block out what happened.
- 41 percent said they have difficulty sleeping.
- 20 percent said they always feel afraid of something terrible happening.
- 16 percent reported thinking that what happened could happen again.
- 39 percent said they feel more nervous and get frightened more easily now than before the war.

- 37 percent said they remember things that happened during the war.
- 35.6 percent said that when doing things their concentration span is short.
- 31.6 percent said that they have heart palpitations.

Although this study did not measure PTSD directly, the results fit the pattern of responses characteristic of trauma—problems sleeping and concentrating, somatic responses such as heart palpitations, and memories of traumatic events. The children's attempts to forget and block out memories of what had happened indicates both the painfulness of the memories and the children's use of a cognitive avoidance strategy to cope with the memories.

Research from other war zones indicates that PTSD rates may be quite high among former child soldiers. Among former child soldiers in northern Uganda, 97 percent of a sample of children who had volunteered to participate in a study showed PTSD symptoms (Derluyn et al. 2004). This rate of PTSD is much higher than the 10 to 20 percent rate that is more typical of civilian children who live in war zones (Cairns 1996). High trauma rates may owe to the particularly brutal nature of the war and the accumulation of severe stresses in such situations. Caution is needed, however, in interpreting these results, since no reliable estimates exist of the prevalence of PTSD in northern Uganda before the war. A common error is to attribute all the traumatic effects observed to the children's war experiences, when there may have been other sources as well. A more compelling methodology is to compare prewar, baseline rates of PTSD in children with the postwar rates. Unfortunately, the baseline rates of PTSD in war zones are seldom known.

One way around this problem is suggested by studies of civilian children, who in war zones also exhibit significant levels of PTSD (Arroyo and Eth 1996; De Jong 2002; Dyregov, Gjestad, and Raundalen 2002; Leavitt and Fox 1993; Miller and Rasco 2004; Mollica et al. 1997; Somasundaram and Jamunanantha 2002; Yule et al. 2003). In war-affected provinces of Angola, nearly two-thirds of all children exhibited PTSD. The limitation of not having prewar, baseline data on PTSD rates has been partly overcome by comparing the rate of PTSD in Angolan children who live in war zones with the rate of PTSD in Angolan children living as refugees in Portugal. These groups exhibit PTSD rates of

69 percent and 18 percent, respectively. This suggests that the high rates of PTSD evident among Angolan children in war-affected provinces owe to experiences of war (McIntyre and Ventura 2003). This method is far from perfect, however, since the refugees could have come from wealthier families and lived in a more supportive environment, which can alleviate trauma (Silove 2006). The extent to which PTSD in war zones is caused by war itself requires much additional research.

Children's trauma has captured attention not only in regard to war zones but also in the aftermath of the devastating tsunami of December 2004 (Foa, Stein, and McFarlane 2006). Although trauma is compelling in part because it is concrete and vividly portrays children's suffering, it is important to avoid overgeneralizations. It is a mistake to assume that all child soldiers are traumatized. A boy who had been abducted and forced to porter for several days but who never saw people killed is in very different psychological terrain than a boy who had been forced to kill friends and family and lived with an armed group for years. Some evidence suggests that the longer children were soldiers, the more strongly they will have been affected (Boothby, Crawford, and Halperin 2006). Children also differ significantly in their genetic makeup, temperament, history, and sources of social support. Because of such differences, two children who experience the same life-threatening events may react in different ways. For example, a sociable girl soldier who fights because she believes in a political cause and who is surrounded by supportive friends may survive an attack by an armed group without developing trauma. A girl soldier who is less sociable, struggles with depression, and finds no meaning in the fighting, on the other hand, might feel traumatized and overwhelmed after surviving an attack by an armed group.

Perhaps most important, trauma is only one of many issues former child soldiers face. For many of these children, a greater concern is their loss of education, lack of training and job skills for earning a living, stigmatization and social exclusion, disability and health problems, and living in chronic poverty (Boyden et al. 2003; Dawes 1994; Peters and Richards 1998; Wessells and Jonah 2006). Although trauma is part of the psychological burden imposed both by child soldiering and by growing up in a war zone, trauma models capture only a small part of a much larger picture of children's life problems. In many war zones, the emphasis on trauma has been excessive and has distracted attention from children's wider psychosocial needs. There are also other strong reasons for challenging trauma models' underlying assumptions, in particular their emphasis on deficits defined by a medical model.

Beyond a Medical Model

Trauma approaches are based on a medical model and therefore emphasize child soldiers' deficits, portraying children as suffering a form of pathology that can have lifelong impacts. This pathology emphasis, which resonates with an older view in psychiatry that childhood experiences lay the groundwork for adult psychopathology, is part of a wider tendency of psychological research and popular writing to view former child soldiers as emotionally scarred and morally damaged. These depictions, although sensational and captivating, do not fit with a growing body of evidence indicating that most former child soldiers function quite well, exhibit complex moral reasoning, and defy stereotypes as predators (Boothby, Crawford, and Halperin 2006; Boyden 2003; Cairns 1996; Straker 1992; Wessells and Jonah 2006). In analyzing how child soldiers have been affected, one must look behind psychological labels and explore child soldiers' adaptability and functionality. Doing this paints a new picture showing that most former child soldiers are more resilient than had previously been understood (Annan and Blattman, 2006). In general, the resilience of young people has been underestimated (Sommers 2006).

The Perils of Labels

Although psychological labels can be useful, they present a plethora of dangers. The PTSD diagnosis categorizes children's reactions as pathological, when in fact they are normal responses to extreme experience. This pathologizing tendency is potentially damaging because it stigmatizes children at a moment in which they are vulnerable and need support (Reichenberg and Freedman 1996). Also, by implying that children are damaged, the trauma label encourages children to step into the role of victim. When children—or adults, for that matter—see themselves as victims, they tend to act in a passive, hopeless manner that impedes their recovery. One of the keys to overcoming trauma is to regain one's sense of control, which would be a difficult prospect for children who have a victim's mindset or believe they are irreparably damaged.

A related problem is the PTSD terminology, with its notion of "post"-traumatic stress, which suggests that the traumatic events have passed. Former child soldiers who have left armed groups face a multitude of stresses associated with fear of revenge attacks or re-recruitment, stigmatization, chronic poverty, and inability to earn a living. Following the signing of a ceasefire, violence in families and communities frequently continues to be a major problem. War frequently makes families a microcosm of the societal violence that surrounds them (Pintar, 2000). In war zones, children who experience family violence are among those who are most profoundly affected psychologically (Garbarino and Kostelny 1996). Heightened levels of family violence continue following the war, placing children at significant risk. Children in many war zones have told me there is no "post-" in regard to their stresses and difficulties, which are ongoing. Instead of "post"-traumatic stress, in war zones it would be far more apt to focus on *continuous stress* (Straker 1987), the lifetime effects of which are poorly understood.

The label *trauma* also invites reduction and overgeneralization. To say that children's problem is trauma is to reduce a complex situation to singular terms. At its worst, the term *traumatized child* creates a universal image that distracts from gender, age, and class issues that affect what happens to children in war and how children interpret their war experiences. The universalizing tendency is most visible and damaging in discourse about the "masses of traumatized children," which overlooks or reduces the enormous amount of individual differences among the children.

Beneath this excessive generalization lies the troubling question whether local people pick up and overuse the term *trauma* not so much because it reveals something fundamental about their situation but because of their destitution and the hidden power dynamics of humanitarian assistance. Local people frequently adopt outsiders' labels and approaches in hopes of keeping the experts happy and obtaining money and help. The trauma idiom has captured the attention of many donors who, eager to assist war-affected children, see trauma healing as a key priority in war zones. What emerges is a system of outside experts, NGOs, donor agencies, and local people who privilege trauma as the major psychological problem, pushing into the background other psychosocial problems facing war-affected children. Lost in the shuffle are local people's own understandings of how they have been affected by war. The privileging of trauma over other psychosocial issues has less to do with science and objectively defined needs than with the politics, economics, and institutional orientations of the humanitarian aid system.

Functionality

Emphasizing deficits, the trauma approach also underestimates children's functionality, which may surpass that of adults in some situations. In Sierra Leone, one young mother told me how her 4-year-old daughter had saved her. Having been captured by the RUF, the mother requested a latrine stop, intending to use it as an escape opportunity. When she tried to escape, soldiers opened fire, leaving her paralyzed in fear, unable to move. Her daughter saved them both by screaming "Run, Mommy, run!" and pulling on her arm, enabling them to run away unharmed.

In war zones worldwide, most children play, learn, do household chores, develop, and get on in difficult life circumstances. The vast majority of former child soldiers I have talked with over the past decade do not show signs of chronic dysfunction but are actively adapting to their new lives and situations. Just as most people naturally find a way to grieve the loss of loved ones and to move ahead with their lives, most war-affected children are not emotional cripples and find a way to get on with their lives. To say that children are resilient is not to imply that they are unaffected by the war (Cairns and Dawes 1996). In fact, many war-affected children who remain functional face significant burdens such as ongoing poverty and the stresses of not knowing how to help their families or what their futures hold. By emphasizing deficits and pathology, the trauma focus distracts attention from children's adaptive capacities, the foundation for programs of reintegration and rehabilitation.

Refocusing on children's functionality reveals unsettling questions about the science behind PTSD research in war zones, which reflects an ethnocentric bias. The definition of PTSD includes dysfunctionality, by which is meant an inability to perform expected daily tasks such as going to school or working. In industrialized countries such as the United States and the United Kingdom, researchers validate their PTSD measures by linking high scores on PTSD scales with problems performing ordinary social roles as workers, students, parents, or children. Typically,

Western-trained clinical psychologists assume the universality of clinical syndromes such as PTSD and its associated social dysfunctions.

In most war zones, researchers use versions of scales developed in Western societies, neglecting the obvious point that in societies such as Angola or Sierra Leone those instruments might not apply. Contrary to the universality assumption, the diagnostic categories of Western societies might not generalize to other cultures, which have their own local or indigenous understandings of mental health and illness (Lee and Sue 2001). One cannot assume that a child who lives in a war zone and who has met the clinical criteria for PTSD, as measured by instruments constructed in the United States or Europe, will be dysfunctional, that is, unable to perform well the age-appropriate roles that are characteristic for children in that child's society. Unfortunately, researchers in war zones have seldom validated their PTSD measures by showing that high scores on PTSD scales correlate with dysfunctionality in the local context. When such correlations have been examined, they have turned out to be quite low, which casts doubt on the validity of the measures. In Angola, many children who were diagnosed according to Western measures as having PTSD function quite well (Eyber and Ager 2004). In Mozambique, too, former child soldiers who exhibited PTSD symptoms over a period of a decade nonetheless functioned well by local standards (Boothby, Crawford, and Halperin 2006).

To assume that the symptom patterns exhibited in societies such as the United States, Angola, and Mozambique have the same meanings is to commit a category fallacy (Kleinman 1987). In fact, Angolan culture has a host of terms indicating mental illness and distress, but none corresponds exactly to "trauma" or "PTSD" as defined in Western, industrialized societies. Those who research the impact of war must be vigilant not to impose outsider categories, which not only would be questionable science but also could silence local people's understandings. When this occurs, psychology becomes a tool of neo-colonialism (Dawes and Cairns 1998; Wessells 1999).

The ethnocentric bias of the trauma approach also reflects distinctly Western ideas of the self and of what it means to heal (Bracken 1998; Summerfield 1999). Western societies, which are steeped in Enlightenment values, tend to view the self as an independent entity. This view makes it natural to think of trauma as an individual affliction deriving from painful, uncontrollable memories, shattered beliefs, and neurological problems that happen inside one's skull. It is equally natural to see healing as an individual process in which war-affected individuals come to terms with their war experiences and integrate the emotional shocks of the past with their current living situation. Although this view admits that social support and social relations are important parts of the healing process, it nonetheless conceptualizes healing in individual terms.

In contrast, many non-Western societies view the self in collectivist, relational terms. Such societies assert the primacy of the group over the individual and regard the self not as an isolated entity but as defined in terms of relations with others (Triandis 2001). This collectivist view has profound implications for understanding the impact of war and for healing. It suggests that the shattering of individual beliefs and emotions, which are central in trauma models, are less important than the relational impacts of war. These relational impacts include the destruction of social trust, the sense of betrayal and fear of attack by one's neighbors and even family members, the abject poverty that forces people to compete grimly rather than share, and the inability to perform roles such as father or mother by providing sufficient food for their families (Pintar 2001; Summerfield 2004; Wessells and Monteiro 2000). In this relational view, healing is less an individual process than a social process of repairing relationships, building social trust, and rebuilding the physical environment in a manner that enables people to act as communities, meet basic needs, and perform their culturally scripted roles (Boyden and Gibbs 1997).

Resilience and Protective Factors

An important but infrequently asked question is why former child soldiers and war-affected children are functional despite all they have endured. To some extent, the answer lies in children's agency and their prodigious abilities to cope with adversity. When children encounter a difficult situation such as abduction or combat, they do not become passive victims and relinquish all sense of control. Rather, they think actively and engage with adversity in diverse ways, using coping strategies as a means of survival and adaptation. Inside an armed group, children cope in part by deliberately choosing to obey orders and avoid dwelling on the bad things they have had to do. Although these strategies may appear passive, they are products of active choice that strengthen children's sense of control and also their awareness that in other situations, other choices are possible. Through their awareness and choices, most child soldiers avoid the trap of becoming robotic killers.

In the postconflict period, former child soldiers continue to use coping strategies, such as avoidance, to deal with their situation and to minimize their exposure to painful memories. Following the Mozambican war, for example, the former child soldiers who functioned well said they deliberately avoided thinking about their bad war experiences. One boy told how he avoided walking past a particular tree where his father had been hanged, because seeing the tree triggered a flood of painful memories (Boothby, Crawford, and Halperin 2006). In Bosnia, too, the teenagers who showed the fewest negative psychological impacts were those who deliberately avoided thinking about what had happened during the war (Jones 2002). Former child soldiers do not always cope through avoidance, however, as many children recall painful memories but cope with their pain by seeking social support. Still, the relatively widespread use of avoidance strategies shakes the prevalent Western view that the best way to deal with traumatic memories is by talking them through.

Child soldiers also remain relatively functional due to the presence of protective factors, which mitigate the effects of potentially harmful experience. The support of family and friends helps child soldiers who have experienced strong emotional effects of violence to maintain moderate to high levels of functionality (Annan and Blattman 2006). A significant protective factor is children's ability to find meaning in violence, particularly in situations in which strong ideologies motivate their participation in violence. In the Israeli-Palestinian conflict, Israeli teenagers who regarded fighting the Palestinians as a patriotic duty and who glorified the war suffered fewer psychological impacts of exposure to violence than did teenagers who lacked such ideological commitments (Punamaki 1996). Among Palestinian youths who engaged in stone-throwing and other political violence aimed at ending the Israeli Occupation, young males who believed they were engaged in a liberation struggle displayed fewer negative impacts than did boys for whom violence was bereft of meaning (Barber 2001). Because many child soldiers find meaning in their participation in political violence, one cannot assume that all child soldiers will be traumatized and haunted by painful memories. As one South African teenager who had fought against the apartheid regime told me:

> I missed out on many things and wish I had a better education. But when I think back, I have mostly good memories of fighting for freedom. If we had not fought, we would have lived as less than people. I'm proud of what we did.

Youths who see themselves as having participated in a liberation struggle not only exhibit pride in their contributions and have positive memories of their engagement in the struggle but also show relatively high levels of psychosocial well-being (Barber 2001). This fits the psychological pattern wherein suicide rates plummet in times of war, as they did in the United States during World War II.

Support from peers and family members are among the most potent protective factors. Child soldiers sometimes fight alongside family members, and in some cases the armed group becomes the children's surrogate family. By talking and being with peers, comrades, and family, child soldiers acquire valuable emotional support, reducing the pain associated with losses, killing, and other difficult experiences. Many child soldiers say that the solidarity and sense of "blood brotherhood" inside the armed group was their most important support. Ironically, departure from an armed group can be very stressful because of the loss of valuable psychological supports. To aid reintegration, civilian life must offer strong social support through family, friends, religious groups, and other means. This theme is developed more fully in Chapters 8 and 9.

Although resilience is typically conceptualized in individual terms, this discussion illuminates the relational nature of children's resilience. In most war zones, where people typically have a collectivist orientation, resilience is best regarded as a fundamentally relational and social process rather than an individual characteristic or process. The ability to find meaning in violence, for example, reflects a group understanding of what it means to live under oppression and a collective belief that only violence can end the injustice. The "struggle for liberation" is inherently collective rather than individual, and the meaning children find in participation in it is equally collective, even if not all members of one's group choose violence as the instrument for achieving liberation.

Two important footnotes to this discussion are warranted. First, it is ill advised to accept romanticized images of liberation struggles suggesting that the violence done in the name of "liberation struggles" is somehow excusable, even condonable. However, it is only when we enter the subjective world of child soldiers and discern their perceptions that we understand why many children enter armed groups. Second, probably the majority of children in armed groups do not find meaning in violence. Many are not parties to the violence, and many have been abducted into situations they abhor. One of the greatest challenges in discussing child soldiers is to avoid implying that what is true of one subgroup of child soldiers is also true of other subgroups.

It is important to move beyond a simple emphasis on deficits and also examine children's assets, such as their competencies in assigning meaning and seeking social support, their coping strategies, and their social networks. The lives of child soldiers embody a dynamic interplay between risk and protective factors, both of which must be understood in order to achieve a comprehensive picture of their psychosocial well-being. This insight has far-reaching implications for research and theory, as it calls for balance in the study of assets and deficits. Practically, it means that the reintegration of former child soldiers is less a matter of helping individual children than of strengthening family and community supports, enabling children to adapt and function well despite difficult past experiences and current living situations.

Moral Development and Behavior

A common stereotype holds that child soldiers show arrested moral development, have little or no sense of right and wrong, and are indifferent to the value of human life. According to the developmental version of this stereotype, child soldiers have been torn away from their families during formative years before they had developed positive morals. In addition to having been robbed of moral tutelage by parents, teachers, and religious leaders, child soldiers presumably develop twisted values by living in armed groups condoning killing and savagery.

This stereotype, like many others, contains elements of truth. In Angola, for example, a former boy soldier said he had acquired a craving for the smell and taste of human blood, the thrill of which made him doubt that he would ever fit into civilian society. This boy's obsession with blood and killing serves a poignant reminder that soldiering can indeed derange a child's values and behaviors. This boy's case is not unique. In countries such as Sierra Leone, former child soldiers have told me of children whose delight in killing and mutilating offended most soldiers. Also, there is good reason to worry about the moral development of children who are born into armed groups, grow up never having experienced civilian life, have had few positive role models, and have experienced violence as a normal part of daily life. How children who are born into groups like the LRA, living all their formative years with them, will learn positive, life-affirming values and morals strains one's imagination.

Also, many former child soldiers do have problems of aggression. A boy from Papua New Guinea said:

> Sometimes now I get very angry, even over small things. Sometimes it's hard to control. I still drink a lot. I might not if I hadn't been a soldier. After the fighting, my life changed. I don't feel good about myself. Yes, I think it's very hard to be normal again. Normal in my case—I get angry. I feel I can murder my enemy or who I get cross with. I want to fight with my father if there's not food for me to eat. (UNICEF 2003, 66)

Like many former child soldiers, this boy tends to act out his bad feelings and show poor impulse control, hinting at a wider problem in self-regulation, evident in excessive drinking. His ability to kill over minor infractions probably stems from having lived with an armed group in which people regularly used violence as a way to handle conflicts. By civilian standards, his aggressive impulses are excessive, adding to perceptions that child soldiers have weak morals.

Beneath such stereotypes, however, lies a more complex picture. The boys discussed above are not the norm—most child soldiers do not show such extreme behavior. The stereotype also disregards the enormous diversity of child soldiers' experiences and situations. Few children spend all their formative years inside an armed group. A child who was abducted by an armed group and exploited for labor for several weeks will probably not show truncated moral development. Also, abducted children have a psychological buffer—attribution—that helps prevent the experience from skewing their values. If they sometimes do bad things while in the armed group, they are likely to attribute their actions to the necessity to follow orders and to survive. This attribution protects them from moral corrosion or seeing themselves as having become bad. Furthermore, someone like the young woman who was the "Mommy Queen," who does not condone killing and oversees the children collected by the armed group in its military sweeps, is unlikely to exhibit bad morals. This enormous diversity cautions against monolithic depictions of child soldiers.

The suggestion that child soldiers are morally lacking sits poorly with evidence that many child soldiers show moral sensitivity before, during, and after their time in armed groups (Boyden 2003; Straker 1992). Often, children's decisions to engage in political violence reflect their ethical sensitivity to injustice, and many are willing to die in a struggle to end oppression. Some children decide to join an armed group out of an ethos of wanting to protect or support their family. Although popular images have suggested that the children who become soldiers are bad seed or enjoy random violence, this view conflates the excesses of a few with the more moderate behavior of the majority. Of the children who join an armed group by choice, many do so to achieve higher goals such as political independence, protection for their villages, or family well-being.

Inside armed groups, children inhabit a different moral space defined by both the moral discourse of the armed group and children's discourse and action within the armed group. A common error is to assume that armed groups have no moral standards because of the horrible things they do. A closer inspection, however, reveals that many armed groups have moral standards, but the standards are inappropriate and sharply at odds with global standards as defined in human rights instruments. For example, groups claiming to be engaged in struggles to end injustice often carve the world into the Good Us fighting against the Evil Them. In this division, which embodies the process of moral exclusion (Opotow, Gerson, and Woodside 2005), only those fighting on the side of good have any claim to morality. In essence, this division shrinks the moral universe. Because those on the side of Evil have no claim to morality and sit outside the realm of ethical concerns, it becomes easier psychologically to mistreat them. It is a short step to the view that the bad things done by the "good" group to the "evil" group are necessary for survival and morally warranted.

Even though this twisting of morals to fit one's political purposes is objectionable, it is effective in influencing children's moral thinking and behavior. Inside an armed group, children may learn to embrace this narrow US–THEM thinking and to see violence inflicted on the enemy as justified and "moral." Generally, their moral sensibilities have not been stunted so much as confined inappropriately to only the in-group. Within their group, children may show strong concern about caring for and protecting their comrades. Following children's exit from an armed group, a major challenge is to redefine the boundaries of their moral universe and ensure that they see all acts of killing and violence as abhorrent and not to be condoned.

At the same time, children are not robots who passively adopt the rhetoric and morals of the armed groups they live within. Teenagers in particular are shapers of political and moral discourse, and they define for themselves the boundary between justified and unjustified violence through their words and actions. During the anti-apartheid struggle in South Africa, black youths in townships developed a strict code of solidarity and prohibited informing on their comrades when captured and tortured by police. They also displayed a sense that there are limits to the justification of violence. In one case, a white welfare worker visiting a township at a highly explosive moment was seized by a mob that intended to kill her. A black teenage leader, no stranger to violence, spared her life, arguing against indiscriminate and unjustified violence, and escorted her safely out of the township (Straker 1992). How extensively this kind of moral thought and leadership occurs in different armed groups is unknown, though one suspects it occurs mainly in armed groups whose survival and success requires having good relations with civilians or maintaining a moral high ground.

The fact that many child soldiers either attempt to escape or actually flee from armed groups testifies to the strength of their moral concerns. A Colombian boy told of his motives for escape from the paramilitaries:

> They give you a gun and you have to kill the best friend you have. They do it to see if they can trust you. If you don't kill him, your friend will be ordered to kill you. I had to do it because otherwise I would have been killed. That's why I got out. I couldn't stand it any longer. (HRW 2003e, 65)

The repugnance this boy felt over having to kill his friend indicates his embrace of civilian values, which would hold the murder of a friend to be an odious act. Similarly, a boy from northern Uganda who had escaped from the LRA told me, "I could not believe the way they [the LRA] killed anyone who broke a rule. And sometimes they killed for no reason at all. . . I could not live with this." Child soldiers attempt escape for a multitude of reasons, of course—they may find life too difficult inside the armed group, fear they will eventually be killed if they stay, or want to return to their families. Still, child soldiers' expressions of horror over the bad things armed groups do, and their willingness to risk their lives to escape, indicate that they had not become mindless killers but had retained some sense of right and wrong.

Child soldiers' moral concerns are evident also in their guilt over particular things they have done. Often, guilt surfaces after they have left the armed group, when the full weight of what they have done comes home to them. A 16-year-old Filipino boy reflected on his experience of killing people:

> We put four hand grenades into a bunker. It made a big destruction. Four soldiers and three resistance forces were killed. My cousin, myself and three others did it. . . That was the first time I saw somebody I had killed. I didn't talk about it. I wanted to keep it to myself. What I saw in reality, how people were dead in those wars, haunts me. If we die from sickness it is good. If we die in wars, in fight, it's not good, it's not right. (UNICEF 2003, 55)

This boy's sense of haunting and guilt reflects not a warrior's code but civilian values disallowing killing. His guilt shows that even as a soldier, he had never let go of the moral standards defined by his community. This guilt is a positive force, because it increases people's adherence to moral standards. A defining feature of communities is their members' sense of personal responsibility to adhere to the morality of the group.

The ugly truth of child soldiers' situation is that they have to negotiate the colliding moral standards of the armed group and their civilian community. Although relatively little is known about how children do this, they probably use diverse strategies to deal with the ambiguities and contradictions of their situation. Some redefine themselves, taking on a new identity and internalizing the values of the armed group so thoroughly that killing becomes as natural as eating. Others use a compartmentalization strategy, marginalizing their civilian morals and thinking instead in terms of the rules of war. This helps them adapt to their new environment and embodies the contextual moral reasoning characteristic of adults (Cairns 1996; Gilligan 1982), who frequently accept the legitimacy of killing so long as the war is just. The compartmentalization strategy bodes well for reintegration, since children's sense of civilian values has not been destroyed so much as bracketed, allowing the children to reclaim their civilian values when they leave the armed group.

Other child soldiers may use a flip-flop strategy in which they experience ongoing tension between civilian and military standards, as if they hopped back and forth between two moral worlds. A child who accepts the armed groups' standards in some situations may be shaken by extreme events such as being forced to kill a friend, bringing civilian values to the fore. This strategy, although commendable for its ethical struggle, can create a heavy burden of stress, leaving children trapped between competing, often incompatible, ideas of right and wrong in a situation where talking ideas through with peers could be very dangerous.

It is not known how prevalent such strategies are, or which strategy yields the most positive outcomes in terms of long-term moral development; these questions warrant much additional research. Given the diversity of children's strategies and reactions, though, we should be cautious about accepting depictions of child soldiers as morally bereft or damaged. Also, relatively little is known about how former child soldiers experience and deal with their past moral transgressions and guilt over the long term. The psychological weight of soldiers' transgressions is evident in the legacy of the Vietnam War, which created lasting wounds in a generation of U.S. soldiers, but it cannot be assumed that children's sense of moral transgressions is grounded in universal moral standards. Culture plays a large role in defining a person's sense of morality. In many societies, spiritual beliefs define obligations to the ancestors as primary moral commitments.

Culture and Spirituality

Each cultural system constructs its own view of the causes and cures of physical and mental illness. In Western societies, most people look to science and mechanistic processes in the physical world to explain things that cause suffering, such as illness, hurricanes, and war. Spiritual life, although not unimportant in the West, frequently takes a back seat to a materialistic, scientific worldview. This emphasis on physical causation shapes Westerners' understanding of their afflictions and also their views about how healing occurs. Headaches are viewed as physical ailments that can be treated with drugs such as aspirin. Increasingly, Westerners see ailments such as depression and attentional disorders as neurological problems treatable with medications that restore the balance among various chemicals in the brain. Viewed through the prism of the medical model, illness, whether physical or psychiatric, is seen as having physical causes and remedies.

In contrast, many non-Western societies place spirituality at the center of life and explain worldly events by referring to the actions of spirits (Honwana 2006). For example, a former boy soldier in Angola displayed trauma symptoms, such as an inability to sleep. His account of why he could not sleep was revealing: "When I sleep, the spirit of the man I killed comes to me and asks 'Why did you do this to me?'" The boy said his biggest stress was being haunted by an angry spirit and pointed out his need to be treated by a traditional healer before he could reenter his community—he believed that the healer could conduct a ritual to clean him and make him acceptable to his family and village. This case also points out the problems of universalized views of mental illness or mental health. For people living in spiritually oriented societies, the greatest stresses are often spiritual rather than physical. In general, concepts of mental health and mental illness are culturally constructed and vary according to the local beliefs about what causes events such as illness and health (Lee and Sue 2001; Swartz 1998).

Beliefs about the spiritual origins of illness are widespread in the developing world, where most armed conflicts occur. The primacy of spiritual causes is evident throughout sub-Saharan Africa, particularly in rural areas less influenced by scientific beliefs and global culture. In Asia, too, people understand many ailments, including mental illnesses, as having spiritual causes and remedies (Eisenbruch 1991; Gielen, Fish, and Draguns 2004; Higginbotham and Marsella 1988; van de Put and Eisenbruch 2004). These beliefs and practices are often referred to as "traditional" because they include ideas and practices handed down over many generations. It is a mistake, however, to view them as fossilized and unchanging. Local beliefs and practices are dynamic and evolve over time in response to changing circumstances and interactions between groups. At best, local practices only partially reflect what had been done centuries ago.

Owing to cultural differences in conceptions of how people have been affected by war, it is useful to take an anthropological approach to the impacts of war on child soldiers. This approach cautions observers against imposing their own understandings, which are products of their own culture, society, and historical moment, and invites us to ask how local people, including children, understand their situation and how they have been affected. This approach recognizes that Western psychology is itself a product of a particular set of cultures and worldviews that may not apply to all societies (Shweder 1990). It also invites a self-reflective stance in which researchers and practitioners criticize their own ethnocentric tendencies and conduct or learn from ethnographic research on the beliefs of people in other cultures.

Western psychologists frequently resist taking the anthropological plunge, in part because they believe it is bad science to support superstitious beliefs about maleficent spirits. This view, however, misses the fundamental point. Whether one agrees with the spiritual beliefs of people in another culture, those beliefs shape that people's behavior, perceptions of the world, and understandings of illness and healing. Learning about such beliefs opens the door to learning about local healing practices and using resources such as rituals to address spiritual maladies. Too often humanitarian agencies view war-affected people as needing healing by outside people and resources, on the assumption that they have no functioning resources of their own. In reality, local people actively engage with the stresses and problems they face, even during the most acute phase of a crisis. Although they may want outside support and may benefit from it, it is arrogant and specious to assume that war-affected people are novices at addressing wars and calamities. By learning how war-affected people have dealt with such hardships in the past, humanitarian agencies stand to uncover and support local resources that provide a platform for supporting people in the current crisis. Local resources usually are most sustainable, because they will remain even after the humanitarian agencies move on to the next crisis.

The Power of the Spirits

Ethnographic research conducted in Angola by the Christian Children's Fund (Honwana 1998; Wessells and Monteiro 2004a) indicates the potency of spiritual beliefs in shaping local people's understanding of the effects of war. Local people believe that when a person dies, his or her spirit continues and wields considerable power. The spirits guide and control events in the visible world, shape people's lives, provide protection against illness and misfortune, and ensure societal well-being. As a *soba*, or traditional chief, from Huambo Province put it:

> The dead are always with us. During the war we walked day and night through the bush, we crossed rivers and nothing happened to us precisely because our ancestors were watching over us. So, for that reason, when a relative dies we have to take good care of the grave, to make him/her happy to help us. (Honwana 1998, 21)

In this belief system, the spirits of the dead—"the ancestors"—protect, support, and are intertwined with the living community. The living community must honor the dead by conducting the appropriate rituals, continuing the unbroken chain of life by having children, and passing on knowledge of traditions. Doing these things establishes a state of harmony between the living community and the ancestors, who, if properly honored, are obligated to protect the living from misfortune and illness.

Burial rituals play a crucial role in maintaining harmony between the living and the ancestors. When a person dies, the conduct of the burial rites enables the dead person's spirit to make transition to the spirit world of the ancestors. Failure to perform the rituals, however, leaves the spirit trapped and angry, leading it to harm the living. Just as the spirits offer protection when they have been honored properly, the spirits can withdraw protection and cause harm such as illness, misfortune, and crop failure when they have not been honored properly.

These beliefs shape how war-affected children experience their situation. For example, an 11-year-old Angolan girl said her village had been attacked and both her parents had been killed, forcing her to flee for her life. Although she showed trauma symptoms such as nightmares, she said her biggest problem was her inability to perform the burial rituals for her parents (Wessells and Monteiro 2000). Being from a rural area, she believed that when people die, they must receive the appropriate rites of burial or else their spirits will linger, causing harm to herself and others.

Sobas, too, speak of the great importance of conducting the burial rituals:

> My mother was killed during the war, and because at that time there was no way of performing the burial, we did not do anything. After

some time, my daughter became ill, and ordinary traditional treatment did not cure her illness. Later a *kimbanda* (diviner) told us that the spirit of my mother had possessed my daughter because since she died we did not do anything. After performing the *obito* [the burial rites], the child's illness disappeared. (Honwana 1998, 25)

The initial failure to perform the burial rites had stirred anger in the spirit of the deceased. Because the girl's illness was viewed as having spiritual causes, there was need for a spiritual cure, in this case performance of the burial rites. Although the psychosocial impact of traditional healing has not been documented well, in this case the conduct of the rituals reportedly healed the girl's illness.

Spirits may also present themselves to living people in order to urge them to conduct the burial rituals needed to allow the spirits to enter the realm of the ancestors:

During the war, my father was killed. I did not perform a burial because I thought that in times of war there is no need for that. But I dreamed of my father telling me that "I am dead but I haven't reached the place of the dead, you have to perform my *obito* because I can see the way to the place where other dead people are but I have no way to get there." (After this dream) I performed the rituals, and I have never dreamed of my father again. (Honwana 1998, 25–26)

In sharp contrast with Western views of dreams as manifestations of unconscious desires, rural Angolans regard dreams as channels for communication with the spirits.

The full power attributed to the ancestors is evident in people's fear of the bad things that unappeased ancestors can cause. As a soba from Huambo Province said:

With this war many people died and did not have proper burials, their heads are in the bush . . . the souls of those who died and were not buried are wandering around and will not let us have peace. The war will continue because the spirits are angry. (Honwana 1998, 65–66)

A person's failure to conduct the burial rites breaches the bond between the spirits and the living, creating a state of discord in which angry spirits cause harm, even war. More than a social norm, the conduct of the rites is an obligation to the ancestors, who can withdraw their protection, visiting destruction on the living.

This belief system casts new light on how war affects child soldiers. Western models portray trauma as a mechanistic reaction to life-threatening events. The role of people's spiritual beliefs in influencing stress, however, suggests a richer, less mechanistic process in which child soldiers actively interpret their life experiences. How they interpret and assign meanings to their experiences determines their stress levels and psychological reactions (Lazarus and Folkman 1984). Children who believe angry spirits haunt them will show much greater psychological impact than those who do not interpret their situation in this manner. From this standpoint, it is vital to ask child soldiers how they understand their experiences and what has been most stressful for them. This approach is the opposite of the usual practice wherein outside psychologists use predesigned scales, which may not measure children's most profound issues.

A closely related issue is the problem of social pollution (Green and Wessells 1997; Honwana 1998, 2006), which reflects an interdependent view of the self. In Angola, people who have witnessed or perpetrated killing are viewed as polluted by the spirits of the dead. Pollution can lead to insanity and loss of control over oneself:

> (A person) can become insane because there (in the war) many things happened: (seeing) the blood of others; carrying dead bodies; killing . . . when he (the soldier) comes back to the village . . . those things haunt him in his sleep, he dreams the things that took place during the war . . . After fighting the war the kazumbi (name of the spirits in Malange) can afflict you . . . my son came back from the FAA (government troops) in 1991 and he was not well, he was very disturbed and even attacked me . . . he was unable to look at any kind of blood because that reminded him or the war . . . I took him for traditional treatment. (Honwana 1998, 67–68)

These problems are communal, because the polluted individuals are portals through which angry spirits can enter the community and threaten or harm anyone. In this respect, mental illness is not an individual problem but a collective malady affecting families and communities. This collectivist orientation stands in sharp contrast to the Western precept that trauma and mental illness are individual afflictions.

Local people believe spiritually polluted people must be cleaned through a cleansing ritual conducted by a local healer. This belief has important implications for the reintegration of former child soldiers, whose return home in a spiritually polluted state could cause many problems for their families and communities. Both the child soldiers and their communities view the problem as spiritual and as collective rather than individual. In this context, what the former child soldiers need is not trauma counseling but spiritual cleansing to appease the angry spirits and enable reconciliation between the living and the ancestors. The reconciliation needed is also between the soldiers and the village, which fears their return in a polluted state. Local communities have a host of purification rituals that local healers perform to clean the returning children, reestablish spiritual harmony, and enable healing and reconciliation.

Traditions and the Impact of War

The spiritual cosmology outlined above hints that war has more subtle yet profound effects than those associated with direct exposure to violence. In particular, an Angolan village's well-being requires that the villagers be in a state of spiritual harmony with the ancestors. Harmony is achieved by honoring traditions such as conducting rituals to celebrate a harvest or performing burial rites following a death. Well-being entails not only physical health but also spiritual and social harmony. Social discord and illness prevail when there is disharmony between the living and the ancestors, when traditions have been disrupted or not practiced, and when the spirits are angry.

When war is viewed through this lens, one acquires a sense of the enormity of its impact on people's health and well-being. By its nature, war breaks down social structures and disrupts patterns of living and practice, making it impossible for people to conduct the rituals that they see as fundamental for their protection and health. Displacement not only uproots people from their homes and destroys crops but also makes it impossible to bury the dead or to do the rituals leading the ancestors to provide the necessary food supply. In these respects, war is a spiritual catastrophe as well as a physical one, and it is clearly collective in nature. In the Mozambique civil war, rural people said that one of the worst parts of the war had been their inability to perform the ceremonies needed to establish spiritual harmony with the ancestors (Nordstrom 1997). The disruption of traditional practices of child rearing in Mozambique during the war not only affected mother–child relationships but also caused the deaths of many young children due to malnutrition (Igreja 2003, 2004). In East Timor following the 1999 attacks by Indonesian paramilitaries, Timorese people reported that one of their greatest stresses was their inability to conduct their rituals and the damage that had been done to their family houses, where they performed their ceremonies (Kostelny and Wessells 2002). The conduct of the traditions gives people a sense of meaning in life, continuity across generations, and protection from harm. War shatters these systems of meaning and protection, creating vulnerability far greater than that which owes to trauma.

The importance of local culture and traditions, however, should not blind one to the damaging effects of some cultural practices. Rituals such as the female genital mutilation practiced widely in West Africa (McKay and Mazurana 2004) are harmful and violate women's rights. Critical thinking and ethical sensitivity are needed to select out the cultural practices supportive of the humanitarian imperative "Do No Harm." Also, traditional beliefs and practices are not equally powerful in all areas. Former child soldiers should not be forced to submit to rituals and practices they neither believe in nor wish to support. In some cases, returning child soldiers oppose the restoration of traditional norms and authority structures that they regard as bankrupt. An enduring lesson for both research and practice is the value of asking children themselves how they understand their situation and what they regard as being in their best interest.

7

Putting Down the Gun

Children's exit from armed groups and integration into civilian life advances a trilogy of priorities: peace, development, and protection. Peacebuilding connects intimately with child soldiering because child recruitment is an engine of contemporary conflict (Singer 2005). In Liberia, child soldiers were the majority of the fighters in bitter conflict during the period 2000 to 2003. In northern Uganda, child recruitment has been the primary means through which the LRA has continued its bloody war. To break cycles of violence and build peace, high priorities are prevention of child recruitment and support for the former child soldiers' reintegration into civilian life.

The urgent link between reintegration and development is clear: war shatters economies, robs children of the education and skills they need to become effective civilians, and creates instability that undermines economic well-being. Reintegration also connects intimately with protection. Children who transition successfully into civilian life are less likely to continue the life of the gun, with its inherent dangers. However, instability in the postconflict environment can put children at grave risk of re-recruitment and thwart their reintegration.

Following armed conflict, many war-torn societies have implemented national programs of disarmament, demobilization, and reintegration (DDR). (In countries such as Liberia, DDR planners have added a second "R" for "rehabilitation, making the process DDRR. DDR is the more widely used acronym and will be used here.) Disarmament is the process of soldiers turning in their weapons, which may be collected and stored safely and subsequently destroyed. Disarmament builds confidence by signaling warring parties' agreement to the peace treaty and their willingness to stand down their armies. Demobilization involves both the formal disbanding of military groups and the release of combatants from a state of military mobilization (Berdal 1996). During the demobilization process, soldiers shed their uniforms and prepare to reenter civilian life. Reintegration, which occurs over a longer term, is a process in which former soldiers transition to civilian life, achieving a viable civilian role that offers an alternative to soldiering (CSC 2004).

Although DDR programs have considerable societal benefits, their success stands also on their ability to address family needs. The need for DDR support rings in the words of former child soldiers, such as an Afghan boy who had fought against the Taliban and who told me:

> At the end of the war we wanted peace but there were no jobs and we did not have any means of supporting our families. In such a situation, why not remain a soldier? At least it's a way of earning some small amount of money.

Providing jobs for former soldiers is a key part of reintegration, both for economic reasons and because having a job enables children to fill culturally defined roles as helpers of their families. Similarly, a girl in Sierra Leone who had been a member of the RUF said: "Before, I was stigmatized and feared as a rebel and bush wife. Because of the [reintegration] program, I can be like other girls, am a respected worker, and provide for my daughter." As this girl's statement testifies, DDR programs succeed when they satisfy former child soldiers' needs to fill their family obligations, avoid stigmatization, and gain social acceptance.

International agencies have learned much about how to structure national DDR processes. However, what remains to be learned far surpasses what is known, and the postconflict landscape is littered with questionable DDR processes offering inadequate assistance to children. Also, significant numbers of child soldiers self-demobilize, and little is known about whether these children fare better or worse over the long term than children going through DDR programs. Some evidence suggests that self-demobilizers reintegrate as well as those coming through official DDR programs (Weinstein and Humphries 2005). Many practitioners believe that nonformal reintegration supports are often a better option than official DDR supports, because they help the many children who are left out of formal processes and they avoid problems, such as the singling out of former combatants, that are commonly encountered in official DDR processes.

It is essential, then, to view DDR processes with a critical eye. Being adult-driven, DDR processes are often out of step with children's needs. Child soldiers' insightful ideas about reintegration have been marginalized in the design, implementation, and evaluation of DDR processes for children. Also, DDR processes for children typically reflect universalized views of children that fail to recognize how children's social class, ethnicity, gender, and particular vulnerabilities and assets shape their needs and experience of the post-ceasefire context (Jareg 2005). The weakness of a one-size-fits-all approach becomes apparent when one considers the distinctive needs of girls, boys, children who have disabilities, children affected by HIV/AIDS, and other vulnerable groups, not to mention the differences in the situations children attempt to reintegrate into. The prominent gender bias visible in most DDR programs has left us having very little understanding of girls' reintegration.

The postconflict emphasis of most DDR programs should not blind us to the fact that many children escape armed groups while fighting continues and have no DDR process as a safety net. In countries such as Burma, Sri Lanka, and northern Uganda, children who leave armed groups face considerable danger of being captured and treated as traitors by their own former group or by opposing groups. If they go home, they are at risk of reprisal attacks or re-recruitment. Lacking official DDR supports, children often attempt to reintegrate, relying on their ingenuity and keeping a low profile lest they be re-recruited. In countries such as Burundi and the Democratic Republic of the Congo (DRC), international agencies have created children's DDR supports while fighting continues. These programs face difficult challenges because the villages children return to can be attacked and may be too unstable to support children's reintegration.

These complexities, however, cannot be allowed to corrode hope, as the majority of former soldiers successfully reintegrate into civilian life (Weinstein and Humphries 2005). This chapter outlines formal DDR processes, reviews particular DDR country programs, and then examines the challenges that arise in situations of ongoing conflict. Because this new field cries out for practical guidance, the chapter ends with suggestions for improvement.

Official DDR

The considerable diversity of DDR processes owes to the need to tailor particular DDR processes to the political, economic, and social situation of that country (Ball 1997; Colletta 1997). DDR processes often begin with a large-scale disarmament in which authorities collect masses of weapons, helping to demilitarize the environment. In Mali, people celebrated the arrival of peace through the symbolic gesture of burning the collected weapons in a Flame of Peace (Poulton 1998). However, societal disarmament is not always feasible. In Afghanistan following the first national election, disarmament was a high priority. As one Afghan man said, "Still people are being threatened by the guns. Many people own guns; you can't talk freely because the commanders will say, 'you just need one bullet'" (Human Rights Research and Advocacy Consortium [HRRAC] 2004, 9). Full disarmament was infeasible due in part to Afghanistan's strong culture of owning and using guns. Also, many Afghans wanted weapons in order to work as armed security guards for various groups.

Demobilization, too, exhibits great variety across situations. In Sierra Leone, where child soldiers had committed some of the worst atrocities, DDR planners included provisions for former child solders to have a relatively long stay, up to six months, in an Interim Care Center (ICC), which provided psychosocial support and allowed staff to trace the children's families so the children could be reunified with them. In contrast, in post-Taliban Afghanistan the demobilization process took only a few days, since the families' locations were known and the emphasis was on family reunification. Many former child soldiers had already returned home outside of a formal DDR process, and it would have made little sense to separate them from their families.

A children's component has been conspicuously absent from many DDR processes. UNICEF and child-focused nongovernmental organizations (NGOs) have pointed out that children have specific needs and, under the U.N. Convention on the Rights of the Child (CRC), are entitled to DDR benefits such as psychosocial assistance. Also, the

U.N. Department of Peacekeeping Operations (1999), which oversees many DDR processes, has official DDR guidelines calling for children's inclusion in DDR processes. Still, numerous pressures work against children's inclusion. An armed group's admission that it has exploited children can decrease its legitimacy and possibly obligate it to shoulder the costs of demobilizing and reintegrating their child soldiers. Sometimes, children themselves object to a children's DDR process, preferring to be demobilized as adults because this would give them greater benefits. Adult bias leads many DDR planners to assume children will be cared for by their families and to see adult demobilization as a higher priority because adults were the majority of soldiers. Whatever the reason, children's exclusion from national DDR processes is an egregious violation of children's rights. Keeping this in mind, it is useful to outline briefly the common elements visible in most children's DDR programs.

Disarmament

In disarmament processes, armies enter secured reception areas or cantonment sites where they surrender their weapons. Typically the authorities register their weapons and give the soldiers a card or written papers documenting their surrender of their weapons. For any soldier, child or adult, putting down the gun symbolizes the end of hostilities and marks the beginning of the transition out of military life. To complement military disarmament, there may also be civilian disarmament processes aimed at standing down militias and demilitarizing society. Civilian disarmament is difficult in war zones, where people frequently equate security with possession of a gun.

Disarmament is both dangerous and confusing. Soldiers might fear that they will be attacked when they enter the reception areas, and they may have heard rumors that give them doubts about their treatment and the prospects for peace. Child soldiers frequently wonder what to believe, particularly if they grew up inside an armed group, have heard empty promises, and have seen previous peace efforts collapse. Rumors about benefits abound, leading some children to expect cash for submitting their weapon. Since failed expectations can unleash riots and undermine the DDR process, disarmament processes frequently include efforts to manage expectations and explain the overall process to child soldiers.

Demobilization

Following disarmament, child soldiers typically enter a demobilization center where they officially exit the armed group and receive an identity card validating their discharge. These coveted cards, which show they are not deserters, protect them from re-recruitment and entitle them to receive demobilization kits. As a boy from Sierra Leone said, "I was so happy once I had my card. Then I knew I was going home and no one would come after me."

For child soldiers, demobilization creates uncertainties about how to reunite with their families, remain safe, and transition to civilian life. Accordingly, international organizations frequently place recently demobilized child soldiers in ICCs, transitional spaces where children live for two weeks to six months or longer, if necessary. To accommodate girls' special needs, agencies usually establish separate ICCs for girls and for boys. ICCs provide a safe space in which the children live while their families are located and preparations made for family reunification. ICCs provide basic health services, addressing the children's significant health issues and reducing the stigma associated with an ill, unkempt appearance. Reproductive health care is particularly important for girls (Barnett 2005; Landry 2005).

Because recently demobilized children are fragile and carry raw emotional wounds, ICCs also provide psychosocial support. Typically this includes an orientation about the overall DDR process and the stages former soldiers go through in transitioning into civilian life. These children need to learn to let go their soldier identities and envision their future life as civilians. Through peer counseling or dialogue, the children discuss their past, present, and future and how they plan to address the challenges ahead. A high priority is to express pent-up feelings and release the energy associated with their war experiences. This is accomplished through engaging children in expressive activities such as drawing, song, dance, storytelling, and other activities conducive to expressing emotions in culturally appropriate ways.

On leaving the ICC, demobilizing soldiers typically receive a kit or transitional allowance that helps them meet their basic needs and aids their reentry into the community. Adult soldiers frequently receive cash to purchase basics like food, clothing, and tools (Colletta 1997). For adult soldiers from rural areas, the demobilization kit typically includes seeds, tools, and related items useful in farming.

Reintegration

Whereas demobilization is a short-term process measured in days, weeks, or months, reintegration is a long-term process measured in years. Reintegration is a reciprocal process that includes not only the adaptation of former soldiers but also the rebuilding of healthy families and communities, without which former soldiers have few positive roles and options.

For former child soldiers, reintegration typically involves five kinds of support. First, family reintegration assistance reunifies children with their families and helps children readjust to living at home and learn to handle family conflict nonviolently. Second, educational opportunities help the children gain the skills and knowledge they missed out on when they were soldiering instead of attending school. Third, psychosocial supports, ideally both Western and indigenous, help quiet their memories of the furies of war and construct civilian identities and roles. To assume civilian roles, former child soldiers need job skills and a means of earning a living. The fourth element, then, consists of training in vocational skills, business management, and income-generating activities, enabling former soldiers to obtain jobs and earn an income.

The fifth element consists of community mobilization to receive former child soldiers and rebuild the spirit of unity that was shattered by war. A high priority is community empowerment and engagement in collective action, which promotes physical reconstruction and helps restore a sense of control following overwhelming experiences. Another key is to reawaken or to establish mechanisms for handling conflict without resort to violence and for addressing any underlying issues of social justice that animated the war. Although these tasks may sound straightforward, they are riddled with complexities, as is evident in particular national DDR processes.

Case Studies of DDR

DDR processes are tidy in concept but messy in implementation. This messiness frequently reflects one or both sides' lack of political will, causing demobilization delays or cheating on the DDR implementation. DDR processes also often labor under competing agendas and political pressures. In some cases the military agendas of standing down troops and restructuring the remaining forces into a unified national army take precedence over reintegration, which ought to drive the entire process. This occurs partly because political leaders gain more political mileage by demobilizing soldiers, which produces immediate gains and bolsters confidence in peace, than by supporting the slower reintegration process. If they channel more funds and effort into demobilization than into reintegration (Landry 2005), they shortchange reintegration, which best serves children's rights, peace, and development.

Unruliness also stems from poor coordination among different actors having divergent priorities. While demobilization is a military exercise overseen by international peacekeeping forces, reintegration is a civilian process guided by U.N. agencies and civilian implementing partners such as governments and NGOs. DDR processes require coordination of the military and civilian elements, and coordination gaps frequently cripple DDR efforts. Such gaps frequently emerge in funding, with more funds being channeled into disarmament and demobilization than into reintegration. Problems of asymmetrical funding haunt children's DDR programs, which too often are poorly funded or relegated to the back burner, a problem doubly true for girls. The country cases reviewed briefly below are not a representative sample, but they illustrate these and other challenges from different parts of the world and unearth valuable lessons for guiding future programs.

Angola

In 1994 in Angola, bitter fighting ended with the signing of the Lusaka Protocol, which called for a national DDR process to restructure armed forces, incorporating many former UNITA soldiers into the Angolan army, and to reintegrate many others into society. Although the Lusaka Protocol had no provisions regarding child soldiers, the subsequently created demobilization commission made children's demobilization and reintegration a high priority (Verhey 2001). This specific attention to child soldiers owed to intensive advocacy by diverse stakeholders and also to learning from neighboring Mozambique, where child soldiers had complained about their denial of demobilization benefits. In Angola, child soldiers received benefits packages equal in value to those received by adult soldiers (Verhey 2001).

The demobilization process had a wobbly start. It was delayed a full year owing to problems in the training and deployment of the staff who were to implement the program. When the demobilization process began, UNITA troops entered fifteen quartering areas, with 8,613 boy soldiers identified for subsequent demobilization and reintegration. No girl soldiers had been identified at that point. Unfortunately, UNITA manipulated the demobilization process by recruiting new child soldiers, whom they presented to meet demobilization targets while keeping more seasoned child soldiers active in the field. Inside the quartering areas, child soldiers stayed alongside adult soldiers, making it possible for the adults and commanders to control the children. Child soldiers languished for ten months in the fifteen quartering areas, where they waited to be registered by a poorly prepared three-person team. Having poor language skills, the team used as interpreters military commanders, who manipulated the children's data in order to re-recruit children. In the end, only 57 percent of the former child soldiers were successfully demobilized and reunified with their families (Verhey 2001).

Interestingly, the demobilization process avoided the use of ICCs. The Angolan DDR planners prioritized family reunification, with the idea that families can best provide psychosocial support and protection for former child soldiers. Also, the prolonged quartering process afforded ample time for UNICEF and NGOs such as Save the Children UK to conduct the identification and tracing needed to reunite children with their families.

The reunification process, however, was plagued by problems. The first several hundred boys released from the quartering areas soon disappeared, creating widespread suspicions that UNITA had re-recruited them. Giving little notice, UNITA repeatedly changed the rendezvous points where children were to meet their families. This shuffling burdened family members, who sometimes walked long distances only to find their children were not at the meeting point; it also burdened the children, who wondered whether they would see their families again. The suspected aim of this shuffling was to leave child soldiers separated, making them easy targets for re-recruitment.

To protect the children from re-recruitment, UNICEF and NGOs such as CCF transported and accompanied the former child soldiers to meet their families. This strategy succeeded, as CCF successfully reunited 2,153 former boy soldiers with their families. The reintegration work, which included supports such as community sensitization, traditional healing, vocational training, income generation, and family dialogues and problem solving (Wessells and Monteiro 2001, 2004a), is described in Chapter 8. When war erupted again in 1998, however, the reintegration work ended and there was another round of mass displacements and suffering.

Following decades of war and intermittent ceasefires, the Angolan war finally ended in April 2002, due in part to the death of UNITA's leader, Jonas Savimbi. A major question was what would happen to the nearly five hundred thousand UNITA soldiers and their families, who had stayed with them, providing logistical support. Another DDR process was designed with the intent of continuing the post-1994 process. Ex-combatants were to receive five months' back pay, a reintegration allowance equivalent to US$100, and a kit containing tools and household items. Hampering the demobilization process were high rates of hunger and malnutrition among former UNITA soldiers, government delays in providing needed food assistance, and frequent changes in the soldiers' release dates (Porto and Parsons 2003).

At best, the situation was dismal for soldiers, who were neither registered as combatants nor eligible for official demobilization and reintegration. The national DDR plan had called for the integration of UNITA soldiers into the Angolan army, followed by their subsequent demobilization. The Angolan army disallowed soldiers under the age of 18, so the process effectively excluded child soldiers (CSC 2004). The situation was even worse for girl soldiers, who mostly had not been combatants, were invisible at the time, and carried enormous economic, psychological, and social burdens (Stavrou 2005).

In the end, boy soldiers were transferred to Family Areas where families lived on land borrowed from the government. Also, boy soldiers were separated from adult soldiers. On the surface, this division protected them from exploitation and re-recruitment, but it also denied them benefits. In the areas where families had gathered and lived following demobilization, aid such as food was distributed according to the number of family members. This created incentives for families to take in "stray" children such as orphans and former child soldiers. Predictably, the family support for former child soldiers evaporated after families left the gathering areas, since they no longer received benefits for supporting additional children, many of whom became separated (Parsons 2004).

The Angolan DDR process faces ongoing challenges. Not least of these is the near complete lack of support for former girl soldiers, whose existence in significant numbers became known only recently. Recent evidence indicates that many UNITA men had two or three girls and women (Stavrou 2005), suggesting the number of girl soldiers is far higher than previously known. Also excluded were former combatants demobilized following 1994. Furthermore, reintegration needs exist not only for child soldiers but also for approximately one-third of the population, the 3.8 million people internally displaced by the war. Many displaced people returned to destroyed villages rather than functioning communities, raising the salient question, what is there for former child soldiers to integrate into?

One of the numerous valuable lessons the Angolan case illustrates is the need for strong advocacy efforts to ensure children's inclusion in the DDR process. Concerted advocacy and program support is needed for girls, a point we return to later in this chapter. Child protection mechanisms also are needed to prevent re-recruitment, monitor and respond to violations, and reduce risks to all war-affected children. The entire process should be driven by an emphasis on reintegration. In the post-2002 period the DDR process emphasized demobilization, probably due to pressures to stand down the UNITA army and convince people the war had ended. An emphasis on demobilization can backfire, though, because reintegration is the true measure of peace. Unhappy former combatants who have not transitioned successfully into civilian life can destabilize the society and undermine development.

Perhaps most important, a DDR process is only a band-aid unless all parties own it and take steps to build peace with social justice. The post-Lusaka DDR process failed because it lacked the backbone of any successful DDR process—political will.

Sierra Leone

When the war in Sierra Leone ended in January 2002, there were more than 135,000 soldiers, most of whom had belonged to the RUF, the opposition group, or the CDF, the pro-government militias that fought against the RUF. More than 48,000 of the soldiers were children, including over 12,000 girls (McKay and Mazurana 2004). Because of the large number of former soldiers, a national DDR program was a high priority. The National Commission on Disarmament, Demobilization, and Reintegration oversaw the program, and UN peacekeepers under UNAMSIL, the UN Mission in Sierra Leone, provided support. In addition to collecting and destroying the weapons surrendered by combatants, the program aimed to demobilize combatants and to prepare them for reintegration. However, the initial estimate of the number of combatants was 45,000, which was far less than the true number of former combatants.

As part of the demobilization process, armies brought their soldiers into reception centers in diverse locations. Soldiers qualified for participation in the DDR program, which was intended for ex-combatants, by turning in an automatic weapon such as an AK-47 and disassembling and reassembling it. Adult soldiers who qualified went next to a demobilization center, which provided a predischarge orientation, benefits packages, and a cash disbursement intended to defray transportation and resettlement costs.

A significant strength of the DDR process was that the peace agreement had included provisions for a separate children's process. This ensured that planning for the children's DDR was initiated from the start rather than being an add-on, and it separated former child soldiers from adult soldiers. Officially, child soldiers were not required to turn in a weapon or to have had combatant status. Demobilized children went to Interim Care Centers, which provided a mixture of orientation and education programs. This was important because, in a study of a convenience sample of one hundred girls reportedly being tracked by NGOs, more than 75 percent indicated education as their greatest need (Mazurana and Carlson 2004). Following demobilization, former child soldiers returned home or to other communities of their choice, where they could choose between vocational skills training or going to school, participating either in regular classes or accelerated classes covering six years of education in three years. National and international NGOs, in partnership with UNICEF and government donors, constructed programs that engaged former child soldiers in peace education, civic reconstruction, income generation, and reconciliation activities.

The DDR program experienced numerous problems related to implementation. Although the weapons test supposedly applied only to adults, most child participants in the DDR process said that they, too, had been required to present and disassemble an automatic weapon (McKay and Mazurana 2004; Mazurana and Carlson 2004). This winnowing practice reduced the number of former child soldiers who were allowed to participate in DDR to just over sixty-eight hundred, which was far fewer than the estimated forty-eight thousand child soldiers. The weapons test discriminated against thousands of children who had not been combatants but who had been laborers, porters, cooks, spies, medics, or sex slaves. It also discriminated against children who had been combatants in the CDF, who had fought mostly with shotguns and pangas (machetes).

The most glaring problem was gender discrimination. Only seven former girl members of the CDF participated in the DDR process, in part because the CDF steadfastly denied having had girl members. Although this denial reflected conventional wisdom, the CDF had in fact included over seventeen hundred girls (McKay and Mazurana 2004). The DDR process also excluded the significant numbers of former girl soldiers who were mothers, who together with their babies had special needs for services such as health care and economic support.

Overall, there were twelve thousand girl soldiers, many of whom had survived rape and abduction. However, only 506—a mere 4 percent—participated in the DDR process, whereas 18 percent of former boy soldiers participated (McKay and Mazurana 2004). Girls' lack of participation owed to discrimination and protection threats, particularly attacks. More than 45 percent of former girl soldiers said they had not participated because they had had no weapon to present (Mazurana and Carlson 2004). Another 21 percent said they feared attacks in the centers by members of opposing forces. These fears were hardly fictitious. In one case, a girl disclosed that she had been a member of the Kamajor, a subgroup of the CDF. Having overheard this disclosure, former child soldiers from the RUF threatened her, leading her to flee the center.

Crowding and insecurity were also issues. One former girl soldier said that she left a demobilization site because "there were too many people crowded in, too many men with nothing to do. The security was bad" (Mazurana and Carlson 2004, 20). Making matters even worse, the centers did not meet basic needs or deliver on promises the girls felt had been made. Only 44 percent of the girls said they had received the promised demobilization benefits; 43 percent said they had not received adequate clothing; 54 percent said they had not received needed sanitation materials; and 23 percent said they had requested medical care but had not received any (Mazurana and Carlson 2004).

Nor did the DDR program meet the needs of other child soldiers who had spent many years in armed groups but who, having reached 18 years of age by the time of the demobilization, demobilized as adults. Evidence also surfaced that between two thousand and three thousand former child soldiers were subsequently engaged in heavy labor under harsh conditions in diamond mines (CSC 2004). It would be foolish to count such heavy labor as reintegration when it merely substitutes one form of exploitative, dangerous child labor for the dangerous labor of child soldiering.

Chief among the lessons to be drawn from the children's DDR process in Sierra Leone is the importance of gender. At every stage, DDR processes need to take into account girls' and women's distinctive needs and risks. Criteria for access to the DDR program should enable rather than deny girls' participation. The services provided in demobilization and reintegration phases should be gender sensitive and include equal benefits, care, and protection for girls and boys. The need for gender sensitivity and equity is by no means limited to Sierra Leone and is evident in DDR processes worldwide. Girls' reintegration is difficult in part because girls who achieved significant status and responsibilities in the military may be reluctant to accept a marginalized status in a DDR program or in the wider society (McKay and Mazurana 2004). To eliminate this gender disparity, children's DDR programs should support girls and boys equally and be part of wider efforts to achieve gender equity in society.

The Sierra Leone experience also shows that all child soldiers should have access to DDR programs and benefits, regardless of whether they had been combatants or had a weapon to surrender. As stipulated in the

CRC (Articles 37 and 39), children have specific entitlements to demobilization and reintegration supports. To refuse child soldiers access to these supports is a violation of their rights.

Liberia

The Liberian war ended with the signing of a ceasefire in 2002 and the departure of President Charles Taylor, who faced charges of war crimes. Approximately twenty-one thousand child soldiers, including large numbers of girls, needed DDR assistance (CSC 2004). The U.N. Mission in Liberia (UNMIL), which provided humanitarian assistance and also international peacekeepers, oversaw the process, working with the National Commission on Disarmament, Demobilization, Reintegration, and Rehabilitation. The DDR plan called for UNICEF to oversee a separate children's process.

The importance of an effective children's DDR process was evident in the legacy of previous failures to support children. Peace agreements that had been established in 1993 and 1994 failed to mention children's needs following demobilization (McCallin 1995). Later, following the pre-1997 war, a national DDR program included only one-third of child soldiers. Despite the large number of girl soldiers, only 78 girls participated in the 1997 DDR program (HRW 2004a; Peters 2003). The DDR program flaws created an environment ripe for children's re-recruitment. One former boy soldier said:

> I went through the program in 1997 and received some assistance but it soon ran out. For a while, I did some small jobs around Monrovia, but there was not much to do and I couldn't afford to go back to school. So two years ago, I decided to join the LURD. I figured it was better to fight and try to get something, than hang around town doing nothing. (HRW 2004a, 39)

This boy's statement leaves little doubt about the inadequacy of temporary assistance and the need for jobs and economic reintegration.

In 2003 and 2004, the DDR process encountered enormous obstacles. Commanders denied repeatedly that children were or had been part of their forces (HRW 2004a). Widespread destruction, displacement, and lawlessness had torn most communities apart, making it specious to talk about community development. Also, the fixation of international attention on the Iraq war dimmed the prospects for achieving the funding needed to support reintegration.

If the aforementioned problems were beyond the planners' control, other problems were of their own making. The attempted start of a children's DDR process in December 2003 was risky because there had been too little research and too little preparation time (Landry 2005). Thousands more soldiers turned up for the initial demobilization than planners had anticipated. Rumors and hearsay about DDR programs in other countries led many soldiers, including children, to expect cash in return for handing over their weapons. Although these expectations had no basis in reality, the soldiers rioted when their demands for money went unmet. The violence, in which about a dozen civilians were killed, scuttled the demobilization process (CSC 2004). This ugly experience underlines the importance of informing soldiers about benefits at the earliest possible stage and managing expectations throughout the DDR process.

Although the official DDR process began in April 2004, poor planning marred the process again. This time, the problem was a decision to provide a cash disbursement, equivalent to US$300, in two payments to each demobilizing child soldier on departure from an ICC. Superficially, cash payments appeared benign because child soldiers would need money to purchase clothing, food, or tools. By equalizing children's and adults' benefits, cash payments promised to prevent squabbling and to reduce youths' desires to demobilize as adults.

However, promise of cash payments to children unleashed a flood of problems that should have been obvious from experience in other war zones. Knowing well how to manipulate and control child soldiers, commanders frequently extorted the cash from the children and used it to recruit additional child soldiers. Local communities tended to see the cash payments as rewards ("blood money") given to the children who had attacked them; this raised tensions and placed children at risk (Landry 2005). An additional problem was that some children used their cash disbursements to purchase drugs or alcohol (Refugees International 2004). As child protection agencies decried the cash payments, UNMIL corrected the problem by designating the second cash payment not for individual soldiers but for their families and communities.

Following this inauspicious beginning, the DDR process got on track.

UNICEF and NGO partners such as CCF, Don Bosco, the International Rescue Committee, and Save the Children constructed and staffed a significant number of ICCs throughout the country, providing separate facilities for girls and boys. By December 2004, approximately five thousand children had been demobilized, and most of their families had been traced, laying the foundation for family reunification and reintegration. A lingering risk, however, is cross-border recruitment. The identification in September 2003 of 168 Liberian child soldiers in refugee camps in Sierra Leone underscored this threat (CSC 2004), which looms large in a region besieged by wars. Still, the Liberian experience yields valuable lessons about the dangers of making cash payments to child soldiers, the importance of advance planning for reintegration, the need to manage soldiers' expectations, and the necessity for regional approaches to the prevention of child recruitment.

El Salvador

The value of DDR programs is evident not only in Africa but also in Asia and Latin America. We can see the need for DDR programs in these areas, because many soldiers there who did not reintegrate became involved in political violence or criminal activities. On numerous occasions in Nicaragua, groups of former soldiers rearmed themselves and resumed fighting (Spencer 1997). In El Salvador, too, many former soldiers find a place not in ordinary civilian life but in urban gangs and organized crime (Verhey 2001). Most practitioners view these former soldiers' engagement in continued fighting and gangs not as an indication that DDR programs are doomed to failure but that much remains to be learned about how to effectively design and implement DDR programs in urban settings.

Following El Salvador's bloody conflict, in which more than 30 percent of the soldiers were girls, consultants hired to assist the demobilization planning recommended specific steps for supporting former child soldiers. Unfortunately, authorities ignored their recommendations, effectively excluding child soldiers from DDR programs. One boy expressed his feeling of betrayal: "We young people were not recognized in any way . . . This was the worst that could have happened to me and my comrades" (Verhey 2001, 8). Exclusion from the reintegration process stings because during the fighting child soldiers had been treated as equals and had fought and sacrificed in the same ways as adult soldiers. No doubt child soldiers' experience of better treatment inside armed groups dimmed their interest in civilian life.

One year later, the authorities partially corrected this problem by providing a few children modest reintegration benefits, mostly education and job skills training. Even this token gesture, though, was riddled with problems. Girls received few, if any, benefits, and many of the former boy soldiers reported difficulties in pursuing education. One said, "I think that housing and education are what I need, but . . . for education, I would like to have a night job so that I could study in the day." Another avowed, "Now they do give classes, but I won't go with those little boys" (Verhey 2001, 19). The children's need to work and contribute to family income frequently prevented them from going to school, as did shame or resentment about having to sit in classes with much younger children. But the program provided very little training in job skills. Only 23 of 293 boys said they had access to training, and there were few job opportunities for those who had completed training. Child soldiers remained disadvantaged, as less than half earned their own income, and of those who did, 85 percent earned less than the minimum wage (Verhey 2001).

Fortunately, these problems were partly offset by high levels of family support for former child soldiers. But the El Salvadoran case underscores the importance of constructing separate children's DDR processes. This lesson also emerges from experience in other countries such as Ethiopia (Ayalew and Dercon 2000).

Afghanistan

Following the Taliban's defeat in November 2001, peace remained a distant hope in Afghanistan. Rival military commanders, or warlords, maintained large private armies, and the country had never been united under a central government. Hamid Karzai's fledgling administration sought to stand down the warlords' armies and integrate selected adult soldiers into a new Afghan army. To achieve this force restructuring and reintegrate many former soldiers, the Afghan government worked with UNAMA, the U.N. Assistance Mission to Afghanistan, in the Afghan New Beginnings Program (ANBP). Although the ANBP had initially included a large adult component and a smaller children's component, UNICEF subsequently assumed responsibility for an independent children's DDR process.

Designed to assist eight thousand child soldiers, the children's DDR process took into account the fact that many child soldiers lived in their home communities but remained in the service of their commanders. Planners recognized the inappropriateness of establishing ICCs, which would have separated children from their families and communities, and opted instead for a community-based approach to DDR. To demobilize child soldiers, UNICEF partnered with international NGOs to create mobile demobilization units that traveled from village to village. Locally elected verification committees worked with local leadership councils (*shuras*) and identified children associated with armed groups. Because local norms regarded children over 14 years of age as adults, the program spoke not of child soldiers but of "minors associated with fighting forces," a more palatable phrase for local communities. Following demobilization, former child soldiers received a medical and psychosocial assessment.

The reintegration process, too, featured a community-based approach. To support reintegration, NGO partners developed community programs to provide education, life skills and vocational training, psychosocial support, and work opportunities. By design, the reintegration programs supported all children, not just the former child soldiers, because all had been affected by war, poverty, and drought. This integrated approach reduced social divisions and the privileging of particular groups. By March 2004, CCF and UNICEF had demobilized more than a thousand child soldiers in the northeast provinces (CSC, 2004).

The children's DDR process suffered due to a delayed start of nearly three years. Such long delays leave children in their commanders' clutches and undermine their hopes for a civilian life. Cheating was also a significant problem, as warlords reneged on their pledges to demobilize particular numbers of child soldiers. Funding was scarce because donors failed to deliver on their promises. Furthermore, many young people who needed assistance received none because they were not considered qualified for the official DDR process. Among the excluded were child soldiers who had turned 18 by the time the official DDR process began, and others who had spontaneously demobilized (left armed groups on their own) years before the process began (Chrobok 2005; Wessells and Kostelny 2002).

An important lesson of the Afghan children's DDR process is that although demobilization frequently captures the public spotlight and garners enormous funding, reintegration is the ultimate goal and requires larger, long-term funding. In addition, effective reintegration requires support for all war-affected children, not just those who have been demobilized most recently.

While Fighting Continues

Nowhere are the challenges of demobilization and reintegration greater than in situations of continued fighting. In ongoing wars, commanders typically do not demobilize their troops. This means that the most likely way a child can exit an armed group alive is by capture or escape. Captured children are regarded as traitors by their former group, and they might be interrogated or imprisoned together with larger, stronger adults, who might abuse them. The prospects are not much better for escapees. In northern Uganda, for instance, escapees from the LRA might be recaptured by the LRA and openly beaten or killed to warn other child soldiers against trying to escape. In Burma, child escapees from the government army are viewed as traitors. Facing mostly negative options, such as joining another armed group, they often seek work illegally in neighboring countries, where they live in fear of deportation.

Many children who return home have no official demobilization papers indicating that they no longer belong to an armed group. Fearing them or remembering the bad things they had done, local people may make reprisal attacks against the children. Risks of re-recruitment may also remain high. In Sri Lanka, children who escape the LTTE and go home are frequently re-recruited by the LTTE (HRW 2004b). Even if they avoid re-recruitment, they may lack access to the reintegration supports available in most formal DDR processes. Euphemisms such as "unofficial demobilization" and "spontaneous reintegration" fail to convey that the children travel uncharted, hazardous terrain and may not reintegrate successfully. Outside formal DDR processes, children's paths are shaped partly by gender and the context into which they seek to reintegrate. These are best illustrated by case studies from northern Uganda and Angola, respectively.

Northern Uganda

In northern Uganda in 1998, a 15-year-old boy from Gulu told me of his exit from the LRA and his attempt to reintegrate into his home village.

> They [the rebels] took me from my village and made me carry heavy loads like the other children. I was big and a good fighter . . . I was promoted to commander and had my own unit. The enemy came, and we fought . . . fought hard. There were lots of deaths and wounded people.
>
> In one battle, the UPDF [government army] surrounded us and a big fight broke out. Everyone was hiding and running, running, trying to get away . . . They captured me and three other boys and took us to their place [compound]. I thought they would kill me since that's what the LRA told us would happen. But they treated us well and took us to a rehabilitation center in Gulu.
>
> I learned to make some things [carpentry] but wanted to go to school . . . I went to school for some days but do not go there now. The children, they called me "rebel" . . . My teacher could not understand and wanted me to obey him. How could I obey him? He has not been in combat and does not know what it is [like] to be a commander and decide for life and death . . .
>
> Now I have no job and am on the street. I don't know what will happen . . . Both sides still fight, but I don't want to be a soldier.

This boy's experience of receiving support from a rehabilitation center is commonplace among former LRA abductees in northern Uganda. Although there is no national DDR program, rehabilitation centers organized by local villagers and international agencies help children transition from the bush and acquire life skills for earning a living. In numerous respects, though, this boy was more fortunate than many other survivors, because he remained outside of armed groups. When children in northern Uganda leave the LRA or other armed groups and attempt to go home, they frequently are reabducted by the LRA or recruited by the UPDF or local pro-government militia groups. He was also fortunate in having had a village to return to. Since the war expanded in 2003, fear of attack has emptied many villages, forcing people to flee into IDP camps best known for their squalor, overcrowding, and pervasive gender-based violence.

This boy's case illustrates the difficulties impeding former child soldiers' reintegration. Stigmatized by other children, this boy was made to feel an outsider and was unable to pursue the education he had wanted so strongly. Respect was an issue, because adults did not treat him with the dignity and respect extended to other villagers, and he did not demonstrate proper respect to local authority figures such as teachers. His unwillingness to obey a teacher who had never made life-and-death decisions suggests that his military identity and thinking remained unchanged. Although he acquired potentially useful job skills, the lack of jobs left him feeling hopeless about the future and idling about town with other unemployed youths.

Despite this boy's problems, it would be a mistake to view him as part of a "lost generation." Many former child soldiers do manage to reintegrate even in the absence of explicit supports such as those provided by official DDR processes. Most likely this boy would have fared better had he received education designed for older children, including former soldiers, and also the opportunity to earn an income. As explained in Chapters 8 and 9, his stigma might have been reduced if the community had been made aware of his situation and had enabled him to perform community service.

In northern Uganda, war is a dual tragedy for children, who are victimized first by being thrust into fighting and second by being denied appropriate reintegration support after they leave their armed groups. The accomplishments of local groups in supporting children's reintegration, although impressive, cannot excuse the continued inaction of the international community. Indeed, this story points out the need for stronger, more comprehensive reintegration supports even as conflict continues.

Girls in Angola

In the Angolan wars, large numbers of girls were taken by UNITA, but even in times of relative peace these girls were denied access to official DDR processes. Many girls who managed to escape or were captured by the Angolan army pursued a self-made reintegration process. CCF/Angola staff listened carefully to a girl who, having spent most of her teenage years inside UNITA, had been captured at age 20 by the Angolan army in 2001. She had recently come to Luanda, the capital city, via Huambo, an inland city.

> Somebody told me that MINARS [a government agency] was sending people to Luanda, and I thought to myself that if I stayed where I was,

with the war still going on, I might be captured again and have to return to the bush . . . But the suffering once we arrived in Huambo was
too great. What with being pregnant, and with small children and
other children, it was too much. I couldn't work . . . When I arrived in
Huambo I was even ashamed to go to the market because I had no
shoes. I walked barefoot and had no skirt to tie about my pregnant
belly. I was ashamed of going to the market—even going to the hospital
for a consultation . . . I felt that the others, the women from the city,
would see us coming from the bush and think less of us because we
were different.

. . . I convinced myself that perhaps by going to Luanda, my life
would change . . . Here I see that the suffering there was too
great; here things are alright because I do my business deals and my
children eat . . . In Luanda, they put us in a refugee camp, where
we are still. I can see my life beginning already to normalize, because
I do my deals . . . With the work I do there are days you go to bed
hungry because you have no money. It's been two months since
they last paid us. You have nothing in the house. What will the children eat?

. . . [Entering Luanda] I was well received . . . The head of MINARS
came round and gave us food. The next day they took us to Viana. Here
in Viana we were well received, and they gave us food, and those of us
with sick children were taken straight to the hospital . . . I felt quite
desperate because the others had husbands who began, during the first
days, to look for work at the small farms. But I was alone, and quite
anxious, because for many jobs, like moving the tent, you needed a
man. (CCF/Angola 2005)

This woman's story, which echoes those of many Angolan girls, illustrates the gendered nature of reintegration concerns. Many of her
stresses arose out of being a mother, reminding us that reintegration is
less an individual concern than a family matter, one inherently difficult
for a single woman having three children. Later in the same interview,
she said she still has bad dreams from her horrible war experiences,
which included having been forced regularly to have sex with older
men. However, her greatest concerns are economic and relate to her
shame at having no decent clothes or being dressed in tatters. Her vacil-
lation between optimism and pessimism indicated the uncertainty of her
situation and her anguish over being unable to feed her children consis-
tently. Her statement about feeling ashamed around other people who

had not been soldiers and who had enjoyed many opportunities illustrates the pain of stigma and lost opportunities.

Although the government provided her some support as a displaced person, the fact that her best option was to live in a crowded camp speaks volumes about the temporary nature of her situation and her lack of long-term reintegration. The government efforts helped but were limited only to survival support—a cruel irony, given that the Angolan government controls immense oil and diamond resources. The limited government aid indicated the need for international DDR supports, particularly gender-sensitive supports, amidst continued fighting. Learning how to provide gender-appropriate supports is a major task for the future (Stavrou 2005).

Democratic Republic of the Congo (DRC)

The DRC offers a useful example of the value of DDR support for child soldiers living in active conflict zones. International agencies such as Save the Children UK offer the support in collaboration with UNICEF (Verhey 2003). Because the conflict is ongoing, the DDR process includes a strong emphasis on prevention of recruitment or re-recruitment through training of military leaders on issues such as children's rights, child protection, armed groups' responsibilities, and what to do if there are children in one's armed group. This training focuses not only on top commanders but also on field commanders, since there is often a gap between what top commanders say and what local field commanders do. Field commanders are often under the greatest pressure to recruit children.

Identified child soldiers are demobilized and taken to ICCs, which provide temporary safety and care and help trace and locate the children's families. The value of these services for children rings in the words of a boy who had been abducted at age 12 by a local militia:

> After many months, in addition to combat between our group and the RCD, there were frequent revolts by our chiefs against the Interahamwe [a Rwandan militia group] in our group. Our chiefs decided to end their solidarity with the Interahamwe and moved part of our group to Mushaki. At Mushaki, by luck, the military authorities demobilised the children in our group.

> After our demobilisation ceremony on 2 April 2002, I was cared for at the Save the Children/DIVAS transit centre and finally, a local NGO took me home to my parents in July 2002.
>
> Unfortunately, when we arrived at my village, we discovered it burned and the neighbors told us that my mother had died and my father had fled. This is why the local NGO took me back to the DIVAS transit centre. Now I am staying in another center in Goma where I am following some training but my greatest hope is that my father will be found so that I can rejoin him. (Verhey 2003, 50)

This boy's story confirms the value of establishing ICCs even in the midst of armed conflict, and it speaks also to the value children attach to rejoining their families.

However, the transit centers encountered numerous challenges. Because the children wanted to return to their families and communities, some were reluctant to participate in center activities such as education. The establishment of an ICC also could spark community tensions. On one occasion, children and staff sitting at an ICC entrance were stoned by neighbors who thought the center-trained children were combatants. Some community members also thought the child soldiers had a better living situation than other children in the community. This episode points out the importance of sensitizing the local community to the purpose of the ICC and developing activities that benefit both former child soldiers and children in the surrounding community. Time was also an issue, as child soldiers stayed in the ICCs for up to several months, creating a debate about whether the center should provide vocational training. Eventually it was decided not to provide vocational training, which could have made centers a magnet for all children hoping to learn marketable skills.

At the village level, the program established community child protection networks, which included local authorities, religious leaders, children, and representatives of diverse community groups and service sectors and contributed to reintegration, protection, and prevention efforts. Avoiding the use of individual benefits, which were so problematic in Liberia, the networks offered reinsertion supports for families rather than individual children. They also monitored recruitment to prevent children's continuing exploitation. Child protection agencies also reached out to former child soldiers who had demobilized spontaneously, that is, without having gone to a center and participated in an official process. The agencies helped former child soldiers obtain the demobilization documents they needed to avoid prosecution as deserters.

This important work, conducted in one of the world's deadliest and least visible wars, testifies to the value of conducting DDR programs while the fighting continues. A valuable lesson is that DDR processes should be part of a wider child protection process protecting all children, including those who demobilize spontaneously.

Strengthening Children's DDR Processes

The international community is very much in a process of learning how to provide effective DDR supports for children. The cases presented above, together with experience from other cases (Kingma 2000; McCallin 1995; Peters, Richards, and Vlassenroot 2003) and evolving guidelines (McConnan and Uppard 2001; UNICEF 2004a), provide valuable lessons and offer practical guidance about how to develop child-friendly DDR processes. These lessons, best regarded as working understandings, include the following.

- *Separate children's DDR process.* Because child soldiers have distinctive needs, children should have their own DDR process, legitimated and codified in the peace agreement.
- *Gender equity.* A high priority is to provide focused supports to girls and women, including mothers, in DDR processes and to ensure equal rights for women in the wider society.
- *Reintegration focus.* Despite political pressures and the military background of many DDR planners, the planning and implementation of DDR programs should have an overarching emphasis on reintegration.
- *Timing.* DDR processes should be implemented immediately following a ceasefire, giving child soldiers access to positive life options and an incentive to abandon war as a way of life.
- *Demobilization and reintegration during armed conflict.* Although DDR is typically organized as a postconflict support, cases such as the DRC indicate the need for demobilization and reintegration during active conflict.
- *Coordination.* Poor coordination, the Achilles' heel of many DDR programs, is frequently visible in problems such as excessive emphasis on demobilization, poor information sharing between agen-

cies, and difficulties managing expectations about soldiers' benefits. An effective DDR coordination process is vital for harmonizing different elements in a manner that supports children's well-being.

- *Education.* Access to quality education is a high priority in DDR processes because war deprives child soldiers of the education to which they have a right and leaves them at a disadvantage in seeking jobs and becoming productive citizens.
- *Job skills and employment.* DDR programs should provide former child soldiers vocational and life skills training that prepares them for jobs. To be effective, the skills training should be complemented by support in obtaining jobs and earning a living.
- *Interim Care Centers.* Although ICCs are valuable transitional devices in some settings, they should be used sparingly and include steps to educate the local community about the Center's purpose, minimize children's length of stay, reduce dependence on the centers, and encourage family and community reintegration.
- *Cash payments to minors.* Cash payments to former child soldiers are damaging and ought to be avoided.
- *Child protection.* DDR processes should include comprehensive efforts to protect children and prevent child recruitment or re-recruitment. The protection of all children is a high priority because the most vulnerable children are at risk of becoming soldiers.
- *Child participation.* Errors occur repeatedly in DDR programs owing partly to failures to learn from children's perspectives. Children's voices should be prominent in all phases of the DDR process—assessment, design, preparation, implementation, and evaluation.

These steps outline an agenda of hope: they can increase protections for children and strengthen macro-level DDR processes, enabling societies to transition out of war and build peace, which is in every child's best interest. These macro-level reforms, however, cannot stand alone. Although they provide a societal framework for supporting child soldiers' reintegration, child soldiers' ability to transition into civilian life depends also on micro-level processes such as how families and communities receive them. These micro-level processes are the focus of Chapters 8 and 9.

8

The Transition to Civilian Life

Getting children out of armed groups is a major accomplishment that ends heinous abuses of children's rights and positions children to rejoin their families and participate in education, jobs, and civilian lives. Child soldiers' safe exit from armed groups frequently evokes a mixture of relief, joy, and hope among families and friends and also among humanitarian agencies.

For child soldiers, however, the situation may be clouded in ambiguity and worry (Mergelsberg 2005). Said a 20-year old from Sierra Leone who had spent many of his formative years with the RUF:

> I know how to be a soldier and to fight. I can use weapons, train, and decide how to attack. I have thought of myself as a soldier for years . . . I haven't been in my village since I was a little boy. My parents saw me last as a child. I have no job, and people look at me like maybe I am a troublemaker.

His concerns about making the transition to civilian life relate to his identity as a soldier and his uncertainties about how he will be regarded in his village. Uncertainties about identity, jobs, and role are among the greatest life stresses for many former child soldiers, who want above all to be normal and like other children.

These concerns are particularly poignant for children who have never lived outside an armed group. For them, "reintegration" is a misnomer implying they are going back to a situation they experienced previously, when in fact they are entering uncharted terrain. Romantic ideas about "going home" are meaningless for them, because their home has been wherever the armed group is. In Angola, children who grew up within UNITA and never interacted with the civilian world had no understanding of how to conduct ordinary transactions such as going to a market and purchasing a loaf of bread. These and similar cases have led many practitioners to prefer the term *integration* over *reintegration.*

Children's psychological residues of their lives as soldiers often dim their hopes for living as other young people do. An East Timorese boy who had joined a militia at age 14 said:

> I had bad dreams and I woke up thinking that somebody wanted to kill me. Now I wake up still from bad dreams. I don't remember my dreams but I feel afraid when I wake up. At this time, I am still constantly afraid. Sometimes I change from feeling happy to feeling sad very quickly. The villagers here don't call me a militiaman but I am the only one who has come back. (UNICEF 2003, 64)

This boy's nightmares and fears indicate the persistence of war's invisible wounds and the need for healing. His awareness of being the only returnee creates a keen sense of difference from others. This sense of difference for former child soldiers, together with their stigmatization as "rebels," "bushwives," or "troublemakers," makes the transition to civilian life a very rocky road.

The diversity of former child soldiers' concerns, which are psychosocial, economic, physical, and cultural, indicates the holistic nature of the reintegration process. The breadth and scope of their concerns caution against singular approaches that assume that a returnee needs only a single form of support, such as a livelihood. Conceived broadly, reintegration is less about reinserting former soldiers back into communities or jobs than about helping children become functional in their society— helping them find meaningful and respected social roles and create civilian identities. Reintegration involves the growth of the whole person and a reconstruction of the child's place and role in the social world. Far from being an individual process, reintegration is an intensely social process of gaining acceptance and developing appropriate relations in families, schools, work lives, and civic groups. Awakening existing social supports or building additional capacities for social support are essential for enabling reintegration.

Family Reintegration

One of the most painful aspects of war for most child soldiers is separation from their families, who typically provided them with social support, love, and, in most cases, protection. An important lesson from World War II and other wars is that children separated from their families exhibit lower levels of well-being than children who had stayed with their families (Cairns 1996; Kinzie et al. 1986). The reunification of child soldiers with their families opens the door to psychosocial support, which families provide in a more effective and lasting manner than professional counseling (McCallin 1998). Family reunification enables children to put war behind them, gain the social support they need for their journey into civilian life, and fulfill their family obligations. Also, a child soldier who is living with his or her family is more likely to be accepted by the community, since family rejection may signal that a child is dangerous or unstable. The importance of family resonates in these words of a boy in the Burmese army: "I want to go home, I want to support my family" (HRW 2002, 161).

Family Tracing and Reunification

An immediate obstacle to family reunification is child soldiers' uncertainty about whether their family survived, where they are, and how they will respond to the child's return. To overcome this obstacle, an essential first step is family tracing and reunification, which may occur spontaneously or with assistance from international agencies such as UNICEF and the International Rescue Committee. This support typically entails documenting the child soldier's identity, collecting information about his or her family and village of origin, and finding out the current location of family members. To trace families in situations of mass displacement, international agencies use diverse tools. They might display children's photos in refugee and IDP camps, distribute videos or radio broadcasts about the children, and circulate maps and pictures drawn by children (de la Soudiere, Williamson, and Botte 2004; DeLay 2002, 2003).

In rural areas, families often walk long distances to meet their children at designated rendezvous points. Usually their reunion evokes joy and celebration through song and dance. In Sierra Leone, one mother described her reaction on rejoining her son, who had been with the RUF for several years:

> I didn't know what to do . . . I had so many tears but was happy to see him. I worried that he would be killed. And some people said the RUF made the children bad. But when I saw him, I thought "He's my son" and gave him a big hug. All the mothers, we sang and danced to show our children how happy we are.

Her concern that her son might have changed and be unable to live with the family resonated with many analysts' gloomy predictions that families would reject their children for having committed brutal acts. In fact, some Liberian children who had committed atrocities decided not to go home (Peters 2003). Although a small number of returning children may have met with rejection, most Sierra Leonean families welcomed their children home, testifying to families' resilience and commitment to their children.

Family reunification, however, is only the beginning of a long, potentially challenging reintegration process wherein children learn or relearn civilian roles. Adult family members usually expect children to obey parents and elders, help with chores such as tending animals and collecting water, and contribute to family income. This can create a clash of expectations since former child soldiers may want to be treated like adults rather than the small children their parents remember. Children and parents must get to know each other anew and negotiate a new mode of relating with each other. It is very likely that there will be conflict in the family. Some former child soldiers, having survived combat or even having been commanders, will defy authority or will be unwilling to obey their parents unquestioningly. Others, with poor self-regulation and weak impulse control, will tend to be aggressive and will vacillate between sullen withdrawal and eruptions of violence. For children who learned in armed groups that fighting is the expected, even necessary, means of dealing with conflict, it can be very difficult to learn to avoid fighting.

Also, family reunification is not universally appropriate. Some children joined an armed group to escape abusive parents, and family reunification could jeopardize their safety. Other children would be returning to very poor families who are unable to feed another person; for these children there is an extremely high risk that they would end up living on the streets or working in dangerous jobs. If rejoining the biological family is clearly contrary to the child's best interests, foster care is a preferred option. However, foster families are just as complex as biological families, and they tend to marginalize foster children, so it is necessary to monitor the well-being and protection of children who have been placed in foster homes (Barnett 2005; Tolfree 2003).

Family reunification is not an option for orphans who have lost both parents and have no extended family who are willing to accept them. Fostering might not be feasible in villages where war and HIV/AIDS have killed most adults. A possible option is to organize youth homes where groups of youths live together and manage as a team household issues such as food security, health, work, and participation in education. This option, although typically viewed as a last resort, has a strong cultural basis in societies in which older children normally care for younger children and derive support and satisfaction from this role (Mann 2004). However, caution is necessary because some youths, whether former soldiers or not, may exploit sexually or economically the younger children with whom they live. Although most former child soldiers have not lost their moral compass, a few bad eggs can be found in any large group of children, making it necessary to monitor and protect children in group living situations. Also, former child soldiers, like other children, need adult models, guidance, and mentoring to develop fully the values and behavior patterns prized in civilian life.

Family reunification presents thorny problems for girl mothers who have survived rape and sexual abuse. In many societies, women regard their baby's father as a husband even if no official marriage has occurred. In countries such as Sierra Leone, this can cause severe conflicts between girl mothers and their biological families, as indicated by the following testimony of a 16-year-old girl whose captor had raped and impregnated her in the bush:

> My husband made me his wife in the bush. He is the father of my baby and is my husband . . . I want to live with him but my parents don't want it. They say I should get a proper husband, not someone from the

bush. I can't live with them. My baby and I live on our own and hope the father will come to us.

This girl's situation was complicated by her parents' rejection of her baby as illegitimate. Also, the "husband," who had returned to the village, showed little interest in living with her, possibly because doing so would have brought increased responsibilities or might have provoked retaliation by the girl's family. For the girl and her baby, the best option lay not in reunification with her parents but in starting her own home, weathering alone the challenges of feeding her baby and earning an income.

Integration into existing families and households may not be a viable option for former child soldiers who return to their villages following years of absence during which they have become adults, as locally defined. Since local people sometimes categorize child soldiers as adults if they have participated in combat, which they regard as adult work, former child soldiers may be expected to move out on their own. Some former child soldiers who return to their villages manage to marry and start a family, which are customary activities for young people. The fact that these young people achieve family integration by starting their own family cautions against the idea that reintegration into existing families is the appropriate solution for all former child soldiers.

These complexities notwithstanding, family reintegration is appropriate and possible for the majority of returning former child soldiers. The reintegration process, which requires the preparation of families for the challenges ahead, is best illustrated by example.

Community Sensitization and Support

In rural Angola following the 1994 ceasefire, CCF/Angola partnered with USAID's Displaced Children and Orphans Fund to support family reintegration. The strategy was to work through the churches, which had long been voices of social justice and peace. A lack of security prevented visits by outsiders, so CCF worked through local church activists (activistas) who were well known and respected in their villages for their work with children. To prepare for their work with families, CCF staff trained the activistas on healthy child development, the impacts of war and violence on children and families, likely problems the returning child soldiers might experience, ways of addressing the problems, and how to gain local support for former child soldiers' safe return.

With the child soldiers awaiting their demobilization from quartering areas, the activistas met with district officials and local chiefs to explain the DDR process, discuss the children's return home, and hear any concerns they had. Winning local leaders' support was crucial since they served as community gatekeepers and would be key figures in addressing any difficulties that might arise. Unsurprisingly, some district officials regarded former child soldiers as troublemakers and feared their return. Citing examples from other war situations, the activistas explained patiently that former child soldiers have a right to reintegration as stipulated by the CRC (Article 39). They also pointed out that most of the children had been abducted and did bad things only because they were forced to. They appealed, too, to the village's responsibility to care for its children. To build confidence, they explained that in other war zones, most child soldiers have reintegrated peacefully, despite leaders' initial doubts. By winning the officials' and leaders' support, these discussions laid an important base of support for the reintegration process and the children's transition.

Gaining the support of community members was also a priority, because family reintegration would surely fail if the returning child soldiers were stigmatized as "rebels" or isolated socially. In this respect, reintegration requires an ecological framework that recognizes the interdependence of children, families, and communities (McCallin 1998; Wessells 2006; Wessells and Monteiro 2004b). In communities, the activistas conducted open discussions to help everyone understand the DDR process, how children had been affected by their war experiences, and the village role and responsibility in aiding the children's reintegration. Also, the activistas met with teachers to discuss the returning children's need for education and the challenges children would encounter in returning to school.

Family Preparation and Problem Solving

These community dialogues set the stage for work with the returning children's families. First the activistas visited the children's families, explained the DDR process, invited discussion about the family's expectations of their child's return, and educated the family about child soldiers' war experiences and current situation. These discussions presented the reintegration process in a positive light, underlined the joy of reuniting with one's child, and kindled a sense of responsibility for children's well-being. The activistas emphasized that returning child soldiers who displayed unexpected or undesired behavior such as talking back to their parents had not "gone bad" but had been affected by their war experiences and would probably recover with their families' support. To help prepare families to address and resolve difficulties, the activistas also engaged families in problem-solving discussions, offering suggestions on how to handle issues such as the returning children's desire for more autonomy than is customary for Angolan children.

The preparatory visits began a six-month stream of visits designed to support families and encourage problem solving. Regular visits proved to be useful, because challenges frequently arose after the initial glow of reunification had faded. In some cases, fathers became angry when their children failed to demonstrate proper respect for parental authority. Heated exchanges frequently escalated, not only because of the clash of parents' and children's expectations, but also because of former child soldiers' impulsivity and difficulty controlling their tempers. These and other difficulties became objects of family problem-solving discussions. If, during their home visits, the activistas saw that families lacked the skills to discuss issues without inflaming tempers, they modeled these skills and taught the families how to manage disagreements in a constructive manner. Family members said they appreciated the activistas' support and had learned from them helpful ways of managing family problems. They also said they had acquired greater understanding of what their children had been through and how to support them.

The apparent success of this model owes to two factors. First was the combination of mediation, modeling, teaching, and family support. The use of a third party—the activistas—served to defuse potentially destructive conflicts and encouraged families to take a problem-solving approach, which mitigated blaming and fighting. This observation fits with increasing evidence that family mediation is essential to the reintegration process (Verhey 2004; Williamson and Cripe 2002). Second was the provision of ongoing support, which is needed because reintegration does not occur overnight. The activistas' teaching of useful skills when the appropriate occasion arose gave families the competencies and confidence they needed to move forward. A key lesson, confirmed in many field programs, is that one-time training sessions or preparatory workshops are severely limited in what they accomplish. Continued training and follow-up support are necessary for enabling the ongoing learning and adaptation at the heart of family reintegration.

Healing and Psychosocial Support

Family reintegration is one of the most fundamental forms of psychosocial support and healing for war-affected children. Beyond the family, too, child soldiers need psychosocial support to meet the challenges of transition. Although former child soldiers are entitled under the CRC to psychosocial assistance and activities promoting recovery and social reintegration, little consensus exists about the best way to address child soldiers' psychosocial wounds (Loughry and Eyber 2003). Adherents of a medical model, outlined in Chapter 6, seek to treat child soldiers for mental illness or problems such as PTSD using predominantly Western methods such as individual or group counseling. No doubt counseling is a useful part of rehabilitation in particular circumstances. However, counseling approaches warrant critical scrutiny because they have been overused or misapplied in many emergencies.

Highlighting the limits of counseling in a situation in which people struggle to meet basic needs, a local chief asked, "How can we heal when we are hungry and have no schools to give children hope for the future?" In a war zone, it is vital to recognize the interrelations between the wounds of past violence and the current life stresses arising from the lack of basic physical items, from food to infrastructure. Often, physical destruction and losses are inseparably fused with local people's feelings in response to the war. Their physical difficulties are an integral part of their psychological suffering. Their lack of good homes or schools embodies and symbolizes their plight, manifests physically their losses, and robs them of a sense of hope and well-being. In such situations, it may be inappropriate to offer psychosocial assistance as a singular intervention. More good will likely come through interweaving psychosocial support with physical construction and assistance in sectors such as health, water and sanitation, and shelter reconstruction.

This insight recommends a more holistic approach focused on the interrelations between children's physical, cognitive, emotional, social, and spiritual development. A holistic approach incorporates also the social dimensions of healing, since it recognizes the power of child soldiers' connection with their social ecologies of families, peer groups, communities, and societies. As discussed previously (Chapter 6), child soldiers' emotional scars and stresses are intertwined with social problems such as stigmatization, social isolation, and inability to earn a living. Soldiering has rewritten children's life scripts, depriving them of the social relations and learning experiences young people need to function well in adult roles. Much of their distress stems from their inability to integrate fully into civilian life and to perform the roles most young people fill in their societies. From this standpoint, psychosocial assistance is less about healing individual wounds or mental illness than enabling former child soldiers to integrate socially, to participate in the rhythms of civilian life, to be functional as defined in the local context, and to redefine themselves as civilians. A holistic approach requires a very large toolkit including not only counseling but also traditional healing, structured group activities, trust-building exercises, nonviolent conflict resolution, livelihood support, reconciliation, substance abuse rehabilitation, and education, among others.

After Demobilization

The need for psychosocial support is visible shortly following demobilization, a time in which children are "crossing a bridge" between military and civilian life (Jareg 2005). On a visit to Gulu in northern Uganda, I watched child survivors of the LRA exit a flatbed truck and enter an ICC run by World Vision. The children's gaunt, unwashed appearance and listless attitudes hinted at their war experiences and the psychosocial challenges ahead. Health problems such as skin diseases were very noticeable, and the staff would test them for the sexually transmitted diseases prevalent in the LRA. Boys and girls went to separate quarters, where they received a wash and much-needed health care. Over the next several weeks they organized themselves and assisted in basic chores such as cleaning. They also participated in a mixture of individual and group counseling conducted by Ugandan staff who are highly familiar with the children's language and situation. As one staff member said, "The children are traumatized and very bad off when they come here . . . But over time and with counseling, they talk about what had happened and they take steps toward recovery." Recovery takes time, and most psychologists measure recovery and rehabilitation in years. Even over a period of months, with the help of the Ugandan staff and participation in group-oriented activities, children showed signs of improvement such as reduced frequency of nightmares and increased hope for the future.

Although counseling can be valuable at this early stage, it is neither the foundation nor the first tier of psychosocial support. When children's wounds are too raw and fresh, talking about painful experiences can leave children in a highly vulnerable state. Less intrusive methods enable former child soldiers to express their feelings in a manner that re-awakens children's inherent capacities for play and joyfulness. At many ICCs, former child soldiers sing songs that most of them had learned at an early age, reconnecting them with memories of their civilian childhood. These memories are strands of a previous life and identity that can be rewoven into the fabric of a new civilian identity following life inside an armed group. Regaining these memories is a useful antidote to the armed groups' indoctrination strategies of cutting children off from their past, and begins the long journey toward being a civilian. Group singing about joy and peace serves as a ritual signaling that the children have crossed the boundary between life as a soldier and life as a civilian.

Songs and dances also provide venues for expressing feelings about the past, present, and future. At UNICEF-supported Grafton Camp in Sierra Leone, I observed teenage boys who had been soldiers sing in rap style, composing lyrics and dancing as others clapped and danced. Their lyrics unfolded stories not only of war but also of their joy to be away from fighting and war and told of their hopes of becoming carpenters or metalworkers who support their families. Their dancing bristled with energy, reaching a fevered pitch when the song touched a nerve of pain or recalled the joy of their family reunions. By enabling youths to vent pent-up feelings, the dancing served also to reduce stress and aid self-regulation. In many cultures, people express feelings through nonverbal means such as dancing and movement rather than the talking method Western counselors use. For former child soldiers, too much talking can be dangerous, because telling the bad things one has done can trigger re-taliation and overwhelming feelings.

For young children whose verbal skills are limited, drawing is a useful way to express feelings. At Grafton Camp, staff gave former child soldiers crayons and paper and invited them to draw a picture, without telling them what to draw. Boys as young as 7 drew nightmarish pictures of villages under attack, people dying, homes burning, and blood spilling in the streets. Their drawings spoke with a power beyond words. Collected over time, children's drawings provide a benchmark of their progress and recovery. Fresh from the battlefield, most children draw deeply disturbing pictures of war and death. Over time and with appropriate psychosocial support, the same children gradually begin drawing colorful pictures of houses, boats, and sports activities of the kind drawn by children their age who had not been soldiers or exposed to war.

The reestablishment of social trust is one of the most basic psychosocial tasks for former child soldiers. At Grafton Camp, staff used games to build trust and also to stimulate children's sense of fun and joy, which had been muted by life inside armed groups. In a game called "the tunnel," boys formed two lines facing each other, and each pair of boys who stood opposite each other joined hands and lifted them overhead, forming a tunnel. The two boys at the front of the human tunnel ducked down and ran through. Having reached the end, they stood up forming the end of the tunnel, whereupon the next two boys at the front ducked and ran through. Amidst great laughter, the boys ran faster and faster, with the tunnel snaking its way around trees and other obstacles. Although a child's game, this was also a means of building trust and a highly symbolic activity (Wessells, 1997). As boys ran through the tunnel, those who were standing could have tripped or harassed them, but they did not. Each boy saw or learned that trust is possible and that it was in his interest not to harm other boys, who could have retaliated subsequently. The tunnel game at once kindled awareness of interdependence and awakened the pleasures of collective joy and cooperation.

Not uncommonly, fighting and bullying are significant problems in children who have recently demobilized (Peters, 2003). Throughout the reintegration process, former child soldiers face a multitude of conflicts, making nonviolent conflict resolution a high priority in psychosocial support. Games like soccer and volleyball can teach children skills for handling conflict nonviolently. With appropriate coaching from project staff, children learn to handle the conflicts through dialogue rather than fighting. The resulting learning or relearning how to follow rules, avoid fights, and manage conflicts in more constructive ways is vital for the transition to civilian life. However, the participation in games can also be destructive, as highly competitive contests can unleash bad tempers and fighting or become theaters of conquest. Whether the games promote psychosocial growth and recovery depends on the manner in which they are conducted. To enable the games to contribute to healthy psychosocial development, trained adults or older children must set the tone, emphasize goals such as communication and teamwork, and use disputes as opportunities for imparting skills of managing conflict without resort to fighting.

Free of the endless drills and duties of life in an armed group and its rigid command structure, former child soldiers must learn to adapt to their new situation of freedom and the rhythms and activities of civilian life. As civilians, they will rely less on external authority to structure their time. They must learn to make choices about how they spend their time, whom to interact with, and how to conduct themselves. Key priorities are to learn new rules of social interaction that comply with civilian norms and accept responsibility for their actions. The children are not starting from scratch, however. Inside armed groups, children frequently learn valuable skills of teamwork and organizing people to perform complex tasks. Well-designed psychosocial programs find a way to engage these skills and transfer them to civilian life.

To provide structure and encourage a sense of responsibility and agency, ICCs frequently invite former child soldiers to help set the house rules and to perform household chores that benefit everyone. Psychologically, it is significant when a group of children who have been immersed in a system of violence decide among themselves to set and obey rules such as "No fighting" and "No name calling." As the youths, together with staff social workers, set the penalties for infractions, they collectively accept a new set of rules that are appropriate to civilian life. By embracing these rules and paying the consequences for violations, the children learn to take responsibility and regulate their behavior in ways appropriate to a civilian mode of living.

Effective social support is the backbone of psychosocial assistance in counseling as well as other modalities. Recognizing this, many ICCs organize daily peer dialogues, sometimes called peer counseling, to permit former child soldiers to express feelings about the group situation, explore the fairness of various rules, and work out their disagreements through means other than fighting. These discussions provide spaces in which children learn to solve problems through talking and reflection and to develop positive relations based on civilian values. Although the interactions are not a form of psychotherapy and the discussion leaders have too little training to be regarded as professional counselors, peer dialogues are useful psychosocial tools because they build important life skills of reflection, empathy, negotiation, and problem solving that aid the transition to civilian life.

Few studies have examined systematically whether a stay in an ICC has a measurable impact on former child soldiers' well-being. In Mozambique, boy soldiers who had stayed in a center organized by Save the Children showed over a two-month period reduced aggression toward adults and other children, less withdrawal behavior, and increased cooperation with children and adults (Boothby, Crawford, and Halperin 2006). Similar improvements have been visible among youths in northern Uganda (MacMullin and Loughry 2002) and Sierra Leone (Peters 2003). A paucity of studies have used a child participation methodology to document how child soldiers view reintegration supports such as ICCs. In one study, children in an ICC said they liked best their opportunities for education and training and also their ability to talk with their caretakers (Peters 2003). Additional participatory research with both girls and boys is needed, not only to offset adult and gender biases in DDR programs, but also to stimulate in the youths a sense of empowerment and agency. This will reduce their feelings of being overwhelmed and enhance their psychosocial well-being.

Rituals and Spiritual Cleansing

In contrast with Western psychologists' emphasis on counseling, former child soldiers frequently say their greatest need is to see a traditional healer who can clean them of the spiritual impurities acquired during the war. Local people view spiritual pollution as a collective threat, so both villagers and former child soldiers are eager to restore harmony between the living community and the ancestors (Honwana 2006). This understanding of the wounds of war as being communal indicates the need for communal as well as individual healing. In rural Africa, this is achieved when local healers conduct communalized rituals that expunge bad spirits and restore spiritual harmony.

In Sierra Leone soldiers raped large numbers of abducted girls, and in some villages a girl had been sexually violated in nearly every household (Kostelny 2002). The situation for the girl soldiers was difficult not only because of the trauma of rape, but even more because of the local mean-ings and stigmas attached to the rape. In rural Sierra Leone, the bush is a sacred place of the ancestors. The villagers saw the rapes as a violation of this sanctity that left the girls in a state of spiritual impurity, which threatened families and community members with misfortunes such as crop failures. Because the villagers feared the girls and reviled them as abominations, the girls frequently suffered ridicule, name calling, and even assault (Kostelny 2004).

Speaking in a group of formerly abducted girls, one girl described their situation to me, evoking much nodding and agreement from the others:

> We are not like other girls, because we were taken in the bush. Our minds are not steady, and we cannot eat off the same plates as our fami-lies. People call us bad names and do not accept us. They call us bad names. How can they do that? We worry about where we will get money to live and feed our babies. Our hearts are heavy even after the war.

In the local idiom, the reference to unsteady minds indicates that the girls cannot think clearly because they are in a state of spiritual impurity. Although mental unsteadiness could be a product of war trauma, it is equally likely the result of believing they were contaminated and also their extreme social isolation, stigmatization, and ridicule. The state-ment "we cannot eat off the same plate as our families" meant their con-tamination barred them from full interaction with their families and also from marriage and business activities. Local villagers confirmed their af-fliction, saying the girls could not conduct business because they would be "sure to fail" owing to their "unstable minds" and "bad luck." The toxic combination of stigmatization, inability to function socially and economically, and belief that one is in a state of impurity that threatens both family and village imposes heavy psychosocial burdens and thwarts recovery.

To address these problems, CCF/Sierra Leone paid the fees for healers, enabling local healers who were acceptable to both the girls and their villages to conduct the appropriate purification rituals for groups of for-mer girl soldiers. Although the rituals varied across regions, they con-tained common elements, such as ritual washing through scrubbing the girls with special leaves and black soap in the river. The scrubbing produced foam that was believed to draw impurities out of the body, allowing the river to wash them away. In one village, healers used a fumigation method in which the girls drank a cleansing mixture of boiled herbs and then inhaled the herbs' vapor while their heads were under a blanket or cloth. The girls' manner of dress was another key element—sitting on a mat covered with cowry shells, the girls wore a white cloth on their heads and a red cloth on their hips. The girls and the healer ate a specially prepared meal together and then danced and drummed all night. In the morning, while the community watched, the girls were wrapped in white cloth, which symbolized purity, and the healer presented them to the village as "new." Following a discussion between the chief and the parents, the villagers welcomed the girls back amidst much drumming, singing, and dancing (Kostelny 2004).

The girls' participation in these rituals had powerful effects on their social acceptance and identity as civilians. Upon completion of the ritual, the girls reported that they immediately felt well and made statements such as "Now my head is clear" and "Now we are like other girls." Over the next several weeks, the girls demonstrated increased social integration and ability to interact freely. One girl said, "Before I was ashamed to mingle with the others—now I mix freely." Another beamed with her newly found ability to integrate: "We stayed apart from the others. Now that we are cleansed, we can do all things together." Several months later, numerous girls said they had married, felt they had achieved civilian identities, and were happy and successful in their roles as wives. Numerous girls also said they had become successful in business and had become respected community members (Kostelny 2004). Community members, too, said the rituals had improved the situation. One put it, "We can do everything with them now—eat, work, and do business. We do not fear them anymore. They have improved behavior."

To speculate a bit, the purification rituals may serve as a gateway or foundation for participation in other activities that support social integration and functionality. Before the rituals had been conducted, it would have been futile to provide access to job training or business activities, because both the girls and their communities regarded this as inappropriate and doomed to failure. In many respects, the conduct of the rituals erased the impurities associated with war experiences, giving the girls a fresh start and an opportunity to participate fully in business and other activities. Although this gateway hypothesis requires additional testing, it suggests that in some cultural settings, traditional healing is a necessary first step in the reintegration process.

The value of local healing rituals indicates that war-affected communities are not blank slates with respect to psychological support but are repositories of knowledge and practices useful in aiding children's well-being. This realization offers a valuable counterpoint to the tendency, often visible in emergencies, of many humanitarian agencies to treat war-affected people as having no psychosocial resources and being reliant entirely on outside support. Although war-affected people frequently need outside support, they have capacities for self-help and valuable local healing resources that fit better the local context and are more sustainable than outside healing methods. In Bosnia, valuable local resources included the women's knitting groups, which served coffee, provided psychosocial support, and were viewed as more appropriate than trauma counseling (Agger 2001). When crises occur, people try to engage local resources, though with varying degrees of success. Humanitarian agencies should learn about and work with these resources, increasing people's access to them, instead of seeking to replace them. Effective assistance to former child soldiers, then, entails a willingness to help the children engage fully with the cultural resources already present in their villages.

Former boy soldiers, too, benefit from participation in local rituals (Annan and Blattman 2006). In rural Angola, two categories of rituals seemed important for cleansing boy soldiers of spiritual impurities. One category consisted of greeting rituals that local villagers perform on the former soldiers' initial return. The CCF/Angola team described the Okupiolissa ritual, which occurred in Huila Province:

> The community and family members are usually excited and pleased at the homecoming. Women prepare themselves for a greeting ceremony . . . Some of the flour used to paint the women's foreheads is thrown at the child and a respected older woman of the village throws a gourd filled with ashes at the child's feet. At the same time, clean water is thrown over him as a means of purification . . . The women of the village dance around the child, gesturing with hands and arms to ward away undesirable spirits or influences . . . They each touch him with both hands from head to foot to cleanse him of impurities . . . When the ritual is complete, the child is taken to his village and the villagers celebrate his return. A party is held in his home with only traditional

beverages . . . The child must be formally presented to the chiefs by his parents . . . The child sits beside the chiefs, drinking and talking to them, and this act marks his change of status in the village. (CCF/Angola 1999)

This type of ritual is conducted for anyone who has been around death and the scourges of war, which are believed to impart dangerous impurities.

A second type of ritual is the purification ritual only healers can perform. It is designed to address the more significant impurities associated with acts such as killing people, which can lead to being haunted by the angry spirits of those who were killed. In one ritual (Wessells and Monteiro 2004a), the local healer used the burning leaves of a sacred herb to define a safe space that bad spirits cannot enter. Using a fumigation method, the healer had the former boy soldier breathe the fumes from specially selected burning herbs. He also scrubbed the soldier's chest and back with special roots that were believed to expunge bad spirits and block their reentry. To appease the angry spirits, the healer made an offering by preparing a banquet of traditional liquor and food, which were placed around the perimeter of the safe space, and by sacrificing a chicken. The ritual ended with the boy leaving the room by jumping through the door. This signified he had left all impurities behind and was clean and acceptable from that point onward.

Following the conduct of such rituals, former boy soldiers typically see themselves as spiritually clean and free to engage with their families and communities. The effects on the boys' social identities and relations are profound, as community members frequently view the soldiers as having been reborn and able to enter civilian life. Some rituals heighten the salience of the child's break with his past as a soldier by including steps such as burning the soldier's clothing (Honwana 1997). In this manner, the rituals help former child soldiers set aside their identities as soldiers and reconstruct their identities as civilians. By cleaning the former soldiers and making them acceptable to the community, the purification rituals set the stage for the soldier's longer-term reintegration. Because of these benefits, practitioners increasingly regard traditional healing as part of the comprehensive assistance to which former child soldiers are entitled (Agger 2006; Annan and Blattman 2006; Wessells and Monteiro 2004a; Williamson and Cripe 2002).

Despite these benefits, purification rituals alone are insufficient for successful reintegration. In a longitudinal study of former child soldiers in Mozambique, demobilized boys spoke of, and showed the benefits of, having undergone traditional healing rituals. However, nearly a third of the former child soldiers showed signs of PTSD ten years following their demobilization. Also, a minority of returning soldiers, particularly those who had only limited family support, functioned poorly (Boothby, Crawford, and Halperin 2006). This suggests the value of providing community-based psychosocial supports after the purification rituals. Also, traditional practices warrant critical scrutiny because some practices are harmful. In Sierra Leone, traditional secret societies may offer psychosocial support to girls who participate in them, but in those groups the girls might also suffer harms, such as female genital mutilation.

Community-Based Psychosocial Support

Reintegration is a dual process of individual adaptation and community acceptance and support. The importance of individual change is visible in many postconflict zones, where formerly armed youths abandon their military swagger, carrying themselves in a more humble, peaceful manner accepted by the community. To make such changes, however, requires community support not only from families but also from peers, teachers, elders, and religious leaders. Much support occurs not through formal psychological or psychiatric treatment but through integration into community rhythms and the activities that are expected of young people, such as participation in schools, youth groups, and religious organizations (Landry 2005; Verhey 2004; Williamson and Cripe 2002). These institutions and groups compose a nonformal system of psychosocial support that community-based approaches seek to mobilize, build upon, and strengthen.

A common error is to assume that all former child soldiers are alike and need the same kind of support. Owing to the wide range in their war experiences and also to differences of temperament and preexisting issues, former child soldiers exhibit considerable diversity in the kind and extent of support they need. Broadly, three groups are discernible. The first is the majority—probably around 70 percent—of former child soldiers, who function well and will benefit from work, play, attending school, and general improvements in economic, political, and social conditions (Hubbard and Pearson 2004; Reichenberg and Friedman 1996; Wessells and Monteiro 2001). Typically these activities are offered to all children in order to avoid singling out former child soldiers, who have a keen sense of their own difference from others and loathe stigmatization and isolation. Some villages organize these activities themselves without external assistance. In other cases, international NGOs facilitate these activities by selecting villagers known locally as helpers of children and providing training on how children have been affected and how to support them. Former child soldiers relish these activities because they provide an opportunity to enjoy activities they were denied when they were in an armed group and that symbolize their civilian status. Singing and playing with others, former child soldiers begin to feel as if they are like other children, accepted socially, and capable of having a civilian life.

The second group—probably around 20 percent, depending on the emergency—of former child soldiers is at heightened risk, and these children need focused supports. This group includes children living on the streets and children with disabilities. Children with disabilities, for example, may suffer from stigmas and need outreach support to participate in activities such as education. Girl soldiers who survived sexual violence may be isolated due to their stigmatization. A key task is to reach out to these at-risk children and reduce the problem of stigmatization. To provide outreach, community-based programs frequently work through networks of community volunteers who make home visits to former child soldiers. These home visits reduce the pain of isolation and also prepare the young person to engage with the community. In the community at large, the volunteers conduct open discussions to sensitize people to the needs and situation of former child soldiers such as those with disabilities. Frequently, these discussions emphasize children's rights, the responsibility of the village to care for its children, and the various ways in which people with disabilities could participate if given the opportunity.

At-risk former child soldiers also benefit from participation in youth groups, which offer a space in which they interact with other children their age, building their sense of normalcy and their confidence that they will reintegrate successfully. Dialogue in youth groups provides important opportunities for learning, both for former child soldiers and for other community youths. Through dialogue, former child soldiers learn how youths who had not been soldiers handle life problems such as poverty and peer conflict. Frequently these dialogues offer former child soldiers valuable spaces for reflection on values and ethics, which figure prominently in the transition process. The community youths, too, learn from the dialogues. Having previously seen child soldiers as dangerous and unfeeling, they come to see them instead as full human beings in a process of redefining themselves and struggling with many of the same life issues that other youths struggle with.

The third and smallest group—usually around 10 percent—of former child soldiers is severely affected and unable to function in a culturally appropriate manner. Some of these children may have had preexisting mental illness or may have had such profoundly disturbing experiences as to render them dysfunctional. These children need specialized services such as psychiatric or psychological care, counseling, or extra attention from traditional healers. Effective community-based support includes networks for referring children in special need to experts who can provide appropriate support.

For those who organize or provide psychosocial support, it is tempting to focus on what can be done to assist former child soldiers. It would be a mistake, however, to overlook the value of what former soldiers accomplish on their own. In some Sierra Leonean villages I have visited, former child soldiers who self-demobilized have formed agricultural cooperatives, youth groups, and community improvement activities on their own initiative. Youth ownership of these activities gives them a life of their own in the community. And the fact that the community benefits and sees youths in a more positive role helps the youths find meaning, identity, and a positive role as civilians. Here again we see that healing is a reciprocal process of self-transformation and social transformation, leading to improved relations between child soldiers and communities.

The most severely affected former child soldiers require specialized support, although which kind of assistance is most useful is contested. Stigmatization is an enormous problem for those whom Western psychologists regard as mentally ill and whom local people regard as "not well" or "crazy." To reduce stigmas, psychosocial workers often educate community leaders and people about the signs of particular disorders and how to help the severely afflicted (Baron 2002). Also, many programs support severely affected people, including former child soldiers, by offering small-group counseling sessions in which groups of approximately five people talk in a safe, confidential atmosphere conducive to support and growth. The provision of effective counseling requires that psychosocial workers receive several months of training and ongoing supervision (Hubbard and Pearson 2004). Persons who have received only a few days or weeks of training hardly merit the label "counselor" (De Jong 2002).

Counseling is inappropriate in some situations, though, and presents risks beyond stigmatization. Soldiers who have completed a purification ritual are typically told not to "look back," that is, to avoid talking about their war experiences or the ritual, lest the bad spirits return (Honwana 1997). For these individuals, counseling and talking about war experiences are neither culturally appropriate nor safe, which cautions against universalized approaches to healing. Also, former child soldiers may fear their talking about their experiences will make them targets for revenge attacks. Counseling can help in some circumstances, but most former child soldiers find it a lower priority than having a job, going to school, and becoming literate.

Livelihoods

Economic issues weigh heavily on former child soldiers, who typically return to situations of chronic poverty wondering how they will obtain food, clothing, and other necessities. These issues loom even larger because jobs are scarce and former child soldiers lack the skills they would need to compete for any existing jobs.

Stigmatization, Role, and Identity

Although returning soldiers' need for money is undeniable, this need intertwines with their burning desire to avoid stigmas and to achieve a modicum of dignity and respect. Said a 16-year-old boy from Sierra Leone who had been part of the RUF:

> When I came out of the bush, I had nothing—no shoes, no shirt, nothing. I could not come into the village this way. People would laugh at me and make fun of me for being so poor. In this situation, I would be nothing, not a person. I had to have a means of living and helping my family.

For this boy, already labeled a "rebel," the thought of bearing the additional stigma of being very poor was too much. His need for money reflected his desire to achieve dignity and recognition as a person capable of helping his family. Fortunately, he received skills training, acquired a job, and earned an income, subduing his fears and winning the respect of his family.

Girls, too, regard livelihoods as pathways toward improved social status. A 15-year-old mother from Sierra Leone said she was highly sought after as a marriage partner because she had received training and obtained a job. In rural Sierra Leone, unmarried girls frequently regard the state of being unmarried as a form of social death. This girl had initially feared she would be unmarriageable because she had been raped and had had a "bush baby." Her job and her ability to earn income had jettisoned her stigma and elevated her to a coveted social status.

Former child soldiers' issues of status are intimately connected to issues of role and social identity. A man who has a job and earns an income is viewed as eligible to enter the roles of husband and father. To marry and start a family means being like other people of one's age and filling the social roles normally expected of young people. Entry into such roles enables young people to redefine their identities, which, as we have seen, are as much about social relations as about personal views. Being a husband and a father, fulfilling the responsibilities of the role of head of family, helps enormously to shift a young man's identity from soldier to civilian. Village people begin to regard a young person who functions well in these roles as a civilian and a member of the village who has a positive contribution to make. In many respects, identity and social role have a reciprocal relationship, since entry into particular social roles sets the stage for identity transformation.

Life Skills and Reintegration

Vocational skills training is often a prominent and much sought-after feature of reintegration programs. Practitioners' field experience has shown that, to be effective, skills training must continue long enough to ensure mastery of the basic skills needed to earn an income. The demand for skills training is understandable in light of former child soldiers' need for marketable skills. In Sierra Leone, former girl soldiers learning tailoring skills from CARITAS, an international NGO, spoke with considerable hope, based in no small part on the skills they were learning. A 17-year-old girl said:

> The war put an end to school, and I was afraid I would have no way to earn a living. In this program, we are learning a skill that will give us jobs. Right now we learn how to design, cut, and sew, but we will also learn how to buy cloth and make our own business.

Also in Sierra Leone, former boy soldiers learning skills of carpentry through a CCF/Sierra Leone program spoke of their pride in their new learning. Said one of the boys, "We were soldiers but now peace has come . . . We must learn a trade. Building gives us hope because we know we can support our families." As this statement illustrates, former child soldiers view vocational training as a portal to a new life, a means of transitioning from their lives as soldiers to the world of civilian life. For them, learning a craft is at once economically necessary and part of the recovery process. To be able to put the war behind them, child soldiers need a way to move forward and a path toward success in civilian life. Their vocational skills enabled them to remake themselves, with the items they crafted serving as monuments to their own transformation and healing.

Vocational skills alone, however, do not enable one to earn a living or to reintegrate in a deeper sense. A classic mistake made in many well-intentioned DDR and job-training programs is to train far more people for a particular job than can be supported by the local economy, which typically lies in shambles. The resulting unemployment stirs frustration and creates economic hardships that can propel youths back to the bush. A market analysis conducted in advance is a useful antidote to this problem. Also, because many former soldiers do not know how to save or keep track of money, many programs teach not only vocational skills but also the fundamentals of running a business. Even such simple skills as how to sell something in a responsible manner may be quite foreign, at first, to former child soldiers, who might never have learned how most people behave in a market. Because most former child soldiers have missed out on education, basic literacy and numeracy skills are frequently included in their business training.

Although job and business training programs offer many benefits, they can also create difficult problems, one of which is jealousy. Often donors designate funding specifically for former child soldiers. This well-intended targeting can create a potentially dangerous privileging of former child soldiers over equally needy villagers. One elder in Sierra Leone asked me, "Why should the soldiers who attacked us get all the assistance, when we all have suffered?" In postconflict situations, many displaced people, who returned home to destroyed villages and abject poverty, wonder why assistance goes to former child soldiers, who might not be the worst off. In fact, many local people regard aid to child soldiers as rewards to those who committed horrible acts. Meanwhile, those who suffered the most—the villagers under attack—receive little or nothing.

Former child soldiers recognize this problem and seek to avoid it. Observed a 19-year-old man in Sierra Leone who had entered the RUF at age 16:

> Because of the DDR, I wore nice shoes and new clothes. I was very grateful because I could never have come out of the bush in the state I was in. But other youths had no nice shoes and clothes. I became stigmatized for a different reason.

Although such jealousies may seem petty, they can erupt into violence, and they sharpen social divisions at a moment when unity is needed. To prevent this problem, well-designed reintegration programs avoid excessive targeting of former child soldiers and invite the participation of all village youths. In Sierra Leone, for example, one program offered support to schools based on the numbers of former child soldiers they enrolled (Williamson and Cripe 2002). In addition to reducing social divisions, this inclusive approach recognizes that many war-affected children—separated children, children with disabilities, and survivors of sexual violence, among others—need support and assistance as much as, or more than, former child soldiers. Reintegration, then, is not a goal for child soldiers only but for all war-affected children.

Education

When children emerge from armed groups, they have many things to grieve, one of which is their loss of education. One teenager who had belonged to an armed group in the DRC for two years said, "I regret it because if I hadn't been a soldier I would have gone further with my studies" (*Child Soldiers Newsletter* 2005, 3). The loss of education embodies a loss of childhood and the opportunities that enable most children to develop into functional, competent adults.

Well-designed education is one of the most empowering experiences for children, including former child soldiers (Castelli, Locatelli, and Canavera 2005). In fact, many youths join armed groups partly because they are disaffected with existing systems of education and have a prevailing sense of hopelessness (Richards 1996). If education will not be available to them when they disarm, child soldiers are likely to see war in the bush as a better option than transitioning into civilian life. Indeed, former child soldiers frequently identify education as one of their top priorities, because having an education expands their life opportunities and creates hope for the future (McKay and Mazurana 2004; Peters and Richards 1998; Williams and Cripe 2002; Women's Commission for Refugee Women and Children 2005). Child soldiers are quick to point out that education helps children understand and participate in the construction of peace. As one Liberian said:

> Most of our brothers, they have been fighting since 1990, so all they think about is war. But if you are educated, you can think of other things. Many do not know right from wrong; they don't know the danger of carrying arms and the damage they have done to our nation for our children and grandchildren. (HRW 2004a, 16)

Also, being in school symbolizes normalcy, being like other children, and the transition to peace.

Numerous obstacles such as lack of schools and teacher shortages make it difficult for child soldiers to receive education in a war zone, however. Even if schools do open, former child soldiers may be unable to participate. Many are stigmatized at school, and 16- and 17-year-olds are often unwilling to sit in school beside 10- or 12-year-olds. A useful strategy in supporting teenagers is to provide accelerated or catch-up education that enables students to complete in three years the equivalent of six years of primary education (Landry 2005). If the curriculum is oriented toward younger children, teenagers might find it irrelevant (Robertson and McCauley 2005). Many child soldiers feel there is an unbridgeable gulf between their teachers' life experiences and their own. Access to education is limited for girls who are forced to stay home to perform household work or who have menstrual problems. And many girls avoid school because of predatory teachers or the high risk of being sexually assaulted when they walk to school or use the latrine at school.

Owing to these and other obstacles, access to education requires much more than enrollment in school (Sommers 2003). Before former child soldiers enter school, there should be training for both children and teachers that increase awareness of child soldiers' situation and reduce issues of stigmatization. Also, teachers need to receive training that enables them to work effectively with this special group of children. In particular, teachers must learn to understand why former child soldiers may act out or isolate themselves in school. Some teachers view children who start fights as being undisciplined or as troublemakers, when the fighting may stem from the children's difficult war experiences. To deal with unruly behavior, teachers need to learn how to use nonviolent, nonpunitive methods that support children at risk. Furthermore, teachers should learn that they are responsible for adhering to a code of conduct that protects children, shielding them from would-be predators. To be effective, such a code would have to be backed by government officials and be enforced in a consistent manner that protects children.

It would be too restrictive, however, to equate education of former child soldiers with going to school. Because economic pressure and cultural expectations require them to work and earn money to support their families, many former child soldiers prefer options like evening literacy courses. Literacy classes might seem a pale substitute for a more comprehensive education, but former child soldiers find them a very practical way to learn basic life skills, such as reading and writing, which give them hope for the future. Literacy classes also give them a way to integrate with other people their own age who had also been denied an education.

This social integration satisfies former child soldiers' most fundamental yearning—to see themselves, and to be seen by others, not as children of the gun but as normal young people accepted by their families and communities. This powerful desire for normalcy and acceptance, in people whose childhood experiences were so far from ordinary, testifies to their resilience, and it reminds us that the journey from soldiering to civilian life is as much social as individual.

9

Community Reconciliation, Justice, and Protection

Reintegration programs assume the existence of relatively peaceful communities into which former child soldiers may integrate. In the long shadows cast by war, however, many people live in a precarious situation somewhere between peace and war. Often, community is more an aspiration than a reality.

For one thing, war shatters communities, forcing displaced people into a survival mode hardly conducive to community spirit. Also, wars like those in Kosovo and Iraq destroyed the sense of law and order, spawning problems of crime and banditry that corrode community well-being. Following war, the intergroup tensions that had led to, and vented themselves during, the war continue to destroy social trust, making a mockery of the collective unity implied by the term *community* (Richards et al. 2005). The quest to rebuild community spirit swims upstream against strong currents of lawlessness and social division.

Although the end of war brings peace on a macro or societal scale, it frequently sets the stage for the eruption of conflicts at a micro level. In villages, land disputes flourish because displaced people return home to find other people living on their land and in their houses. People displaced for years may decide to stay where they are, adding to that area's competition for food and other scarce resources. At war's end, people from previously fighting political factions and ethnic and religious groups may return to the same villages, stirring fears and creating conflicts conducive to continued fighting and renewed recruitment of child soldiers. Mired in local conflicts, local villagers frequently see peace as far removed from their lives and do not see their connection with the societal peace process.

To repair the torn social fabric and increase unity, community reconciliation is a high priority following war. Nowhere is the need for community reconciliation greater than in regard to former child soldiers, who in countries such as Sierra Leone and Liberia identify as one of their greatest concerns about returning to their villages their fear of revenge attacks (Utas 2004), which add to their formidable problems of stigmatization and social isolation. It is vital, then, to reconcile community members with the returning child soldiers and to enable people who fought on or supported different sides to live together without fighting and animosity (Staub and Pearlman 2006). An inspiring, if hard won, lesson from conflict-torn countries like South Africa is that peace is achieved not only by signing formal agreements but also through reconciliation work at the grassroots level (Marks 2000).

If community reconciliation is lofty in principle, it is vexing to achieve in practice. Following the adage "No peace without justice," some villagers might reject particular child soldiers or want to hold them accountable for their crimes. Justice is elusive in the best of times, but it is particularly elusive in postconflict countries with overcrowded jails and paralyzed legal systems beset by corruption and low capacity. Reconciliation can also be thwarted by problems concerning child protection. Even during DDR processes, the risk of children's re-recruitment may remain high. Also, children who have left armed groups may be at risk due to protection threats such as sexual violence and drug abuse. To achieve reintegration and peace at the micro level, it is necessary to interweave elements of community reconciliation, justice, and child protection.

Community Reconciliation

There is much disagreement over how reconciliation can best be achieved, and the world is in a continuing process of learning how to reconcile fractured societies and communities following armed conflict. Even the definition of reconciliation is debated. One influential model (Lederach 1997) depicts reconciliation as a long-term process linking elements of mercy, truth, justice, and peace. Other models (e.g., Kriesberg 1999; Rouhana 2004) depict mercy and forgiveness as desirable, but not necessary, and place greater emphasis on achieving justice and restructuring social and political relationships. For present purposes, I will define reconciliation broadly to mean the rebuilding of positive relationships following destructive conflict. The nature of the reconciliation process as applied to child soldiers and war-affected communities is best illustrated by an example from Sierra Leone.

Community Mobilization

In Sierra Leone's northern province, the site of the RUF headquarters toward the end of the war, people had suffered profoundly and had been preoccupied with finding food, watching out for RUF attacks, and preparing to flee at a moment's notice. Many people lived in IDP camps more notable for their squalor than for their sense of community. When the war ended, masses of people returned to their villages homeless and destitute. Owing to war's displacement and chaos, former habits of collective planning and action had become dormant. Villages seldom held meetings, and aspirations of rebuilding community spirit were overshadowed by fears, jealousies, and pressures to restart farms and rebuild homes. Many neighboring villages viewed each other as rivals because they competed for the same scarce resources such as useable farmland and the charred remains of schools and health posts. Feeling cynical and disconnected from the societal peace process, one local leader said, "We were hungry before the war, we were hungry during the war, and now we are still hungry."

To reweave the fabric of community, CCF/Sierra Leone used a strategy of building positive relations through cooperative activities in twenty-six communities. These activities helped people come to terms with the past and begin planning their future together, resolving local conflicts using local means, and helping former child soldiers enter positive roles in their villages. The strategy was implemented through a community mobilization process, which is a highly participatory process wherein local people define their own goals and take ownership for projects that help them attain these goals, with external agencies playing a facilitating role (Boothby 1996; Donahue and Williamson 1999). A frequently used method of mobilization is to work through already existing community groups that have community-wide networks and opinion leaders who can spread key messages and motivate people to participate. Using this tactic, CCF's Sierra Leonean staff identified local groups called "Kankalay Committees" or "togetherness groups," which had experience in planning and action. Where no such committees existed, the staff conducted dialogues with local people, who then formed committees including representatives from various community subgroups. Because they worked on projects of development, the committees named or renamed themselves Community Development Committees (CDCs).

The CDCs, which served as catalysts for collective planning and action, facilitated a series of open meetings for all villagers. The initial meetings provided a reflective space in which people stepped back from the war and took stock of their experiences and situation. This reflection enabled them to begin planning a way forward. Local people told of their families' suffering during the war, which they had been loathe to do previously because they feared that talking would evoke retaliation. Villagers spoke most passionately about their current needs for shelter, water, health care, and other necessities. Out of these discussions emerged a sense of common pain and struggle and a spirit of safety in collective dialogue. As people became aware that the problems were too big to be addressed individually, they affirmed their need to work together to address the problems and strengthened their sense of community.

Later on, the CCF staff, together with the CDC members, brought the subsequent community discussions around to children's needs and situation. Ironically, although children are among the most vulnerable, their needs typically receive scant attention owing to adults' preoccupation with survival. In animated discussions, people expressed grave concern over the lack of schools and health posts, which were vital for their children's health and future. Teenagers and children also spoke of their strong desire for education and a life without war. The discussions of children not only catalyzed thinking about the future but also stimulated planning aimed to meet children's needs. General statements such as "Our children must have education" gave way to practical discussions of how villagers could work together to plan and build a school. In this manner, villagers mobilized themselves for constructive action. The discussion of children was helpful also because it drew attention away from potentially divisive political issues, such as who in the village had supported the RUF. As people affirmed their concern about children, they created a discourse emphasizing that the children were not to blame for the war. The focus on children kept villagers looking forward, which encouraged a sense of hope and enabled people to put the war behind them.

A key task in the community meetings was to prioritize the various ideas about which community rebuilding projects benefit children the most and also help the village achieve its long-term goals. The identification of the top three ideas occurred naturally as people repeatedly identified projects such as school or health post construction as vital for children. Playing a facilitative and boundary-setting role, CCF staff sought to narrow this list to a single project, based on funding restraints and the potential benefits of building a single, unified project. The group process of identifying the community project was challenging and evoked passionate debates. People feared initially that the debates would spark fights, because the norms of peaceful debate had all but disappeared during the war. Fortunately, the villagers were eager to learn nonviolent ways to manage their differences. Through prolonged discussions, the villagers selected a single project, which in most cases consisted of refurbishing a school or building a health post. The process itself had positive outcomes, as people learned or relearned the norms of peaceful dialogue and decision making that aid community integration and reconciliation.

Discourses of Empathy, Unity, and Nonviolence

After the project had been decided upon, community-selected teams set about designing the structure and planning the construction. A key part of the plan, one owing mostly to CCF, was for former child soldiers and other youths to do the construction. The importance of this plan was visible in the local treatment of former child soldiers. Some recently demobilized children had returned home and had blended in by being highly respectful to others and carrying themselves without a trace of military swagger. Others, however, had been labeled "rebels" and felt isolated. As one boy soldier said, "It was like I was invisible—no one wanted anything to do with me. Even my friends stayed away." Formerly abducted girls suffered particularly harsh treatment, as some community members called them names or attacked them.

To reduce these problems and make good use of the time needed to deliver the construction materials, CCF staff opened community reconciliation dialogues, setting the stage for former child soldiers' reintegration. The initial dialogue, a four-hour workshop conducted for groups of thirty local chiefs, elders, senior women, youths, and other opinion leaders, addressed local perceptions of former child soldiers. A prevalent misperception was that child soldiers had not themselves suffered. The CCF staff sought to correct this misperception by telling stories of how child soldiers had been abducted and forced to attack their own people. To avoid singling out former child soldiers, the staff framed the dialogue in terms of human rights and highlighted the suffering of all children during the war. They also pointed out the need for nonviolent conflict resolution and reconciliation. During the dialogues, local people affirmed the suffering of former child soldiers by telling stories of children they knew or had heard about.

The main point of this dialogue, and the wider community discussions it stimulated, had been to awaken empathy, which Martin Luther King Jr. (1986) described as the ability to walk a mile in other people's shoes. Empathy is one of the most useful psychological tools for reducing destructive conflict; it replaces hatred with understanding, and it reestablishes the humanity of the people formerly seen as demons (Hoffman 2000; Smith 2004; Staub 2003; White 1984). As villagers empathized with former child soldiers, they abandoned their dehumanized images of the children as unfeeling perpetrators. Increasingly, they saw former child soldiers as victims of exploitation, and viewed the commanders, not the children, as responsible for the killing and looting.

The community dialogues also aimed to awaken local people's natural resilience and spirit of unity, which, remarkably, the war had not destroyed. Asked whether they could accept the peace and now live together without fighting, local people said repeatedly, "We are one people." Using a mixture of traditional proverbs and songs, they demonstrated their unity and awakened Sierra Leonean norms of "forgive and forget" (Shaw 2005). Many people told stories of the past and how the community had previously succeeded in putting war and social divisions behind them. Although this rhetoric was rosy, it helped unveil ideals and images of unity and forgiveness that war had obscured, if not trampled. The recovery of positive ideals and aspirations is a fundamental part of the reconstruction process, because it feeds the moral imagination and whets people's desire to build a better social order.

Empathy alone, however, cannot end destructive conflict or contain those who bear grudges and continue to taunt or pick fights. Recognizing this, community members decided to form conflict resolution committees that consisted of people elected by the community and that served a dual role of conflict prevention and resolution. To prevent harassment and fighting, the committees established clear rules that prohibited undesired behavior and imposed fines on violators. This activity not only ended the mistreatment of former child soldiers but also helped reestablish, at the village level, norms of decent behavior and lawfulness that the war had corroded. The committees also ameliorated other conflicts by mediating disputes between people who had conflicts over such issues as land and water. Local people regularly sought out the committees for advice, treating them as the point of first contact in handling disputes. Following traditional practice, the committees referred particularly difficult cases to community elders, who heard the cases and decided the appropriate settlement.

The Power of Cooperation

The project sought to reduce tensions between villagers and former child soldiers by using the well-established psychological principle that cooperation toward the achievement of shared goals is one of the best ways to reduce conflict and improve relations between former adversaries (Deutsch 2000; Sherif et al. 1961). To enable cooperation between village youths and former child soldiers, the CDCs formed work teams composed of former soldiers and village youths, in a 60–40 ratio. The former soldiers included children and also older people in their twenties and thirties, who fall into the expansive category of "youth" in Sierra Leone (Wessells and Jonah 2006) and who in many villages were among the neediest people. The youths were selected according to criteria such as high motivation and ability to do heavy labor. Willingness to stay in the community was also an important criterion, because the point of the project was to enable reintegration.

Preparation was needed to prepare the youths for working together. In some communities, tensions ran high between former soldiers and the village youths, or between youths who had fought on different sides. To reduce the risks of fighting and name calling, the CCF staff conducted in each community a two-day reconciliation workshop for the mixed group of youths. Using cultural activities such as songs, proverbs, and local stories, they emphasized the importance of unity and reconciliation. Having called attention to the suffering by all youths, they encouraged the youths to put the war behind them and to think about how to move forward together toward the future. Through modeling and games, they also encouraged the youths to interact with each other in a respectful manner, providing concrete pointers about gestures and remarks that were likely to trigger fighting or animosity.

Having completed the preparatory workshop, the communities stood ready to do the construction. With CCF having procured the materials and local contractors having designed the projects, the work teams in the twenty-six communities built the civic works projects—mostly schools, health posts, small bridges, and latrines—that the communities had selected previously. For twenty days of labor, each worker received the local equivalent of US$27. Although this is a small sum by international standards, it enabled local people to purchase necessary items such as clothing and food.

This immediate employment and urgently needed income kept the former soldiers from returning to the bush and helped restore their dignity. Observed one former soldier in his twenties who had been with the RUF as a child:

> In my village, when you are very poor, you are nothing . . . I cannot stand being treated that way, because I suffered during the war. This work made me feel proud again, and other people treated me very well because they know I earn money.

For the returning former soldiers, earning money helped them not only avoid humiliation and shame but also win respect. Living without money and wearing very shabby clothes only proves to villagers that one has wasted years fighting and has little promise for the future (Utas 2004). With money in hand, young people can enter roles such as helping their families and providing food.

Beyond the monetary benefits, the project encouraged reconciliation by rekindling a common sense of humanity and decreasing stereotypes. A village youth who had not been a fighter said about the former child soldiers:

> Before I thought they were like animals. I heard such horrible stories . . . But we worked together in building the school. We helped each other, laughed together, and made something very good that helps our village a lot . . . Now I see they are like us in so many ways. It is time to stop the fighting.

In the mixed group in which this young man spoke, the faces of every former soldier beamed with a smile at the treasured words "Now I see they are like us." In the heart of every former child soldier lies a powerful desire for peer acceptance and the ability to be like others. Although the changes did not occur immediately, over time the cooperation strategy weakened demonic images and fears and planted the seeds of mutual acceptance and hope of living together in peace. Remarkably, relations also improved between warriors who had fought on opposite sides. Although their ability to collaborate stemmed in part from their weariness with the war and pressures imposed by the communities, their cooperation reestablished their sense of common humanity and conferred on them a hope of peaceful coexistence.

A significant challenge for the youths was to move beyond temporary employment, which can create false expectations and manifold frustrations unless it leads eventually to long-term employment and a steady income. Following the construction of the civic works, the youths who had shown the highest levels of motivation during the construction received occupational counseling to decide which kind of work suited them best. These discussions also provided information on which skills were most marketable. Next the youths took part in vocational training in which they learned skills in local crafts such as tailoring, tie-dying, carpentry, and metalwork from local artisans, who also served as reintegration mentors. The training, which varied in length according to the amount of time required to achieve mastery, was valuable not only because it promised future employment but also because it offered spaces in which the youths reflected on their war experiences and received mentoring from the master artisans. As discussions often turned to issues of guilt or uncertainty about the future, the mentors provided adult advice and a caring orientation that touched the former soldiers. Following the learning of vocational skills, selected youths formed solidarity groups, the members of which received loans and small business training followed by paid employment.

No less significant than the skills that the youths learned in this process were the things the youths learned about finding a direction in life. Observed one former boy soldier:

> When I came out of the bush, I didn't know what I would do, how I would live—nothing. I didn't know if it's possible to live in the village or maybe I should go fight again. But I was so tired of fighting, I decided to try another way. When I was a little boy, my grandfather

helped me build things . . . Now I am learning to be a carpenter, and I know what to do.

Carving out direction in their lives and achieving the skills and the confidence to follow it are significant, because they enable the youths to shift their identity from soldier to civilian. The fact that villagers had learned to see the youths not as troublemakers but as productive earners and potential breadwinners for their families enabled the soldiers to reconstruct their identities and gain social acceptance.

There were also discernible benefits for the larger peace process. Earlier sentiments that the peace process was remote, even extraneous, to villagers' lives gave way to the insight that each community has a part in the overall process. As one elder said, "Our peace is good for Sierra Leone, and Sierra Leone's peace is good for us." The former child soldiers themselves also understand very well the connection between community reconciliation and societal peace. As one boy put it, "If our villages reject us, we will fight war again." Of course, peace is not synonymous with the absence of war, and reconciliation and peace also require attention to issues of justice.

Justice

Although combatants frequently see violence as necessary for the achievement of justice, the irony is that life in most postwar zones is teeming with injustices. One significant form of injustice is the inappropriate detention of child soldiers without charging them or giving them access to a fair trial, as has occurred for the Afghan child detainees held in the U.S. military camp at Guantanamo Bay. In many countries, juvenile justice issues cause stress and harm to former child soldiers (UNICEF 2002a). Another source of injustice is that following many conflicts, the former victims assault their former dominators. In Kosovo, following NATO's bombing of Serbia, the Kosovar Albanians returned home and assaulted Serbs in much the same manner as Serbs had assaulted them. In Rwanda, Tutsis who had survived the 1994 genocide subsequently returned home and conducted reprisal killings of the Hutus whom they believed had orchestrated the genocide.

Injustices are often less visible, and even mundane. Displaced people frequently return home to find squatters occupying their homes. Returnees who lost everything might eye with envy other families whose property remained unscathed or who were known to have profited from the thriving grey business activities permeating war zones (Nordstrom 2004). Local people not only have a keen sense of who is better or worse off but also harbor strong feelings about who deserves to be better or worse off. In some villages, people who had stayed during the fighting regard "leavers" as traitors or less deserving of good things (Peters 2003).

Former child soldiers who attempt to return home enter a difficult terrain awash in unhealed grievances, vigilante justice, and contested privileges. In some cases, villagers' strong feelings of injustice block child soldiers' attempts to reenter the community. In Sierra Leone, boys who had fought in the RUF, said, when asked whether there were some child soldiers who could not return:

> One boy from this village did many terrible things during the war. He smoked a lot of weed [cannabis], took drugs, and did crazy things. The thing he liked to do most was kneel on people and use a razor blade to carve the letters "RUF" on their chests. No one ordered him to do these things . . . He can never return to this village.

Discussions with village adults echoed his sentiments, and some people felt that he "would only be attacked." Others said his return "wouldn't be right" because his actions had severed his bonds with the community. Fearing retaliation or harsh treatment, former child soldiers who have committed atrocities may decide quietly never to go home, preferring instead to live in the anonymity of a large city such as Freetown. Concerns about justice weigh heavily on former child soldiers, but their situation is made more complex by the existence of rival models of justice—retributive and restorative.

Retributive Justice

A retributive model of justice seeks to hold wrongdoers accountable for their crimes through punishment, the severity of which is proportional to the seriousness of their crimes. As one elder in Sierra Leone said, "Bad crimes must be punished, even when children did the wrong." A retribution model asserts that the failure to punish perpetrators creates a climate of impunity, enabling more fighting and wrongdoing and tacitly encouraging horrible acts because perpetrators know they will escape punishment (Clark 2003).

Proponents of this view point out that child soldiers, particularly those who committed heinous crimes they were not directly ordered to commit, must be held accountable by being punished for their actions. An important qualification is that selected child soldiers should be tried and incarcerated not as adults but as children. In many developing countries, children who are convicted of crimes are detained in adult prisons, where they suffer rape, discrimination, beatings, sexually transmitted diseases, and psychological issues associated with their mistreatment. The separation of juvenile justice from the adult justice system is intended to reduce such problems associated with the treatment of children as adults (UNICEF 2002a).

The retributive justice model for dealing with former child soldiers resonates with the policy in many U.S. states of permitting children to be tried as adults and to receive severe penalties. Advocates of this policy typically argue that older children know right from wrong and must be prosecuted as criminals because they deliberately chose to break the law. The literature on postconflict reconstruction is replete with arguments that without punishment and accountability, neither peace nor justice is possible. This philosophy is conspicuous in Rwanda, where the government decided to prosecute the leaders of the 1994 genocide through the official criminal justice system and to apply the death penalty where it was warranted.

The retribution model, however, faces daunting problems in regard to former child soldiers. If, as argued throughout this book, adult exploitation of children lies at the heart of the problem of child soldiers, should it not be adults who are held accountable for what child soldiers have done? As a young Burundian girl put it, "Why should we be the martyrs of these stupid, ridiculous conflicts?" (UNICEF 2002b, 115). The trial of child soldiers as criminals also risks stigmatizing them, reducing their chances of successful integration. Particularly regarding children who were abducted and forced to commit atrocities by armed groups, it seems wiser to regard the children as pawns rather than as willful perpetrators. Recognizing this, the Acholi people, whom the LRA has attacked repeatedly in northern Uganda, routinely classify escapees from the LRA as children who are not responsible for their actions. This de facto amnesty, which extends even to young people who are over 18 years of age, indicates a collective belief that young people who have been abducted and terrorized should not be held accountable for their actions (Mawson 2004).

The retribution model also raises difficult questions about where to draw the line between victims and perpetrators. Even though some child soldiers kill and commit atrocities without direct orders or visible coercion, their actions may owe to the combination of brutalizing experiences and commanders' indoctrination of them into an alternate moral universe in which killing and atrocities are condoned. Commanders' culpability is conspicuous in the practice of giving children drugs that promote wild behavior and blunt moral inhibitions. Standing in the shadows behind many a child perpetrator is a manipulative adult leader.

Although the retribution model seeks to diminish violence by ending impunity, retribution can fuel ongoing cycles of violence. When children who were forcibly recruited are treated as criminals, this can rouse in them anger and defiance that can lead them to commit more violence. As one boy from northern Uganda said: "I did what I had to do to stay alive inside the LRA. I attacked villages and killed people—it is true. But I didn't want to do those things, only I had to do them . . . It makes me angry when people call me 'rebel.'" A former boy soldier in the RUF in Sierra Leone put it eloquently: "Before people blame me, they should ask who started the war. I can tell you it was not the children . . . I am sorry for what I did during the war, but if people treat me as a criminal, I will go back to the bush." Such sentiments indicate that former child soldiers see their prosecution and punishment not as brakes on cycles of violence but as warrants for additional fighting. Legal approaches seeking justice through punishment can also thwart peacebuilding efforts in areas recently emerged from war (Mawson 2004), a point we will return to in Chapter 10.

Difficult practical issues also besiege the retribution model. For example, well-intentioned plans to incarcerate juvenile offenders separately from adults frequently run aground on the lack of separate facilities for children and a paucity of trained personnel to staff and manage prisons in ways that protect children's rights. Also, retribution approaches attempt to distinguish victims from perpetrators who bear the greatest responsibility for atrocities and war crimes. The distinction between victims and perpetrators, however, becomes blurred in regard to child soldiers, since children who were forced to kill are at once perpetrators and victims (UNICEF 2004b). In practice, it is vexingly difficult to distinguish between victims and perpetrators. The protected status of children and the transitional status of teenagers, coupled with the fact that young children and teenagers can be manipulated fairly easily, add complexity to the assignment of culpability. Many courts have proven unwilling to hold children accountable for their actions during war.

A case in point is the Special Court in Sierra Leone, which was established to try those "who bear the greatest responsibility" for war crimes (Cohn 2004). In 2006 the Special Court began its prosecution of former Liberian president Charles Taylor for war crimes. When the Special Court was being established, acrimonious debate erupted over whether to try child soldiers who had participated in brutal violence without obvious coercion. The U.N. Office for the Special Representative for Children and Armed Conflict argued that the Court's jurisdiction should include the most feared young offenders who were unable to go home and who were unlikely to have sought rehabilitation and reintegration services on their own. Proponents of children's prosecution contended that bringing the youths into a credible system of justice was their best chance for accessing the rehabilitation and reintegration services that the CRC guarantees. UNICEF and many NGOs, however, pointed out that prosecution would violate local cultural norms of forgiveness and also stigmatize the children and increase their chances of re-recruitment (Cohn 2004). Eventually the Special Court was granted the power to prosecute people between the ages of 15 and 18. However, the Court's prosecutor decided to focus on adult leaders and has taken no action against children (Singer 2004). Perhaps it would be too extreme a position to hold that children should never be tried, but the difficulties faced by the Special Court recommend the use of alternate means of achieving justice.

Restorative Justice

A restorative model of justice attempts to make restoration, or repair relational damage, through the offending party's offering goods or services that signal recognition of and remorse for the wrongs it has done. The goods or services are reparations intended neither as punishments nor as full compensation for losses. After all, what payment could possibly compensate someone whose family has been killed? Still, the reparations, if appropriately constructed and agreed to by the disputing parties and the community, symbolically recognize the injustice and provide a means of redressing it. In contrast to the retribution model, the restorative model recognizes that legal interpretations and penalties seldom satisfy the people most affected by violence (Stover and Weinstein 2004).

Following armed conflict, the international community frequently establishes a Truth and Reconciliation Commission as a transitional mechanism for the restoration of justice through a mixture of truth telling and reparations. However, this mechanism does not always fit the local culture and may overlook local, indigenous mechanisms for the achievement of restorative justice (Shaw 2005). A case in point is Sierra Leone, which had its own Truth and Reconciliation Commission (UNICEF 2004b).

In Sierra Leone, a CCF staff member told me how the local chief promoted justice in the case of former boy soldiers.

> When the child soldier returns home, he tells his story to his family. In Sierra Leone, children tell their parents everything . . . The parents then go to the chief and ask him to talk with the boy. If the chief agrees, the boy lies face down on the ground and holds the chief's ankle. In this position, he tells everything he did during the war. If the chief believes him and thinks he can come back, he can tell the boy to do a job that helps the village. He may tell the boy to talk with a particular man who is like a guide and support.

Further discussion revealed that the chief frequently sizes up the veracity of the former child soldier's statements by comparing the boy's story with information gleaned from other sources. Also, the chief judges the boy's remorsefulness by observing his posture of submission and listening for signs of guilt, shame, and regret. The "jobs" assigned are a form a community service, such as cleaning common areas or helping to repair communal buildings such as meeting places. Typically, the greater the wrongdoing, the greater will be the community services the chief requires. The man whom the boy is asked to talk with serves as a mentor and moral tutor who listens to the boy and understands his challenges in readjusting to civilian life. In addition to supporting the boy, the mentor also guides by giving advice, helping the boy understand how villagers perceive him and what it will take on the boy's part to reintegrate fully. Whether similar processes exist for girls is an open question deserving additional research.

It is worth unpacking this chief's approach, which resembles some of the best practices Western social services have devised. Broadly, it reflects a sophisticated system of diagnosis and action that collects evidence from multiple sources. This evidence is used to make decisions regarding remorse and the likelihood of rehabilitation, and to assign mentoring and community service. The boy's prostration before the chief signals his complete submission to local authority, and, by implication, his willingness to obey local rules. This gesture is also a ritualized means through which the boy breaks with his past as a soldier and reformulates himself as part of the civilian community. The boy's remorse and willingness to make reparation with the village finds expression in his community service, which is a widely used means of developing community spirit and positive relations between youths and community (Flanagan and Van Horn 2003; Hamburg and Hamburg 2004). Since the service is public, the villagers can see for themselves the boy's demeanor and desire to help the village, which increases their willingness to accept him without stigmatizing or isolating him. The boy's entry into the mentoring process signals his commitment to develop civic values and redefine himself as a civilian. Mentoring is a potent means of enabling youths to negotiate their new identities and to transition from one moral universe into another (Roffman, Suárez-Orozco, and Rhodes 2003). Ingeniously, this approach combines elements that at once aid him as an individual and restore his relationship with the community.

A frequently overlooked point is that former child soldiers are actors, many of whom develop their own ways to restore positive relationships with and repay their moral debts to their villages. In the Small Bo chiefdom in Sierra Leone, youths had been pawns in adult power struggles and had fought for many years. According to one youth:

> Between 1982 and 1984 there were political rivalries here in town between various members of the political party APC who were competing for seats in parliament. The young people were used and manipulated in these rivalries and were set against each other. Fighting took place and houses were burned. (Peters 2003, 27)

Following the war, youths, including former child soldiers, established the Small Bo Youth Community Development Organization as a means of contributing to their communities (Peters 2003). The youths organized a farm cooperative and also donated volunteer labor for community projects, such as repairing schools and roads. One youth expressed a keen sense of pride:

> The whole idea behind it is to develop the place, and we, the youth, are the energetic ones. If we could involve ourselves in rehabilitating the place, it would not make sense to go back to the bush or to destroy the place. (Peters 2003, 27)

As this project illustrates, both justice and rehabilitation involve repairing the torn social fabric at the village level and children's demonstrating their willingness to make amends with the community by aiding in its restoration and development.

In contrast with the retribution model of justice, which often conflicts with local cultural norms, the restorative justice approach fits many African societies' norms of justice and restoration, which are rooted in the concept of Ubuntu, meaning "A person is a person through other persons" (Tutu 1999, 31). From this standpoint, justice for child soldiers is less about imposing penalties on them than about defining reparations and group processes that heal the social wounds between the children and the villages they attacked. An important task for future research is to document more fully the local processes of justice and their role in supporting the reintegration of former child soldiers.

Child Protection

The reintegration process requires a strong foundation of child protection, a term used frequently but seldom defined clearly. Child protection consists of two interconnected elements: reducing harm to children, and strengthening children's resilience. Both entail the creation of a protective environment and require a bit of explication. The term *child protection* often evokes images of a protector standing between a child and a person armed with a gun. However, in a war zone some of the greatest dangers to children are not physical harms but the psychosocial and spiritual risks associated with social exclusion, stigmatization, humiliation, spiritual contamination, and denial of access to positive life options (InterAction Protection Working Group 2004; Save the Children

2005). In light of this holistic array of risks, efforts toward child protection should be equally holistic.

Many conceptualizations of child protection display a deficits emphasis, underestimating children's resilience. In fact, children's protection stems as much from children's resilience and coping as from the construction of external protection programs. Most children naturally engage with risks and threats, finding ways to deal with them in a positive manner supporting healthy development. Children's positive coping often stems from the presence of protective factors, primary among which is a strong relationship with parents or caretakers. Another key protective factor is access to social support from family members and neighbors. Since resilience has a strong social foundation, it makes sense to think in terms of building social supports for children in families, schools, peer groups, and community groups. Together, the combination of these two elements—reductions in vulnerability and risks, and increases in the sources of resilience—help create a protective environment for children (UNICEF 2005).

The intimate connection between the reintegration of former child soldiers and child protection becomes clear in cases of former child soldiers who have escaped armed groups. As a 16-year-old girl from Sri Lanka said, her life is riddled with fears of re-recruitment or punishment for having defected:

> The LTTE came looking for me, but I was hiding in the forest. I slept in the forest close to my home, because the LTTE comes at night. The LTTE has come to my village two times. They did not take anyone yet, but they are looking. Someone else released by Karuna showed them my home. When they came to my home, no one was there. I heard that if the LTTE comes to my home and asks me to rejoin and I refuse, they have an order that they can shoot me. I don't want to go back. (HRW 2004b, 40)

This girl's fears were compounded by her knowledge that the LTTE would take one of her siblings if they could not find her.

Child protection processes are vital not only to prevent girl soldiers' re-recruitment but also to aid their reintegration. Following their return home, girls who have been in armed groups often face formidable obstacles of stigmatization and social isolation, adding to their economic and psychological burdens. Well-designed protection programs reduce problems of stigmatization and social isolation and also offer the holistic supports outlined in Chapter 8.

It is not only former child soldiers, however, who require protection. Many other vulnerable children—such as orphans, separated children, children with disabilities, and children at risk of early marriage—may face situations more harmful than those faced by child soldiers and are entitled to protection under international law. That commanders frequently recruit new child soldiers from the ranks of vulnerable children makes it all the more important to interweave reintegration and child protection efforts at all levels, including local communities.

Community Mechanisms of Child Protection

In light of children's vulnerability, one might expect that children would be among the most cared for and visible members of war-affected communities. In fact, the opposite is true—following armed conflict, children are frequently invisible and poorly cared for. This odious situation occurs because war shatters families, and adults are psychologically overwhelmed or preoccupied with finding food and other necessities. Also, war disrupts or destroys community protection mechanisms such as women's groups or religious groups. Following armed conflict, many rural villages lack community activities and structures that protect children and guide them toward a positive future.

An essential step toward children's well-being is to mobilize communities for the care and protection of children. In the DRC, for example, Save the Children (SC) established Community Child Protection Networks, each of which provides "a forum where community members meet, discuss child protection problems and research solutions" (Verhey 2003, 19). The networks aim to protect children from all forms of abuse and advocate for children's protection. To mobilize the community for child protection, SC staff approached local authorities, including traditional leaders, and explained their work on child protection. Local authorities were also invited to organize subsequent meetings with local people. At these meetings, with various community groups present, SC staff discussed the needs for child protection and the purpose of the networks. Next, an open community meeting decided the criteria for participation in the network. Typically, the networks consisted of twenty-five to forty people, including local authorities, religious leaders, children, members of women's associations and other local groups, and people involved in social services, mainly health and education. SC staff then trained the participants on child rights and how to recognize and respond to abuses of children. The training also covered how to gather information about children's well-being and needs, and how to organize community projects that will support children's protection.

Following the training, the networks focused on salient local issues of protection. One network, for example, brought different armed groups into local peace negotiations, facilitating access to humanitarian services. Through direct negotiation with local authorities and commanders, the networks successfully redressed specific cases of recruitment and re-recruitment (Verhey 2003). The benefits to individual children ring clearly in the case of a boy recruited at age 10:

> I fought a long time at the front. In 1999, as part of a group of malnourished children, I was taken to the hospital in Kisangani. There were around 80 of us originally from North and South Kivu. The ICRC negotiated our demobilization with the chief military officer and organized our transportation. We were received by SC in Goma.
>
> I was finally reintegrated with my parents in November 2001, but there was a land dispute between a commander in our area and my parents. This commander started harassing me because our demobilization orders from Kisangani had not been countersigned in Goma. I fled to the bush.
>
> Three months later I found a community child protection network in a nearby village. This network brought me back to Save the Children in Goma. In August 2002, having learned that this commander left our village, the network went to see my family and the local authorities. Finally, I was able to go home and all the neighbors were very happy. (Verhey 2003, 20)

This case illustrates the benefits of having a community structure that pressures local commanders and provides ongoing support for children's protection.

Beyond the benefits to individual children, child protection networks or groups bring children out of the margins, making their well-being a central focus of community life. As this occurs, parents frequently become more attentive to their children, and community groups launch initiatives to assist children through the construction of schools and other facilities supporting children. The heightened focus on children can also promote peace by increasing awareness of the damage done by war and the need to support all survivors. As previously warring subgroups rally around children, they begin to reframe their situation, focusing less on their political differences and finding common ground in their desire to protect their children. In this manner, community-based child protection aids the reconciliation process.

Child Participation and Agency

Worldwide, discussions of child protection have emphasized the responsibility of states and adults to protect children. Ironically, these discussions depict protection as something one does to or for children, when in fact the CRC asserts child participation as a core principle. Although child participation is a universal aspiration often recited in mantra-like form, it is seldom achieved in practice—child protection remains mostly an adult-led activity. This adult bias may reflect adults' legitimate concern that asking children to participate in their own protection will burden them with the task of halting their abuse, which they had been powerless to prevent in the first place. A more likely source of children's lack of participation in child protection is adults' reluctance to share power with children (Boyden 2003). This reluctance notwithstanding, it is important to recognize children's agency as a potential resource in child protection efforts.

A case in point comes from the work of ChildFund Afghanistan, the Afghan arm of CCF, in the northeast provinces of Kunduz, Takhar, and Badakshan. Due to decades of war and chronic poverty, Afghanistan presents a cornucopia of risks to children, including land mines and unexploded ordnance, gender and ethnic discrimination, food insecurity, dangerous child labor, disease, early marriage, and child soldiering. Having met with village elders and the mullahs, ChildFund Afghanistan (CFA) initiated dialogue with community people about these risks. Following cultural norms, the participants were mostly adults, who expressed deep concern for their children's well-being. Although the adults said they knew very well the risks faced by young girls or young boys, or by teenage girls or boys, a different picture emerged from discussions with children. Girls, for example, reported a high level of stress due to the lack of private latrines, though adult men showed little awareness of this situation. The girls' stress reflected the cultural norms that required women to cover themselves in public and treated any display of skin as a profound dishonor and a punishable offense. Badly needed was a method for eliciting children's views and participation in the child protection process, without sidelining adults.

To address this need, ChildFund Afghanistan staff constructed a process of child-led risk mapping that paved the way for the formation of a community Child Well-Being Committee. First, the staff convened groups of approximately ten boys or girls between the ages of 7 and 13. Following the strict Afghan gender norms, male staff worked with male children, and female staff worked with female children. Asked to create a picture of their village or camp, the children drew all the houses and main landmarks. Next, the staff asked the children to draw in the dangerous places or places where accidents happen to children. The ensuing discussion and excitement revealed the children's delight in having their voices heard and telling their situation as they viewed it. With conspicuous enthusiasm, the children drew pictures of uncovered wells toddlers had fallen into or open ditches containing human refuse. The pictures also showed young boys trying to cross powerful rivers using makeshift bridges in order to get to school, often with disastrous consequences. Interestingly, the girls' pictures focused more on issues like forced early marriage and problems of staying covered, whereas boys' pictures focused on environmental threats such as damaged bridges and open wells.

The following day, the children presented their findings to the village in the form of a skit or play in which they acted out scenes such as a child drowning while attempting to cross a dangerous river. Being the only show in town, the children's performance captivated villagers' attention and sparked animated discussion about how to reduce the risks the children had identified. The different priorities identified by the girls' group and the boys' group provided eloquent testimony to the gendered nature of the risks to Afghan children and left many Afghan parents asking themselves why they hadn't been aware of those risks before.

Playing a facilitative role, the ChildFund Afghanistan staff steered the questions and discussions away from self-flagellation toward the formation of two community committees in each village, one composed of girls and women and the other of boys and men. The purpose of the committees was to monitor local risks and catalyze action to reduce them. The staff emphasized the value of including in the committees a mixture of children and adults and also of representatives of any sub-groups in the village that had not participated recently in community decision making. This focus on inclusiveness aimed to build full partici-pation in civil society and to avoid discrimination. Discrimination, itself one of the main risks to children in war zones, can lead aid to flow only into the hands of a particular clan or power elite within the village. Subsequently, each village organized male and female Child Well-Being Committees consisting of ten people, half of whom were children. The committees not only monitored risks to children but also facilitated vil-lage groups' use of small grants to conduct civic works projects such as repairing bridges or installing wells and latrines. Typically, the main workers on these projects were teenage boys who either attended school in the morning or who participated in literacy classes in the evenings. In this manner, the project avoided pulling teenagers away from edu-cation, which itself is a significant source of protection (Nicolai and Tripplehorn 2003). An ongoing issue, however, is teenage girls' partici-pation in education, which remains limited owing to cultural norms dic-tating that girls do not need as much education as men. To address this issue, CFA organizes literacy courses for both teenage girls and boys.

The pride children felt working as members of the Child Well-Being Committees was conspicuous in my visits to villages, such as one where I was greeted by both an elder and a smiling 14-year-old boy who looked me in the eye and took me around to see the fruits of the various child protection activities. He explained that the children not only had done much of the work but also felt more highly respected as a result. Alone with elders subsequently, the skeptic in me wondered whether the chil-dren's activity and pride detracted from adults' sense of leadership and power. Reflecting a collectivist view, one elder answered this concern by saying, "We have always been for our children, and now we see that they are for us. We learn together and our village becomes stronger. Our chil-dren are our future." Other elders echoed these sentiments, and some admitted the project had given them new understanding of children's views and abilities. Having myself been reared in the United States at a time when the dominant view was that "children should be seen and not heard," it was humbling to see poor Afghan villagers learning from their children and nourishing children's leadership in ways that have often eluded developed societies.

The monitoring of child soldiering is one of the most significant accomplishments of the Child Well-Being Committees. At the village level, the committees serve as the eyes and ears of the community, collecting information on children's recruitment from diverse sources. This watchfulness is valuable in itself because it reduces commanders' hopes of hiding their recruitment of children. Also, the committees have raised villagers' awareness of the plight of vulnerable children and helped create circumstances that reduce the likelihood of recruitment. In some villages, the committees have been instrumental in identifying for participation in income-generation programs very poor children who might otherwise have been lured into armed groups by commanders who promised to pay them as soldiers. Although the reduction of child soldiering owes much to the national DDR process spearheaded by UNICEF (Chrobok 2005), the committees complement the national DDR program, not only through monitoring and prevention but also by engaging children as people who have leadership abilities.

A key lesson of this project is that in work on child protection and reconciliation, children's leadership is a precious resource. That it remains largely untapped illuminates an important path for future efforts toward child soldiers' reintegration and the postconflict reconstruction of war-torn societies.

10

Prevention

Preventing the exploitation of children as soldiers is one of the monumental challenges of our time. It makes little sense to stand back and allow the damage to occur, picking up the pieces afterward. A former child soldier from Burma who had been captured by an opposition group highlighted the importance of prevention: "My life would be very different. If I hadn't been arrested maybe now I'd be a good person. Instead I'm a bad person. It makes me sorry. If I hadn't been a soldier I would have continued and finished high school, then university, and I could have found many good jobs" (HRW 2002, 160). A proactive approach is needed to keep children out of armed groups to begin with and to ameliorate the problem of child soldiering on a large scale. Effective prevention on a large scale requires sustained attention to the multiple causes of child soldiering.

There is more consensus on the importance of prevention than on how to achieve it. This is perhaps understandable in light of the diverse causes of child soldiering and the tendency of specialists to focus on only one or another of the factors that propel children into armed groups. From a broad perspective, one can discern three prevention strategies. First is the legal strategy, which is most visible in efforts to strengthen and enforce international legal standards and to criminalize child recruitment. Second is the conflict prevention strategy, which seeks to address the core problem by preventing the armed conflicts that draw children into the ranks of armed groups. Unlike the legal approaches, this strategy views an exclusive focus on child soldiers as too narrow and attempts to address the problem of war itself. Third is a systemic prevention strategy, in which key actors work at different levels to prevent children's recruitment. This strategy addresses the push and pull factors that exist at family, community, societal, and international levels and animate child recruitment.

Although practitioners and policy analysts often focus on one of these strategies, the tasks of prevention are too large and multifaceted to be addressed successfully by any single strategy. Comprehensive prevention requires attention to legal, political, economic, social, cultural, and psychological issues. In this chapter, I will argue that effective prevention is possible but is best achieved by interweaving the legal, conflict prevention, and systemic prevention strategies.

Legal Standards and Criminalization

The logic of the legal strategy is to construct international norms against the recruitment of children, using the standards as a means of holding violators accountable. To date, however, the international community has achieved greater success in developing high standards than in enforcing them. Vigorous efforts are under way to close this accountability gap.

Raising the Standards

Numerous international legal instruments, such as the 1977 Additional Protocols to the 1949 Geneva Conventions, ban child recruitment. However, the most comprehensive and explicit legal prohibitions against child recruitment are set forth in the 1989 CRC, which defines the minimum rights to which children are entitled and has been endorsed by over 190 states. Article 38 of the CRC set 15 years as the minimum age for combat participation and recruitment into armed groups. The adoption of the 15-year minimum was both a holdover of the minimum established earlier under the Geneva Conventions and also a political compromise. Gaining political acceptance of an 18-year minimum was difficult, because in the 1990s, governments such as the United Kingdom, the Netherlands, the United States, and various developing countries recruited significant numbers of 15- to 17-year-olds, who, even if they were not combatants, received military training and entered the stream leading to combat.

Although the 15-year minimum prohibited the exploitation of the youngest, most vulnerable children, many analysts, myself included, criticized it for not protecting older children, who are the most frequent targets of recruitment. Also, the 15-year minimum created a painful imbalance by permitting people to fight and die at an age at which most countries denied them the right to vote.

To correct these limits, the global CSC spearheaded an international campaign to establish 18 years as the minimum age of recruitment. A highly significant achievement was the adoption of the Optional Protocol to the CRC on the Involvement of Children in Armed Conflict, which entered into force in 2002. The Optional Protocol set 18 years as the minimum age for direct participation in hostilities and for compulsory recruitment by governments. By elevating the minimum age for combat participation to 18, the Protocol at once protected older children and made it harder to recruit younger children, whose small size betrays recruiters' claims the children are old enough to join. Also, the Optional Protocol completely banned nonstate actors' recruitment or use in hostilities of people under 18 years of age. Along with these achievements, however, came a compromise wherein governments are allowed to recruit people between the ages of 16 and 18 years provided that the recruitment is voluntary and backed by the informed consent of the child's parents or legal guardians. This compromise notwithstanding, the Optional Protocol succeeded in raising the bar for children's participation in hostilities.

The quest for higher international standards gained an additional boost from the establishment of the International Labor Organization Convention 182. Ratified by over 150 governments, Convention 182 defines the compulsory or forced recruitment of children under 18 for use in armed conflict as one of the most dangerous forms of labor. This linkage between dangerous child soldiering and exploitative child labor is significant because in many societies, children are expected to work and to help support their families. The Convention draws a line between moderate, acceptable forms of labor, in which children do chores to help their families, and extreme, dangerous forms of labor that jeopardize children's health and violate their rights.

In addition to these global standards, the CSC and other actors have encouraged the construction of numerous regional agreements to limit or ban the use of children as soldiers. Significant regional declarations include the Maputo Declaration on the Use of Child Soldiers (Africa, 1999), the Montevideo Declaration on the Use of Child Soldiers (Latin America, 1999), the Berlin Declaration on the Use of Child Soldiers (Europe, 1999), the Kathmandu Declaration on the Use of Child Soldiers (Asia, 2000), and the Amman Declaration on the Use of Child Soldiers (Middle East, 2001).

These and other standards have helped to define a set of benchmarks according to which behavior can be judged, and they provide legal levers that societies may use to prosecute offenders. The process of establishing the higher standards is also significant because it has raised awareness about the damage caused to children and established a consensus that child recruitment is a fundamental violation of children's rights. Commenting on the impact for children, Jo Becker (personal communication, Aug. 16, 2005), former chair of the CSC Steering Committee and a leading international analyst of child recruitment, said, "While governments and groups may still engage in the practice, few if any now defend it. It was not that many years ago that I remember discussions where government representatives and others would defend the use of child soldiers. This rarely happens anymore." The success of the Optional Protocol is visible in the altered practices of governments such as the United States, which no longer deploys people under 18 years in combat.

An obvious problem facing the legal strategy, however, is that outlaws do not obey the law. The adoption of higher standards has not led to large reductions globally in the use of child soldiers. This situation has evoked cynicism among many children, who have grown weary of the enormous gap between lofty policies and the hard realities of their lives. Cynicism is often heard among youths in Iraq, where children had been recruited by both the government under Saddam Hussein and Kurdish armed opposition groups in the years before the 2003 U.S. invasion. Said a 17-year-old Kurdish girl who had fled northern Iraq before the 2003 Iraq war: "I don't want to hear any more speeches. I want to know what they're going to do for us, I want to know how they're going to take action" (UNICEF 2002b, 107). This girl's concerns resonate with the fact that child recruitment remains widespread. In some countries, the government recruits children; in many others, it is the nonstate actors, opposition groups—UNITA, the LTTE, the RUF, among many others—and paramilitaries that recruit children. Under international law, these nonstate actors are bound by the legal instruments outlined above. Worldwide, armed groups frequently pay little more than lip service to issues of child soldiering, even though they are obligated to obey international law. To address this problem, advocates have sought increasingly to shame and prosecute child recruiters.

Naming and Shaming

In the international arena, moral standing carries greater weight than many people realize. States perceived as rogues lose not only their moral standing but also the goods and trading privileges extended regularly to states or groups that are perceived as having good values. One strategy for limiting child recruitment, then, is to publicly shame those who continue to recruit and exploit children.

A prominent architect of this tactic has been Olara Otunnu, who formerly held the position of Special Representative of the U.N. Secretary-General for Children and Armed Conflict. A watershed event was the passage in 2001 of Security Council Resolution 1379, which ordered the creation of a list of the groups who recruit or use children as soldiers. Following this call, Secretary General Kofi Annan listed twenty-three offending parties in his November 2002 report to the Security Council. This naming of the offenders was intended to shame them into compliance with their treaty obligations.

By the following year, when it was clear that those charged had neither stopped nor slowed their recruitment of children (Cohn 2004), steps were taken to sharpen the tactic of naming and shaming. In 2003 the Security Council passed U.N. Resolution 1460, which created an enlarged list of child recruiters. To boost the pressures for compliance, the Security Council demanded that the violators develop clear plans to end the practice and provide information about the steps they had taken to end child recruitment. It also urged member states to limit the trade of small arms to the violating states. To date, however, the Security Council has not taken concrete actions against violators, which many analysts believe it should do in order to obtain greater compliance. A hopeful step, however, is the Security Council's adoption in 2005 of a new resolution—resolution 1612—requesting a systematic monitoring and reporting system to document violations against children in armed conflict, including child recruitment. Resolution 1612 also establishes a Security Council working group that will receive information about such violations and make recommendations to the Security Council about appropriate action.

Unfortunately, these and related efforts have been only minimally successful thus far, raising doubts about the Security Council's ability to bring armed groups into compliance with international standards. Out of the public spotlight, many groups that have pledged not to recruit children have reverted to their old habit of recruiting and exploiting children. In Afghanistan, shortly after Mullah Omar, a Taliban leader, had promised to punish any commander who used child soldiers, the U.N. reported the Taliban's use of thousands of children as soldiers (International Rescue Committee 2001). Similarly, in Sri Lanka the LTTE has reneged repeatedly on its pledges to end its recruitment and use of child soldiers (HRW 2004b). During the time period in which the naming and shaming approach was used, child recruitment increased in places like northern Uganda, Burundi, and the DRC (Cohn 2004).

These observations lead to the inescapable conclusion that stringent legal standards alone cannot stop children's recruitment. Cynically, child recruiters have either ignored the standards while enjoying impunity or have given the public appearance of supporting the treaties while secretly recruiting children. According to an emerging global consensus, the problem lies not in the shortage of useful standards but in the lack of compliance with the standards. For the standards to be effective, they must be supplemented by strong enforcement measures that add teeth to the law and end recruiters' impunity (CSC 2004; Singer 2005; Vandergrift 2004).

War Crimes, Punishment, and Deterrence

Various means exist for the criminalization of child recruitment and the administration of penalties to punish and deter recruiters. One of the most prominent is the legal prosecution of child recruiters as war criminals. A hopeful step was the establishment through the 1998 Rome Statute of the International Criminal Court, which is intended to be a permanent court investigating and prosecuting genocide, crimes against humanity, and war crimes that national courts have been unable or unwilling to prosecute (CSC 2004; UNICEF 2002a). A significant legal milestone was reached when the Rome Statute defined as a war crime the recruitment or active use in hostilities of children under the age of 15. The negotiators of the Statute agreed in their preparatory discussions that it is a war crime to use children, not only in combat but also in military activities such as spying, scouting, or serving as decoys or as guards (CSC 2004). The serious intent and the global scope of the International Criminal Court became apparent in 2004, when it launched investigations into crimes under international law in the DRC and northern Uganda, sites of extensive child recruitment.

The idea of prosecuting child recruitment as a war crime has also taken root in Special Courts established by the United Nations. In June 2002 the Special Court for Sierra Leone handed down indictments of people even in high posts, including former Liberian president Charles Taylor, on grounds of having recruited and used in hostilities children under the age of 15.

It is an open question whether the prosecutions by the International Criminal Court and the Special Courts will in fact deter child recruitment. To succeed, the courts will need the moral support and resources of countries worldwide, but the United States has revoked its signature on the treaty that established the Court. Also, it is questionable whether the Courts can manage the number of cases needed to deter child recruitment on a large scale. By nature, the Court moves slowly, operating in historical time that perhaps is not well suited to the timely prosecution of significant numbers of offenders.

Legal prosecution of individuals, however, is not the only means of punishment and deterrence. A potentially useful alternative tactic is to isolate child recruiters by blocking their supplies and imposing sanctions against their trading partners. An essential first step is to cut off military assistance and stop the flow of small arms to states and groups that recruit children (Vandergrift 2004). This is a task of considerable magnitude, because states in which child recruitment occurs receive weapons and aid from a daunting array of countries, including states that do not exploit children as soldiers. For example, countries such as China, India, Malaysia, and Canada gave military aid to Sudan during its pre-Darfur civil war, in which thousands of children were recruited (HRW 2003c). The United States, which has supported numerous policies and legal mechanisms against the use of child soldiers (Southwick 2004), is subject to criticism on this point. During the 1990s, the U.S. government gave billions of dollars in military training and weapons to states whose armed forces were known to be regular recruiters of children (Stohl 2002). Also, the United States has poured enormous amounts of aid into Colombia, where child recruitment by pro-government paramilitaries is well documented, but it has set no conditions on the government of Columbia regarding children's exploitation.

To effectively criminalize groups that recruit children, strong compliance mechanisms are needed, such as targeted sanctions against the leaders and the groups by freezing their assets, preventing trade with them, or imposing travel restrictions and boycotts of their goods (Singer 2004). Many wars that exploit children run on profits from illegal sales of precious resources (Cilliers and Dietrich 2001; Klare 2001), so a vital step is to block the illicit trade in materials like "blood diamonds" through international boycotts and campaigns.

As important as the criminalization strategy is, it is vital to acknowledge its practical limits. For one thing, sanctions are easier to impose than to target accurately. Often the burden of sanctions weighs most heavily on the backs of the poor. Also, the black and gray markets that move many of the materials used to conduct wars are notoriously difficult to control. The relative ease with which small items such as diamonds can be smuggled makes it difficult to penalize recruiters on a scale likely to offset the potential gains achieved through child recruitment. It is unrealistic to assume that the U.N. Security Council could rapidly achieve tight control over these markets. In addition, the criminalization strategy can trigger intergroup animosities that foreclose other options for resolving conflict and decreasing child recruitment.

A case in point is the 2004 decision by the International Criminal Court to prosecute LRA leaders in northern Uganda for war crimes such as the abduction and use of children as soldiers. Although this step received a warm reception in international circles, it evoked a mixed reaction from the Acholi people, who have suffered the brunt of the LRA attacks (Allen 2005; Pham et al. 2005) and have their own indigenous means of handling conflict (Baines 2005). Seeing the war as rooted in a regional conflict wherein the Ugandan government privileges the people of the south, many Acholi people viewed amnesty for soldiers and a negotiated settlement with LRA as their best hope for ending the war. Unfortunately, the announcement of the Court's intent to prosecute LRA leaders reduced the LRA's willingness to negotiate (Refugee Law Project 2005), although LRA leaders reentered negotiations with the government in July 2006. It is difficult to foresee what the effects will be of the multiple indictments handed down thus far. This case shows the need to consider the wider implications of using the criminalization strategy in any particular situation.

The criminalization strategy also cannot offer comprehensive prevention. The fact that many children join armed groups as a way to earn money cautions against the idea that penalizing recruiters will end child soldiering. At the grassroots level, children's disaffection with the political system and their inability to meet basic needs, access education, or obtain paying jobs creates conditions that are ripe for child soldiering. Even if the criminalization strategy helps stop recruiters and commanders from enlisting and using children as soldiers, it does not accomplish the parallel task of reducing children's motivation to become soldiers. Nor does it address the need to prevent war itself. Because war frequently comes to children, drawing them in as warriors, comprehensive prevention efforts must include efforts to prevent armed conflict.

Conflict Prevention

The value of taking a conflict prevention focus came home to me during discussions with former child soldiers in Sierra Leone. A former member of the RUF said excitedly:

> People blame all the bad things that have happened on the soldiers or the commanders. But I can tell you, the problem is the war itself. You see, when war comes, all the good goes out and people act crazy. You will never stop children from fighting unless you stop the war.

In war zones, youths resonate with this view, regardless of whether they had been involved in armed groups. In fact, war-affected youths identify peace as one of their top three needs (Women's Commission for Refugee Women and Children 2005). Youths' call for peace reminds us of children's suffering in war and how war skews values, making unthinkable acts such as child abduction seem normal. Youths' call for peace also points out the need to look beyond the problem of child soldiering, which is only one form of the damage war inflicts on children.

Since war allows the destruction of children, and adults as well, it is necessary to take tasks of conflict prevention seriously. Conflict prevention includes multiple components, such as analysis of the roots of conflict; the establishment of systems of early warning and crisis management; improvements in governance and justice systems; and methods of resolving or transforming conflict through mediation by third parties, problem-solving dialogues, and unofficial diplomacy, among others. Rather than discuss this vast array, I will focus on three aspects that pertain most directly to youths: structural injustice, the normalization of violence, and youths as peacebuilders.

Addressing Structural Injustice and Youth Disaffection

Terms like *conflict prevention* tend to evoke images of getting people who are about to fight to talk out their differences and reach a peaceful agreement. The richer meanings of the term, however, relate to the transformation of the longer-term, insidious conditions leading to destructive conflict.

One such condition is structural injustice, in which a category of people are denied their rights and suffer discrimination and inability to meet their basic needs. Structural injustice is a form of psychological violence evoking humiliation and shame (Christie, Wagner, and Winter 2001), and it is has contributed to many conflicts. In Northern Ireland, British domination, coupled with Catholics' high rates of unemployment and poor housing, helped foment civil war (Cairns and Darby 1998). In Kosovo, Serb discrimination against Kosovar Albanians planted the seeds of armed conflict. The East Timorese struggle for independence was prompted by the brutal Indonesian domination of East Timor. In Sudan, the historic domination by the northern, Muslim peoples led to a bloody civil war against the predominantly Christian people of the south. In Rwanda, the Tutsi domination of Hutus under the Belgian regime set the stage for the ascent to power of a Hutu regime that discriminated against Tutsis and eventually orchestrated a genocide against them. Structural injustice is a prominent source of nearly all the conflicts discussed in this book.

With few exceptions, the conflict prevention literature has paid scant attention to children, though there are many reasons why it should. To begin with, children constitute a significant part of armed groups and are increasingly important actors in contemporary conflicts. Also, the weight of structural inequality falls hard on youths, particularly teenagers, who are at a stage in life in which they are defining their place in society and making decisions about their life paths. When youths have few positive options, they feel cheated, abandoned, and hopeless. Feeling disaffected and disenfranchised, they become susceptible to the lure of radical ideologies, making it easier for political leaders to manipulate them and leading them to see war as promising a brighter future.

In my observations, youths' disaffection in war-affected countries has three main sources, the first of which is political marginalization. In most countries heading down the perilous slide into war, failed or failing governments rule, and youths feel powerless and voiceless. In countries such as Sierra Leone, youths saw the government as having failed to provide them with the education and other advantages they needed to build a positive future. Yet they felt powerless to change it. Their sense of powerlessness to change the system from within, together with their frustration over flawed government policies or corruption, led many youths to turn to violence as a way to establish a new, better government.

Poor economic conditions also stir youths' sense of disaffection. Worldwide, 1.2 billion people, approximately half of whom are under 18, live on less than the equivalent of US$1 per day. Living in abject poverty and facing high rates of unemployment that are unlikely to abate in the near future, many youths see little chance that they will be able to earn an acceptable income, purchase land and animals, and start a family. At a moment when they experience their political awakening, youths notice that economic hardships are not distributed evenly but fall disproportionately on particular minority groups. Their anger over unfair treatment and their sense of political powerlessness create an explosive mixture that political leaders can easily ignite.

A second source of youth disaffection is the social exclusion many impoverished youths experience (Boyden et al. 2003). The presence and seeming inescapability of poor economic conditions make war a psychologically attractive opportunity space in which youths can gain money, power, and respect. Youths do not simply step into the space called war and realize only then its advantages. Many youths seek the coming of war because it means they will have guns and the power to loot and achieve riches they had only dreamed of previously (Delap 2005). For girls, disaffection may stem from their marginal status and their desire for greater equality. For both boys and girls, imagination of the better life ahead not only sours their taste for the present but also spurs their disaffection, whetting their appetite for fighting. Although most war-engaged youths eventually tire of war and seek peace, their initial, rosy view of war invites many into armed groups.

Disrespect is the third source of youth disaffection. In the developing countries where most contemporary wars occur, adults expect youths to be subservient and respectful at the same moment in which the youths are also expected to demonstrate increased autonomy and to earn money to support their families. These conflicting role expectations, together with youths' inability to earn money, frequently lead youths to behave in ways that stir adults to perceive them as troublemakers. For example, many dejected, frustrated youths spend time idling with other youths, showing little respect for parents and elders. Adults react to this behavior with anger and criticism, which shades easily into disparagement and contempt. From the standpoint of the youths, who typically feel invisible already (Women's Commission for Refugee Women and Children 2000), adults' criticism stings with disrespect and a lack of appreciation of youths' difficult situation. Whether real or perceived, adults' disrespect only adds to the disaffection and rage many youths feel over the failure of the system, which, after all, adults had created.

These sources of disaffection add up to hopelessness about their current state of life and an inability to find meaning within the existing system. When this occurs, youths are more likely to find meaning in revolution and violence. Although youth disaffection is not a cause of war per se, it is nonetheless a significant contributing factor and is likely to become influential in societies that have a "youth bulge," that is, a large cohort of youths in conditions of low employment and hopelessness (Urdahl 2004). Disaffected youths are easily manipulated by extremist political leadership and ideologies, which lead children into armed groups. Although youth disaffection has many sources, I have attempted to highlight the importance of structural injustices.

Fortunately, the structural sources of youth disaffection are not inexorable and may be addressed through numerous actions, such as the establishment and implementation of the following:

- National government policies against discrimination, including discrimination based on gender
- National programs for job creation and income generation for youths, including those from marginalized groups
- Dialogue and conflict mitigation processes that stop the fighting between states and nonstate actors
- Policies and programs that support the participation in governance of youths from diverse subgroups
- Youth programs of community service

These steps reflect the importance of youths' full economic and political participation and embody the idea that youths who have positive opportunities and life options are more likely to become good citizens rather than soldiers. Also, youth participation and visible youth engagement in community are antidotes for issues of disrespect. By helping their communities, youths come to be seen not as troublemakers but as promising citizens, and they find meaning in being part of a larger cause without recourse to violence.

Ending Normalized Violence

The pervasiveness of violence in war zones is an obstacle to peace because it renders normal the abnormal and horrific. It is natural for children who grow up in war zones—who see armies fight, family members join armed groups, fights in families and schools, and romanticized media images of warriors—to think of fighting as the main way to deal with conflict, and to develop values conducive to military participation.

A key step toward ending the normalization of violence is to provide training on violence reduction at multiple levels, beginning with families. Many families living in war zones inflict harsh corporal punishment on their children daily. These children often see their main role models—their parents—use violence. In Angola, CCF staff initially believed that corporal punishment was too deeply rooted to be susceptible to change, but the staff managed to reduce it by using an approach that taught empathy and reflection. First, a group of mothers were asked to close their eyes, and think back to a time in their own childhood when they had done something bad and were being punished by one or both parents. Asked to describe their feelings, the mothers said they felt badly, powerless, or scared of the parents who were beating them. Next, the CCF trainer provided a quiet space for reflection. Examining their own experiences, one or two mothers typically exclaimed, "Oh my God, that's what I'm doing to my own children!" This "Aha!" experience came as a bolt of lightning for the mothers, many of whom pledged on the spot to stop beating their children. This exercise sparked mothers' willingness to learn nonviolent methods, such as time-outs, to manage undesired behavior. Several years later, both children and mothers reported a reduced frequency of corporal punishment.

Numerous methods are also available for reducing violence in schools.

For example, in northern Afghanistan, beatings by teachers were a leading cause of school dropout in 2003. To reduce such beatings, the Child Well-Being Committees formed by ChildFund Afghanistan designated a trusted person to whom children reported instances of beatings by a teacher. Following the occurrence of a beating, the Committee members visited the teacher who had administered the beating and discussed the need to use alternate, nonviolent methods of behavior management. Subsequently, both teachers and children reported a reduced frequency of beatings, and the number of dropouts attributable to corporal punishment decreased as well. This work is complemented by efforts at the national level by the Afghan Ministry of Education, ChildFund Afghanistan, the International Rescue Committee, and Save the Children to ban the use of corporal punishment in schools.

At the community level, youth-led radio programming is a useful tool for decreasing romantic images of violence and promoting nonviolent means of conflict resolution. In Sierra Leone, for example, Search for Common Ground enabled local youths in rural villages to create their own radio show, "Talking Drum," which uses drama to show the harmful effects of violence and teach children that education is more valuable than carrying a gun. In countries such as Rwanda and Burundi, Search for Common Ground has also used radio drama as a way to reduce entrenched stereotypes of enemies, which had been transmitted as a prelude to the 1994 Rwandan genocide. The use of radio fits Africa, where most people own a radio and well-designed programs attract huge audiences. A significant challenge is to spread the use of such nonviolent programming not only through radio but also through other media such as television, film, and computers.

Youths as Peacebuilders

Peacebuilding refers to efforts to establish peace before, during, or following armed conflict. A useful, if underutilized, conflict prevention strategy is to engage youths as peacebuilders. Youths' motivation to perform this role was evident at the International Conference on War-Affected Children, which the Canadian Government conducted in Winnipeg in 2000. Youths from around the world dialogued in the no-nonsense style of teenagers who have grown weary of adults' rhetoric and inability to stop children's slaughter. As one youth put it, "We are tired of only being the victims; we want to be the ones who make a difference" (UNICEF 2002b, 123).

Youths' ability to make a positive difference is visible in conflict prevention activities worldwide. Following the Serb attacks on Kosovar Albanians, large numbers of people lived in refugee camps in Tirana, where the recent wounds and pain of war were etched on people's faces and had left them feeling overwhelmed and hopeless. In partnership with UNICEF and the Albanian Youth Council, young refugees held weekly discussions to identify problems and examine how to resolve them without recourse to violence. Rekindling the spirit of community, the youths organized camp cleanups and sports activities, and raised funds to support the poorest families (Women's Commission for Refugee Women and Children 2005). When they returned home, many of the youths participated in the Kosovar Youth Councils, which strove to keep youths out of the Kosovar Liberation Army and prevent attacks on Serbs.

Children and youths have also raised awareness of peace and children's needs through the conduct of national campaigns. Living in one of the most war-torn countries in the world, Colombian children organized in 1996 a national exhibit of children's letters, poems, and pictures on peace. The assembly, which drew five thousand participants, drafted a declaration in which they asked the armed factions for "peace in our homes, for them not to make orphans of children, to allow us to play freely in the streets and for no harm to come to our small brothers and sisters" (UNICEF 1999, 42). This activity led to the formation of the national Children's Movement for Peace (Cameron 1998), which drafted a national children's referendum in which nearly three million children voted to make their highest priorities peace and the rights to survival, family, and freedom from abuse. Due in part to the children's referendum, peace became a significant issue in the subsequent presidential campaign. Mayerly Sanchez, who at age 14 was one of the leaders of the organization, said, "Children are the seeds that will stop the war" (UNICEF 1999, 43). Although no single group can achieve peace in a country like Colombia, it is significant that children raised national consciousness about the damage being done to children and established a venue that encouraged young people to contribute to peace rather than war.

At the grassroots level, Colombian children have organized numerous initiatives to staunch the flow of children into armed groups. In Medellín, children in poor neighborhoods organized musical bands. Using slogans such as "When you hold a violin in your hands you'll never hold a gun," these bands have encouraged music participation over fighting, using music as a medium of peacebuilding (Hart and Mojica 2006). Creative art is another means grassroots groups have used to encourage youths to stay out of armed groups. In the Workshop for Life (Tailler de Vida), displaced youths, some of whom had participated in violence, use theater, dance, wall painting, and rap to portray their life experiences and express publicly their hopes for a peaceful life. The strength of their message rings in the title of one of their videos—"This War Is Not Ours and We're Losing It!" (Hart and Mojica 2006). This promising activity raises public awareness of youths' situation and aspirations, and also enables peer education supporting norms of peace. To convert cultures of violence into cultures of peace, policy changes are useful but insufficient by themselves. If peace is to take root, youths themselves must acquire a strong orientation toward peace and establish norms against fighting.

In Afghanistan, too, youths became a significant voice for peace when in December 2004 they assembled thousands of children from diverse ethnic groups and regions at a National Children's Forum, which President Karzai addressed. The children drafted a National Children's Manifesto, calling for adults to make badly needed improvements in children's health, education, and economic circumstances. The Manifesto rang with the youths' commitment to doing their part to build peace:

In our villages, returnee camps and communities, we have formed networks of children's groups. When children in our communities have a problem, we work together to find solutions. We do this all over Afghanistan so that we can contribute to the future of our country and our brothers and sisters . . .

Children who are with commanders should be released. The commanders don't treat us well and don't allow us to go to school. The government should take weapons away from commanders and others who don't protect us but threaten and scare our families and us . . .

We will do all we can to rebuild our beloved country; we will use our education to reconstruct our country, we will promote peace amongst our brothers and sisters; we will continue to help children in need in our communities and include them in our lives. We will listen to the government and help them improve our lives.

Youths have also contributed to peacebuilding through their actions at the highest levels of the United Nations. In 2002, UNICEF organized the U.N. Special Session on Children in which children from different countries voiced their concerns to U.N. leaders, calling for action on a wide range of issues concerning peace and justice. The Special Representative to the Secretary-General on Children and Armed Conflict has been instrumental in helping to deploy Child Protection Advisors in U.N. peace operations in countries such as Sierra Leone and the DRC and in making children and armed conflict an item on the Security Council agenda. These efforts have forged valuable connections between children's issues and the international peace and security agenda at the United Nations.

A Systemic Prevention Strategy

Children are enveloped by social subsystems, such as the family, community, society, region, and global community. So it makes sense to focus prevention efforts on strengthening the shielding mechanisms at these diverse levels. This systemic, ecological approach reminds us that building a comprehensive prevention system is a bit like building a bicycle wheel, which contains many spokes, a weakness in any one of which can weaken the wheel or cause it to collapse. To be sure, there is great need for effective legal and conflict prevention mechanisms. However, we need also to think about the other elements—supportive families, education, cultural mechanisms, leaders who act on behalf of children's protection, and so on—that contribute to a comprehensive system of prevention. These elements are visible in initiatives ranging from the family to the international levels.

Local Initiatives

Local initiatives are necessary in part because, in war zones, commanders continue to recruit children despite their countries' verbal support of legal instruments such as the CRC and the Optional Protocol. In Sri Lanka in April 2004, the LTTE split into warring factions, both of which recruited children. To prevent the armed groups from keeping their children, villagers confronted LTTE commanders, demanding the return of their children. Said one villager:

> All the people came to fight, even children . . . More than 1,000 people were fighting [to demand the return of their children.] . . . We spoke directly with the assistant political leader. He told us, "We came to protect you." At the same time, our people asked them—both Prabhakaran's and Karuna's people, "You took our children from us and now you are shooting those children . . . Why are you shooting these children? You say you are Tamil leaders so why are you killing Tamil people? Please give us our children back and then you can go away. (HRW 2004b, 35)

Although some LTTE people threatened to shoot the protestors, the villagers persisted, eventually winning the release or return of many children.

Prevention efforts are seldom so heroic, and frequently they involve quiet labor out of the public spotlight. Much excellent work on prevention occurs in families. Many Sierra Leonean teenagers have told me they had not joined armed groups because their families had forbidden them to join or to fight. One boy said, "My mother made me stay away from fighters and watched out for me." Also, many families protect their children from recruitment by fleeing their village with their children when rebel forces are near or sending children away to safer areas. Families' watchfulness over their children and prohibitions against joining armed groups is a valuable counterweight to the practice in other families of encouraging sons and daughters to enlist as a way to earn money or restore family honor. Families can also prevent recruitment through the creation of a caring, supportive environment that gives children many reasons to stay with their family (Delap 2005). If abuse propels many children into armed groups, family love and support are potent forms of prevention.

However, family prevention efforts require effective community supports. Desperate to save their children, some families try to protect them through questionable means, such as compelling their daughters to marry very young since armed groups such as the LTTE prefer not to recruit married girls (HRW 2004b). In Sri Lanka, some children, including those who had formerly been recruited and want no part of military life, agree to enter the LTTE in exchange for letting their brothers and sisters go free. Although these attempts at prevention are well intentioned, they trade one risk for another. A stronger tactic is for communities to rally around their children, compelling commanders both to release current child soldiers and halt their recruitment of children. This tactic is not feasible in all situations, but it stands a good chance of success in situations where the armed groups depend on local people's moral or material support.

Even where armed groups exploit and attack communities, local initiatives may nonetheless contribute to prevention. In northern Uganda, the parents of abducted children formed the Concerned Parents Association in order to prepare local villages for the return home of their children and to work on a peaceful resolution to the conflict (Women's Commission for Refugee Women and Children 2005). Through international advocacy campaigns, the Association helped raise international awareness of the fact that children were being abducted by the LRA, and helped obtain funds to meet the children's rehabilitation needs. This shining example of the global village phenomenon illustrates how prevention can be strengthened by working at multiple levels simultaneously.

Some of the best steps toward prevention come at the community level. It is vital for community leaders and other members to send out effective messages warning children and parents of the dangers associated with recruitment. That these dangers are not always understood by children is clear in the statement of a 12-year-old Liberian girl who had decided to join an armed group:

> I will not go back because the first time God spared my life. Maybe the next time I will die. There is nothing good in war for children. Some go back to their families crippled or half crazy because of the drugs they used. I will not go back and I don't want to be part of it again. (Delap 2005, 14)

If girls such as this and community leaders spread the message that living with armed groups is far more difficult and damaging than one might expect, the result can be strengthened prevention at the local level. Also, communities can support prevention by ensuring that people's most basic needs are met, because the risks of children's recruitment increase when children are hungry or families have no livelihoods (Delap, 2005).

The cultural influences on recruitment are often addressed most effectively at the community level. A tradition in many rural villages is for young people, particularly teenage boys, to join local militias as a way to protect their villages, or serve their families, or both. Humanitarian agencies have frequently attempted to transform such cultural norms by teaching local people about children's rights, using pocket versions of the CRC translated into the local language. This approach, however, often fails because local understandings of childhood collide with those enshrined in universalized legal instruments.

This collision is not inevitable, particularly if one is willing to take a pragmatic approach. In an Angolan village, CCF staff had met with elders to gain support for the idea that no children should be soldiers. The elders, however, contested the label *child soldiers* as applied to gun-wielding 15-year-olds, whom local people regarded as adults. Wanting to respect local cultural views, but also children's rights under international law, the CCF staff took two steps to break the impasse. First, they gained elders' acceptance of the idea that young people should not fight or serve in armed groups. Acceptance came easily because the elders felt responsible for the protection of young people and agreed that people under 18 years would better serve the village by starting and supporting their own families than by fighting. Second, the staff negotiated the use of the term *underage soldiers,* which everyone accepted because law treated people under 18 years as minors and prohibited their recruitment. In this manner, the staff balanced respect for local culture with the need to protect children's rights. This episode illustrates that respect for children's rights is better achieved through a process of dialogue and negotiation than through the imposition of legal instruments for which local people feel little ownership.

Local cultural practices have sometimes been portrayed as the enemies of prevention. Although cultural resources such as healers and rituals have sometimes been subverted as tools of war, there is no need to view local practices as the cultural bogeyman. As we saw in Chapter 8, local cultural resources such as healing rituals are useful supports for the reintegration of former child soldiers. In my experience, traditional leaders, healers, religious leaders, influential women, and other people who are keepers and embodiments of local culture often help prevent child soldiering by engaging young people in nonmilitary pursuits and even, when feasible, pressuring leaders of armed groups not to recruit children. Prevention requires support for child protective cultural practices and opposition to harmful cultural practices.

At local levels, prevention should also include efforts to:

- Promote methods of positive parenting, which involve teaching children values of nonviolence and reduce the likelihood that children will join armed groups as a way to escape an abusive family
- Strengthen community protection mechanisms for monitoring, reporting, and acting on abuses of children, including child recruitment
- Improve community services for children, particularly vulnerable children such as displaced children, whom recruiters frequently target
- Use traditional song, dance, and related cultural activities to spread important protection messages, such as the need to avoid places and activities where armed groups recruit children
- Educate children, families, and community people, including local officials, about the harm soldiering causes to children and means of preventing recruitment
- Encourage in children a sense of civic responsibility and engagement in community activities, which will earn them respect
- Support youth groups through which girls and boys develop positive competencies, learn to manage conflict without recourse to violence, and create peer pressure for peace
- Make education for girls and boys highly accessible, engaging, and a stepping stone to positive life options
- Provide literacy and numeracy courses and other training venues to older children who missed out on school earlier in life
- Use collective grassroots action to reduce economic and social marginalization

Societal Initiatives

At the societal level, universal birth registration is a decisive step toward prevention. By documenting children's age, official IDs make it easier to identify violations of the Optional Protocol and also undercut recruiters' claims not to have known that a recruit was a child.

It is also necessary to establish stronger national mechanisms of accountability to prevent child soldiering. An essential first step is universal adoption of the CRC. The failure of the United States to ratify and accede to the CRC is a highly visible and noteworthy gap, since progress in protecting children's rights requires the support of the world's most powerful nation for the foundational child rights instrument. The refusal of the U.S. Congress to ratify the CRC reflects deep mistrust of international law and a wider belief of U.S. citizens that U.S. law trumps international law. Ironically, the CRC does not require outright adoption of all articles of the CRC but permits states to create a legal process for bringing their national law in line with international law. Unwillingness to ratify stems also from political pressures to allow U.S. states to use corporal punishment in schools and impose harsh penalties on underage lawbreakers. For U.S. readers of this book, this situation cries out for a national campaign to ratify and abide by the CRC.

As long as war creates an opportunity space for young people, children will continue to join armed groups as a way to meet basic needs, obtain wealth, power, and prestige, or find meaning in radical ideologies. To prevent child recruitment, we must shrink this opportunity space, if not by preventing wars then by providing children with civilian opportunities and services, thereby reducing their motivation to join armed groups. The provision of education even during armed conflict is a step that many former child soldiers say would have kept them from joining an armed group.

Prevention at the societal level also requires efforts to:

- Monitor child recruitment by national armies and related paramilitary groups
- Develop agreements between the government and nonstate actors in the country not to recruit children, and impose U.N. sanctions against governments and armed groups that violate these agreements
- Provide appropriate protections for at-risk children, such as displaced children, separated children, and others who are often targets for recruitment
- Integrate peace education into the national education curriculum
- Provide vocational training and jobs for young people

- Halt the flow of small weapons into the country
- Redress the massive economic disparities and forms of marginalization that lead many youths to join armed groups
- Educate all citizens about their rights

Regional Initiatives

Excessive reliance on country-specific approaches has limited prevention efforts. Too often, governments, donors, and international agencies have reified state boundaries and constructed systems of aid and prevention that are ill equipped to address regional issues. Disrespecting state borders, child recruitment and the welter of associated problems—war, weapons flows, illicit economic activities, chronic poverty, and HIV/AIDS, among others—spill over into neighboring countries (HRW 2005; Landry 2005). Governments in countries such as Rwanda or Liberia often have deliberately destabilized or invaded neighboring countries, such as the DRC and Sierra Leone. The importance of regional influences on armed conflict suggests the need to focus less on country wars than on regional conflict systems.

Regional conflict systems have created a thriving market for itinerant former child soldiers. Although most children enter armed groups to fight a particular war, usually in their own country, some become mercenaries in wars in neighboring countries. A former RUF fighter from Sierra Leone who went on to fight in LURD in Liberia said:

> In 2001, I disarmed with the RUF in Bo and got training to be a carpenter, and at the end, they gave me a set of tools. But after the six month course, I couldn't get work. There were so many workshops—all over Bo. All over Kenema. Too many carpenters. After about seven months of trying, S ran into me on the street in Bo and told me, "Hey, I want you to be with me in Liberia." She said they were paying $200 to go. I was fed up and since she used to be my general, I told her I'd go. (HRW 2005, 68)

The emphasis of training over jobs and income generation dooms many DDR programs, planting the seeds for mercenary activity in which youths "graduate" from one war and move on to others. Morally, this system is an eerie counterpart to the educational system in which young people graduate from one school and advance to others.

The mercenary system indicates the need to reduce the regional opportunity space that actively draws children into armed groups. No matter how strong country-specific DDR programs are, the children who fall through the cracks or feel frustrated over the lack of opportunities will likely become the troops fighting the next wars in neighboring countries. Also, the regional nature of conflict suggests the limits of country-specific approaches to conflict prevention. Because regional problems require regional solutions, steps toward the prevention of child soldiering should include the creation or strengthening of regional systems for:

- Monitoring, reporting, and acting on cases of child recruitment
- Tracking children's movement across national boundaries
- Demobilizing and reintegrating former child soldiers
- Ensuring that jobs are available for trained former child soldiers
- Enabling children to achieve greater gain through peaceful activities than through fighting
- Training commanders and military groups in child rights and the importance of enforcing a strict ban on child recruitment
- Prosecuting child recruiters
- Boosting public awareness of children's rights

Global Initiatives

In the global village, the expanding levels of interdependence and interconnectedness offer many opportunities for generating global initiatives that have significant impact at other levels. The value of marshaling global pressures should not be underestimated. After all, international pressures had a significant impact in ending the apartheid regime in South Africa and also in reducing the mistreatment of political prisoners in countries worldwide. Global steps that should be taken to prevent children's abuse as soldiers include:

- Global youth initiatives that enable youths to take leadership on issues of child soldiers, war prevention, the creation of jobs, and access to quality education
- The imposition of U.N. Security Council penalties on countries that trade weapons with, or allow the flow of illicit materials into, countries in which children are exploited as soldiers

- Building into international peace agreements provisions for children's DDR and prevention of further child recruitment
- Campaigns to strengthen the International Criminal Court and its prosecution of child recruiters
- Global poverty reduction initiatives in which youths are central actors
- Worldwide campaigns to strengthen child protection
- Action research that identifies effective program practices for supporting all war-affected children and preventing child recruitment

Perhaps the most important step is the expansion of a global grassroots campaign to end children's exploitation as soldiers. The pioneering efforts of the Coalition to Stop the Use of Child Soldiers (see www.child-soldiers.org) have begun the campaign and laid the foundation for wider efforts. What is needed now is greater engagement by citizens from many different countries and the systematic exchange of tools and lessons learned by different communities. If a global campaign is to avoid the adult biases that have hampered many programs, then children must play a central, leadership role. A children's leadership approach fits not only with the principle of child participation but also with the enduring lesson that adults are more likely to listen to the children than to other adults.

If this vision of a global campaign led by children seems nebulous, picture children in schools worldwide learning about the issue and organizing youth groups to support via email their counterparts in war-torn countries and writing to political leaders. Picture local groups sharing via the Internet ideas for prevention campaigns and for programs that create positive opportunities for youths outside of armed groups. Picture youth groups linked with regional and global youth associations whose primary purpose is to end all forms of youth exploitation and to make their voices heard in the public arena. Picture youths at the center of local, national, regional, and global child protection campaigns.

Adults, too, have an important part to play in a global campaign. Picture parents and other adults advancing the campaign through their advocacy for education and jobs for young people and support for children in peaceful pursuits. Adult leaders control the political strings of power, so they, too, need to be brought into a global, collective effort.

Our greatest challenge in regard to prevention is one of hope, and it is one to which we must rise together. Through the ages, visionaries and agents of social change have been told they were powerless to effect global change. Early advocates of ending massive problems such as slavery were dismissed as mad or contemptuous of civilization. However, those advocates turned out to have been right, and their hope and courageous action freed countless people.

It lies within our power to stop the wanton exploitation of children as soldiers and the theft of their childhood. The knowledge and the tools for accomplishing this historic task are at hand. Now the question is whether we will commit ourselves to the protection of our most precious heritage, our children.

References

Agger, I. 2001. Reducing trauma during ethno-political conflict. In *Peace, conflict, and violence,* ed. D. Christie, R. V. Wagner, and D. Winter, 240–250. Upper Saddle River, NJ: Prentice Hall.

———. 2006. Approaches to psychosocial healing: Case examples from Lusophone Africa. In *Handbook of international disaster psychology,* vol. 2, ed. G. Reyes and G. Jacobs, 136–155. Westport, CT: Praeger.

Allen, B. 1996. *Rape warfare.* Minneapolis: University of Minnesota Press.

Allen, T. 2005. *War and justice in northern Uganda.* London: London School of Economics.

Amnesty International. 2000. *Rape and other forms of sexual violence against girls and women.* Downloaded July 21, 2004, from web.amnesty.org/library/print/ENGAFR510352000.

———. 2004a. Darfur: Rape as a weapon of war. Downloaded July 21, 2004, from web.amnesty.org/library/print/ENGAFR540762004.

———. 2004b. Rape—the hidden human rights abuse. Downloaded July 21, 2004, from web.amnesty.org/library/.

Annan, J., and C. Blattman. 2006. The psychosocial resilience of youth in northern Uganda. Survey of War Affected Youth, Research Brief 2. Downloaded May 12, 2006, from www.sway-uganda.org/SWAY.RB2.pdf.

Arroyo, W., and S. Eth. 1996. Post-traumatic stress disorder and other stress responses. In *Minefields in their hearts,* ed. R. Apfel and B. Simon, 52–74. New Haven: Yale University Press.

Ayalew, D., and S. Dercon. 2000. "From the gun to the plough": The macro- and micro-level impact of demobilization in Ethiopia. In *Demobilization in sub-Saharan Africa,* ed. K. Kingma, 132–172. New York: St. Martin's.

Baines, E. 2005. *Roco Wat I Acoli.* Gulu: Liu Institute for Global Issues and Gulu District NGO Forum.

Ball, N. 1997. Demobilizing and reintegrating soldiers: Lessons from Africa. In *Rebuilding war-torn societies,* ed. K. Kumar, 85–105. Boulder, CO: Lynne Rienner.

Barber, B. 2001. Political violence, social integration, and youth functioning:

Palestinian youth from the Intifada. *Journal of Community Psychology* 29(3): 259–280.

Barnett, K. 2005. Home truths for girls returning from the armed forces and groups. *Child Soldiers Newsletter,* no. 13, 4–5.

Baron, N. 2002. Community based psychosocial and mental health services for Southern Sudanese Refugees in long term exile in Uganda. In *Trauma, war, and violence,* ed. J. de Jong, 157–203. New York: Kluwer.

Berdal, M. 1996. *Disarmament and demobilisation after civil wars.* Adelphi Paper 303. London: International Institute for Strategic Studies.

Bhabha, J. 2005. Destroying childhood. *Harvard Magazine,* Sept.–Oct., 23–28.

Bloom, M. 2005. *Dying to kill.* New York: Columbia University Press.

Boothby, N. 1996. Mobilizing communities to meet the psychosocial needs of children in war and refugee crises. In *Minefields in their hearts,* ed. R. Apfel and B. Simon, 149–164. New Haven: Yale University Press.

Boothby, N., J. Crawford, and J. Halperin. 2006. Mozambican child soldier life outcome study: Lessons learned on rehabilitation and reintegration efforts. *Global Public Health* 1(1): 87–107.

Boothby, N., and C. Knudsen. 2000. Children of the gun. *Scientific American* 282: 60–66.

Bowlby, J. 1969. *Attachment and loss.* Vol. 1: *Attachment.* New York: Basic Books.

Boyden, J. 1994. Children's experience of conflict related emergencies: Some implications for relief policy and practice. *Disasters* 18: 254–267.

———. 1997. Childhood and the policy makers. In *Constructing and reconstructing childhood,* ed. A. James and A. Prout, 184–215. London: Falmer.

———. 2003. The moral development of child soldiers. *Peace and Conflict: Journal of Peace Psychology* 9: 343–362.

Boyden, J., and J. de Berry, eds. 2004. *Children and youth on the front line.* New York: Berghahn.

Boyden, J., C. Eyber, T. Feeny, and C. Scott. 2003. *Children and poverty: Voices of children.* Richmond, VA: Christian Children's Fund.

Boyden, J., and S. Gibbs. 1997. *Children and war.* Geneva: United Nations.

Bracken, P. 1998. Hidden agendas: Deconstructing post-traumatic stress disorder. In *Rethinking the trauma of war,* ed. P. Bracken and C. Petty, 38–59. London: Free Association Books.

Brett, R. 2003. Why do adolescents volunteer for armed forces or armed groups? Paper presented at the Spanish Red Cross international conference "Adding Colour to Peace," Valencia, Nov. 5–7.

Brett, R., and M. McCallin. 1996. *Children: The invisible soldiers.* Vaxjö, Sweden: Radda Barnen.

Brett, R., and I. Specht. 2004. *Young soldiers.* Boulder, CO: Lynne Rienner.

Bronfenbrenner, U. 1979. *The ecology of human development.* Cambridge, MA: Harvard University Press.

Brown, I. 1990. *Khomeini's forgotten sons*. London: Grey Seal.

Brownmiller, S. 1975. *Against our will*. New York: Bantam.

Cairns, E. 1996. *Children and political violence*. Cambridge, MA: Blackwell.

Cairns, E., and J. Darby. 1998. The conflict in Northern Ireland: Causes, consequences, and controls. *American Psychologist* 53(7): 754–760.

Cairns, E., and A. Dawes. 1996. Children: Ethnic and political violence—a commentary. *Child Development* 67: 129–139.

Cairns, E., and M. Roe. 2003. *The role of memory in ethnic conflict*. Houndsmills, Basinstoke, UK: Palgrave Macmillan.

Cameron, S. 1998. *Making peace with children*. Bogota, Colombia: UNICEF.

Carpenter, C. In press. War's impact on children born of rape and sexual exploitation. In *Children and armed conflict*, ed. A. Knight. Alberta: University of Alberta Press.

Castelli, L., E. Locatelli, and M. Canavera. 2005. *Psycho-social support for war affected children in northern Uganda*. London: Coalition to Stop the Use of Child Soldiers.

Child Soldiers Newsletter. 2005. Former child soldiers learn discipline of school. Spring.

Christian Children's Fund/Angola. 1998. *Final report: Project on reintegration of child soldiers in Angola*. Luanda.

———. 1999. Unpublished field research notes.

———. 2002. *Free to play in peace*. Luanda.

———. 2005. Unpublished interview conducted as part of the *Breaking the silence* report. (See Stavrou 2005.)

Christie, D., R. Wagner, and D. Winter, eds. 2001. *Peace, conflict, and violence*. Upper Saddle River, NJ: Prentice Hall.

Chrobok, V. 2005. *Reintegrating Afghanistan's young soldiers*. Bonn: Bonn International Center for Conversion.

Cilliers, J., and C. Dietrich. 2001. *Angola's war economy*. Pretoria: Institute for Security Studies.

Clark, C. 2003. Juvenile justice and child soldiering: Trends, dilemmas, challenges. *Child Soldiers Newsletter*, Mar. Accessed at www.child-soldiers.org/cs/childsoldiers.nsf/.

Coalition to Stop the Use of Child Soldiers. 2001. *Child soldiers global report 2001*. London.

———. 2002. *Child soldiers 1379 report*. London.

———. 2004. *Child soldiers global report 2004*. London.

Coghlan, B., R. Brennan, P. Ngoy, D. Dofara, B. Otto, and T. Stewart. 2006. Mortality in the Democratic Republic of Congo. *Lancet* 367: 44–51.

Cohn, I. 2004. Progress and hurdles on the road to preventing the use of children as soldiers and ensuring their rehabilitation and reintegration. *Cornell International Law Journal* 37(3): 531–540.

Cohn, I., and G. Goodwin-Gill. 1994. *Child soldiers*. Oxford: Clarendon.

Cole, M., and S. Cole. 1993. *The development of children*. 2nd ed. New York: Freeman.

Colletta, N. 1997. Demilitarization, demobilization, and the social and economic integration of ex-combatants. In *Conference on promoting human rights, democracy, and reintegration in post-conflict societies, Oct. 30–31, 1997*. Washington, DC: USAID.

Collier, P., V. Elliott, H. Hegre, A. Hoeffler, M. Reynal-Querol, and N. Sambanis. 2003. *Breaking the conflict trap*. Washington, DC: World Bank.

Dawes, A. 1994. The emotional impact of political violence. In *Childhood and adversity*, ed. A. Dawes and D. Donald, 177–199. Cape Town: David Philip.

Dawes, A., and E. Cairns. 1998. The Machel study: Dilemmas of cultural sensitivity and universal rights of children. *Peace and Conflict: Journal of Peace Psychology* 4(4): 335–348.

Dawes, A., and D. Donald. 1994. *Childhood and adversity*. Cape Town: David Philip.

———. 2000. Improving children's chances. In *Addressing childhood adversity*, ed. D. Donald, A. Dawes, and J. Louw, 1–25. Cape Town: David Philip.

de Jong, J. 2002. Public mental health, traumatic stress and human rights violations in low-income countries. In *Trauma, war, and violence*, ed. J. de Jong, 1–91. New York: Kluwer.

Delap, E. 2004. *No place like home?* London: Save the Children UK.

———. 2005. *Fighting back*. London: Save the Children UK.

de la Soudière, M., J. Williamson, and J. Botte. 2004. *The lost ones*. New York: UNICEF.

De Lay, B. 2002. *Mobility mapping and flow diagrams*. New York: International Rescue Committee.

———. 2003. *Family reunification, alternative care, and community reintegration of separated children in post-conflict Rwanda*. New York: International Rescue Committee.

Derluyn, I., E. Broekaert, G. Schuyten, and E. De Temmerman. 2004. Post-traumatic stress in former Ugandan child soldiers. *Lancet* 363: 861–863.

De Temmerman, E. 2001. *Aboke girls*. Kampala: Fountain.

Deutsch, M. 2000. Cooperation and competition. In *The handbook of conflict resolution*, ed. M. Deutsch and P. Coleman, 21–40. San Francisco: Jossey-Bass.

Doná, G. 2001. *The Rwandan experience of fostering separated children*. Stockholm: Save the Children Sweden.

Donahue, J., and J. Williamson. 1999. *Community mobilization to mitigate the impact of HIV/AIDS*. New York: Displaced Children and Orphans Fund.

Dyregov, A., R. Gjestad, and M. Raundalen. 2002. Children exposed to warfare. *Journal of Traumatic Stress* 15: 59–68.

Eisenbruch, M. 1991. From post-traumatic stress disorder to cultural bereavement. *Social Science and Medicine* 33(6): 673–680.

Elbe, S. 2002. HIV/AIDS and the changing landscape of war in Africa. *International Security* 27(2): 159–177.

Ellis, S. 1999. *The mask of anarchy*. London: Hurst.

Erikson, E. 1968. *Identity, youth, and crisis*. New York: W. W. Norton.

Eth, S., and R. Pynoos. 1985. Developmental perspective on psychic trauma in childhood. In *Trauma and its wake*, ed. C. Figley. New York: Plenum.

Eyber, C., and A. Ager. 2004. Researching young people's experiences of war. In *Children and youth on the front line*, ed. J. Boyden and J. de Berry, 189–208. New York: Berghahn.

Flanagan, C., and B. Van Horn. 2003. Youth civic development. In *Community youth development*, ed. F. Villarruel, D. Perkins, L. Borden, and J. Keith, 273–296. Thousand Oaks, CA: Sage.

Foa, E., S. Stein, and A. McFarlane. 2006. Symptomatology and psychopathology of mental health problems after disaster. *Journal of Clinical Psychiatry* 67: 15–25.

Foster, G., C. Levine, and J. Williamson, eds. 2005. *A generation at risk*. Cambridge: Cambridge University Press.

Frank, D., P. Klass, F. Earls, and L. Eisenberg. 1996. Infants and young children in orphanages. *Pediatrics* 97: 569–578.

Garbarino, J., and K. Kostelny. 1996. The effects of political violence on Palestinian children's behavioral problems. *Child Development* 67: 33–45.

Garbarino, J., K. Kostelny, and N. Dubrow. 1991. *No place to be a child*. Lexington, MA: Lexington Books.

Garfield, R. M., and A. I. Neugut. 1997. The human consequences of war. In *War and public health*, ed. B. S. Levy and V. W. Sidel, 27–38. New York: Oxford University Press.

Gielen, U. P., J. Fish, and J. G. Draguns, eds. 2004. *Handbook of culture, therapy, and healing*. Mahwah, NJ: Erlbaum.

Gilligan, C. 1982. *In a different voice*. Cambridge, MA: Harvard University Press.

Green, E., and M. G. Wessells. 1997. *Evaluation of the province-based war trauma team project*. Washington, DC: USAID.

Grossmann, K. E., K. Grossmann, and E. Waters. 2005. *Attachment from infancy to adulthood*. New York: Guilford.

Gurr, T. 1993. *Minorities at risk*. Washington, DC: U.S. Institute of Peace.

Hamburg, D., and B. Hamburg. 2004. *Learning to live together*. New York: Oxford University Press.

Hart, R., and R. Mojica. 2006. Building citizenship in the face of violence: Opportunities for the agency and social participation of children in Colombia. In *International perspectives on youth conflict and development*, ed. C. Daiute,

Z. Beykont, C. Higson-Smith, and L. Nucci, 245–264. New York: Oxford University Press.

Herman, J. 1997. *Trauma and recovery.* New York: Basic Books.

Higginbotham, M., and A. Marsella. 1988. International consultation and the homogenization of psychiatry in Southeast Asia. *Social Science and Medicine* 27: 553–561.

Hoffman, M. 2000. *Empathy and moral development.* Cambridge: Cambridge University Press.

Holland, D., S. Skinner, W. Lachicotte, and C. Cain. 1998. *Identity and agency in cultural worlds.* Cambridge, MA: Harvard University Press.

Honwana, A. 1997. Healing for peace. *Peace and Conflict: Journal of Peace Psychology* 3(3): 293–305.

———. 1998. *"Okusiakala O'Ndalu Yokalye": Let us light a new fire.* Luanda: Christian Children's Fund.

———. 2006. Child soldiers. In *International perspectives on youth conflict and development,* ed. C. Daiute, Z. Beykont, C. Higson-Smith, and L. Nucci, 225–244. New York: Oxford University Press.

Hubbard, J., and N. Pearson. 2004. Sierra Leonean refugees in Guinea. In *From clinic to community,* ed. K. Miller and L. Rasco, 95–132. Upper Saddle River, NJ: Erlbaum.

Human Rights Research and Advocacy Consortium. 2004. *Take the guns away.* Islamabad, Pakistan: Army Press.

Human Rights Watch. 1998. *Sowing terror.* New York.

———. 2001. *Reluctant recruits.* Washington, DC.

———. 2002. *"My gun was as tall as me."* New York.

———. 2003a. *Forgotten fighters.* Washington, DC.

———. 2003b. *Stolen children.* New York.

———. 2003c. *Sudan, oil, and human rights.* New York.

———. 2003d. *Uganda: Child abductions skyrocket in north.* Geneva.

———. 2003e. *You'll learn not to cry.* New York.

———. 2004a. *How to fight, how to kill.* New York.

———. 2004b. *Living in fear.* New York.

———. 2005. *Youth, poverty and blood.* New York.

Human Security Centre. 2005. *The human security report 2005.* New York: Oxford University Press.

Igreja, V. 2003. The effects of traumatic experiences on the infant–mother relationship in the former war zones of central Mozambique. *Infant Mental Health Journal* 24(5): 469–494.

———. 2004. Cultural disruption and the care of infants in post-war Mozambique. In *Children and youth on the front line,* ed. J. Boyden and J. de Berry , 23–41. New York: Berghahn.

InterAction Protection Working Group. 2004. *Making protection a priority.* Washington, DC.

International Rescue Committee. 2001. *Watchlist on Children and Armed Conflict Newsletter,* Nov.

ISIS–Women's International Cross-Cultural Exchange. 1998. *Documenting women's experiences in armed conflict situations in Uganda 1980–1986.* Kampala.

Janoff-Bulman, R. 1992. *Shattered assumptions.* New York: Free Press.

Jareg, E. 2005. *Crossing bridges and negotiating rivers: The rehabilitation and reintegration of children associated with armed forces.* London: Coalition to Stop the Use of Child Soldiers.

Jones, L. 2002. Adolescent understandings of political violence and psychological well-being. *Social Science and Medicine* 55: 1351–71.

Kagitcibasi, C. 1996. *Family and human development across cultures.* Mahwah, NJ: Erlbaum.

Keairns, Y. 2002. *The voices of girl child soldiers: Summary.* New York: Quaker United Nations Office.

———. 2003a. *The voices of girl child soldiers: Colombia.* New York: Quaker United Nations Office.

———. 2003b. *The voices of girl child soldiers: Philippines.* New York: Quaker United Nations Office.

———. 2003c. *The voices of girl child soldiers: Sri Lanka.* New York: Quaker United Nations Office.

Kelman, H. C., and V. L. Hamilton. 1989. *Crimes of obedience.* New Haven: Yale University Press.

King, M. 1986. *Stride toward freedom.* San Francisco: HarperSanFrancisco.

Kingma, K. 2000. *Demobilization in sub-Saharan Africa.* New York: St. Martin's.

Kinzie, J., et al. 1986. The psychiatric effects of massive trauma on Cambodian children. *Journal of the American Academy of Child Psychiatry* 25: 370–377.

Klare, M. 1999. The Kalashnikov age. *Bulletin of the Atomic Scientists* 55(1): 18–22.

———. 2001. *Resource wars.* New York: Henry Holt.

Kleinman, A. 1987. Anthropology and psychiatry: The role of culture in cross-cultural research on illness. *British Journal of Psychiatry* 151: 447–454.

Kostelny, K. 2002. *Sealing the past, facing the future.* Richmond, VA: Christian Children's Fund International.

———. 2004. What about the girls? *Cornell International Law Journal* 37(3): 505–512.

Kostelny, K., and M. Wessells. 2002. *Mapping local cultural resources for psychosocial support in East Timor.* Richmond, VA: Christian Children's Fund International.

Kriesberg, L. 1999. Paths to varieties of intercommunal reconciliation. In *Conflict resolution*, ed. H. Jeong, 105–130. Aldershot, UK: Ashgate.

Laeeq, A., and Jawadullah. 2002. Flowers on the frontline. *Child Soldiers Newsletter*, Sept.

Landau, S. 1993. *The guerilla wars of Central America*. New York: St. Martin's.

Landry, G. 2005. *Child soldiers and disarmament, demobilization, rehabilitation and reintegration in West Africa*. Dakar: Coalition to Stop the Use of Child Soldiers.

Lazarus, R., and S. Folkman. 1984. *Stress, appraisal, and coping*. New York: Springer.

Leavitt, L., and N. Fox, eds. 1993. *The psychological effects of war and violence on children*. Hillsdale, NJ: Erlbaum.

Lederach, J. 1997. *Building peace*. Washington, DC: U.S. Institute of Peace.

Lee, J., and S. Sue. 2001. Clinical psychology and culture. In *The handbook of culture and psychology*, ed. D. Matsumoto, 287–305. New York: Oxford University Press.

Loughry, M., and C. Eyber. 2003. *Psychosocial concepts in humanitarian work with children*. Washington, DC: National Academies Press.

Machel, G. 1996. *The impact of armed conflict on children*. New York: UNICEF.

———. 2001. *The impact of war on children*. Cape Town: David Philip.

MacMullin, C., and M. Loughry. 2002. *An investigation into the psychosocial adjustment of formerly abducted child soldiers in northern Uganda*. New York: International Rescue Committee.

Mann, G. 2004. Separated children. In *Children and youth on the front line*, ed. J. Boyden and J. de Berry, 3–22. New York: Berghahn.

Marks, S. 2000. *Watching the wind*. Washington, DC: U.S. Institute of Peace.

Marsella, A., T. Bornemann, S. Ekblad, and J. Orley, eds. 1994. *Amidst peril and pain*. Washington, DC: American Psychological Association.

Marsella, A., M. Friedman, E. Gerrity, and R. Surfield, eds. 1996. *Ethnocultural aspects of posttraumatic stress disorder*. Washington, DC: American Psychological Association.

Masten, A. 2001. Ordinary magic: Resilience processes in development. *American Psychologist* 56(3): 227–238.

Mawson, A. 2004. Children, impunity and justice: Some dilemmas from northern Uganda. In *Children and youth on the front line*, ed. J. Boyden and J. de Berry, 130–141. New York: Berghahn.

Mazurana, D., and K. Carlson. 2004. *From combat to community*. Boston: Women Waging Peace.

Mazurana, D., and S. McKay. (2001). Child soldiers: Where are the girls? *Bulletin of the Atomic Scientists* 57(5): 30–35.

Mazurana, D., S. McKay, K. Carlson, and J. Kasper. 2002. Girls in fighting forces and groups. *Peace and Conflict: Journal of Peace Psychology* 8: 97–123.

McCallin, M. 1995. *The reintegration of young ex-combatants into civilian life.* Geneva: International Labor Office.

———. 1998. Community involvement in the social reintegration of former child soldiers. In *Rethinking the trauma of war,* ed. P. Bracken and C. Petty, 60–75. London: Free Association Books.

McCann, I., and L. Pearlman. 1990. Vicarious traumatization: A framework for understanding the psychological effects of working with victims. *Journal of Traumatic Stress* 3: 131–150.

McConnan, I., and S. Uppard. 2001. *Children not soldiers.* London: Save the Children UK.

McIntyre, T., and M. Ventura. 2003. Children of war: Psychosocial sequelae of war trauma in Angolan adolescents. In *The psychological impact of war trauma on civilians,* ed. S. Krippner and T. McIntyre, 39–53. Westport, CT: Praeger.

McKay, S. 2006. How do you mend broken hearts? In *Handbook of international disaster psychology,* vol. 4, ed. G. Reyes and G. Jacobs, 45–60. Westport, CT: Praeger.

McKay, S., and D. Mazurana. 2004. *Where are the girls?* Montreal: International Centre for Human Rights and Democratic Development.

Mergelsberg, B. 2005. *Crossing boundaries.* Sydney: Ben Mergelsberg.

Miller, K., and L. Rasco. 2004. An ecological framework for assessing the mental health needs of refugee communities. In *The mental health of refugees,* ed. K. Miller and L. Rasco, 1–64. Mahwah, NJ: Erlbaum.

Mocellin, J. 2006. Reintegrating demobilized militia and former combatants: Lessons learned in Somalia. In *The psychology of resolving global conflicts: From war to peace,* vol. 3, ed. M. Fitzduff and C. Stout, 216–241. Westport, CT: Praeger Security International.

Mollica, R., C. Pole, L. Son, C. Murray, and S. Tor. 1997. Effects of war trauma on Cambodian refugee adolescents' functional health and mental health status. *Journal of the American Academy of Child and Adolescent Psychiatry* 36: 1098–1106.

Nicolai, S., and C. Tripplehorn. 2003. *The role of education in protecting children in conflict.* London: Humanitarian Practice Network.

Nordstrom, C. 1997. *A different kind of war story.* Philadelphia: University of Pennsylvania Press.

———. 2004. *Shadows of war.* Berkeley: University of California Press.

Opotow, S. 1990. Moral exclusion and injustice. *Journal of Social Issues* 46(1): 1–20.

Opotow, S., J. Gerson, and S. Woodside. 2005. From moral exclusion to moral inclusion: Theory for teaching peace. *Theory into Practice* 44(4): 303–318.

Pape, R. 2005. *Dying to win: The strategic logic of suicide terrorism.* New York: Random House.

Parsons, I. 2004. Beyond the silencing of guns: Demobilization, disarmament and reintegration. In *From military peace to social justice? The Angolan peace process*. Accessed at www.c-r.org/accord/ang/accord15/08.html.

Peters, K. 2003. *When children affected by war go home*. London: Save the Children UK.

Peters, K., and P. Richards. 1998. Fighting with open eyes. In *Rethinking the trauma of war*, ed. P. Bracken and C. Petty, 76–111. London: Free Association Books.

Peters, K., P. Richards, and K. Vlassenroot. 2003. *What happens to youth during and after wars?* Amsterdam: Netherlands Development Research Council.

Petty, C., and E. Jareg. 1998. Conflict, poverty and family separation. In *Rethinking the trauma of war*, ed. P. Bracken and C. Petty, 146–169. London: Free Association Books.

Pham, P., P. Vinck, M. Wierda, E. Stover, and A. di Giovanni. 2005. *Forgotten voices*. Berkeley, CA: International Center for Transitional Justice and Human Rights Center.

Pintar, J. 2000. Anticipating consequences: What Bosnia taught us about healing the wounds of war. *Human Rights Review* 1(2): 56–66.

Porto, J., and I. Parsons. 2003. *Sustaining the peace in Angola*. Paper 27. Bonn: Bonn International Center for Conversion.

Poulton, R. 1998. *The peace of Timbuktu*. Geneva: UNIDIR.

Price-Smith, A., and J. Daly. 2004. *Downward spiral*. Peaceworks no. 53. Washington, DC: U.S. Institute of Peace.

Prunier, G. 1995. *The Rwanda crisis*. New York: Columbia University Press.

———. 2006. Willful impotence: Darfur and the international community. *Current History* 105: 195–202.

Punamaki, R. 1996. Can ideological commitment protect children's psychosocial well-being in situations of political violence? *Child Development* 67: 55–69.

Pynoos, R., and S. Eth. 1985. Developmental perspective on psychic trauma in childhood. In *Trauma and its wake*, ed. C. Figley, 36–52. New York: Brunner/Mazel.

Pynoos, R., A. Steinberg, and A. Goenjian. 1996. Traumatic stress in childhood and adolescence. In *Traumatic stress*, ed. B. van der Kolk, A. McFarlane, and L. Weisaeth, 331–358. New York: Guilford.

Radda Barnen [Save the Children Sweden]. 2002. *Children of war*, Mar. Stockholm.

Rashid, A. 2000. *Taliban*. New Haven: Yale University Press.

Reardon, B. 1985. *Sexism and the war system*. New York: Teachers College Press.

Refugee Law Project. 2005. *Whose justice?* Working Paper no. 15. Kampala.

Refugees International. 2004. *Demobilization in Liberia*. Washington, DC.

Reichenberg, D., and S. Friedman. 1996. Traumatized children: Healing the invisible wounds of war; a rights approach. In *International responses to traumatic stress*, ed. Y. Daniele, N. S. Rodley, and L. Weisaeth, 307–326. Amityville, NY: Baywood.

Reis, C., and B. Vann. 2006. Sexual violence against women and children in the context of armed conflict. In *Handbook of international disaster psychology*, vol. 4, ed. G. Reyes and G. Jacobs, 19–44. Westport, CT: Praeger.

Renner, M. 1999. Arms control orphans. *Bulletin of the Atomic Scientists* 55(1): 22–26.

Richards, P. 1996. *Fighting for the rain forest*. Oxford: International Africa Institute.

Richards, P., S. Archibald, B. Bruce, W. Modad, E. Mulbah, T. Varpilah, and J. Vincent. 2005. *Community cohesion in Liberia*. Social Development Papers: Conflict Prevention and Reconstruction, no. 21. Washington, DC: World Bank.

Robertson, C., and U. McCauley. 2005. The return and reintegration of child soldiers in Sudan. *Child Soldiers Newsletter*, Spring, 12–13.

Roffman, J., C. Suárez-Orozco, and J. Rhodes. 2003. Facilitating positive development in immigrant youth. In *Community youth development*, ed. F. Villarruel, D. Perkins, L. Borden, and J. Keith, 90–117. Thousand Oaks, CA: Sage.

Rosen, D. 2005. *Armies of the young*. Brunswick, NJ: Rutgers University Press.

Rosenberg, T. 2005. AIDS: Think again. *Foreign Policy*, Mar./Apr.

Rouhana, N. 2004. Group identity and power asymmetry in reconciliation processes: The Israeli-Palestinian case. *Peace and Conflict: Journal of Peace Psychology* 10: 33–52.

Rubin, J., D. Pruitt, and S. Kim. 1994. *Social conflict*. 2nd ed. New York: McGraw-Hill.

Rutter, M. 1979. Protective factors in children's response to stress and disadvantage. In *Primary prevention of psychopathology*. Vol. 3: *Social competence in children*, ed. M. Kint and J. Rolf, 49–74. Hanover, NH: University Press of New England.

———. 1985. Resilience in the face of adversity. *British Journal of Psychiatry* 147: 598–611.

Save the Children. 2005. *Protecting children in emergencies*. Policy Brief 1(1), Spring. Westport, CT.

Save the Children UK. 2002. *HIV and conflict: A double emergency*. London.

———. 2003. *When children affected by war go home*. London.

———. 2005. *Forgotten casualties of war*. London.

Schafer, J. 2004. The use of patriarchal imagery in the civil war in Mozambique and its implications for the reintegration of child soldiers. In *Children and youth on the front line,* ed. J. Boyden and J. de Berry, 87–104. New York: Berghahn.

Shaw, R. 2005. *Rethinking truth and reconciliation commissions.* USIP Special Report 130. Washington, DC: U.S. Institute of Peace.

Sherif, M., O. Harvey, B. White, W. Hood, and C. Sherif. 1961. *Intergroup cooperation and competition.* Norman, OK: University Book Exchange.

Shweder, R. 1990. Cultural psychology—What is it? In *Cultural psychology,* ed. J. Stigler, R. Shweder, and G. Herdt, 1–43. New York: Cambridge University Press.

Silove, D. 2006. The impact of mass psychological trauma on psychosocial adaptation among refugees. In *Handbook of international disaster psychology,* vol. 3, ed. G. Reyes and G. Jacobs, 1–17. Westport, CT: Praeger.

Singer, P. 2004. Talk is cheap. *Cornell International Law Journal* 37(3): 561–586.

———. 2005. *Children at war.* New York: Pantheon.

Smith, A. 2002. *HIV/AIDS and emergencies.* Network HPN paper 38. London: Overseas Development Institute.

Smith, B. 2004. Realistic empathy. *Peace and Conflict: Journal of Peace Psychology* 19: 335–339.

Smith, D. 2003. *The atlas of war and peace.* London: Earthscan.

Somasundaram, D., and C. Jamunanantha. 2002. Psychosocial consequences of war: Northern Sri Lankan experience. In *Trauma, war, and violence,* ed. J. de Jong, 205–258. New York: Kluwer.

Sommers, M. 2003. *Education in emergencies.* Washington, DC: Creative Associates International.

———. 2006. *Youth and conflict.* Washington, DC: EQUIP3/Youth Trust. Downloaded May 19, 2006, from www.equip123.net.

Southwick, M. 2004. Political challenges behind the implementation of the Optional Protocol to the Convention on the Rights of the Child. *Cornell International Law Journal* 37: 541–546.

Spencer, D. 1997. *Demobilization and reintegration in Central America.* BICC paper 8. Bonn: Bonn International Conversion Center.

Spiegel, P. 2004. HIV/AIDS among conflict-affected and displaced populations. *Disasters* 28(3): 322–339.

Staub, E. 1989. *The roots of evil.* Cambridge: Cambridge University Press.

———. 2003. *The psychology of good and evil.* Cambridge: Cambridge University Press.

Staub, E., and L. Pearlman. 2006. Advancing reconciliation. In *Psychological interventions in times of crisis,* ed. L. Barbanel and R. Sternberg, 213–243. New York: Springer.

Stavrou, V. 2005. *Breaking the silence.* Luanda: Christian Children's Fund.

Stohl, R. 2002. *Children in conflict: Assessing the Optional Protocol.* Accessed at www.cdi.org/document/attachment/Stohl.pdf.

Stover, E., and H. Weinstein. 2004. Conclusion. In *My neighbor, my enemy,* ed. E. Stover and H. Weinstein, 323–342. Cambridge: Cambridge University Press.

Straker, G. 1987. The continuous traumatic stress syndrome. *Psychology and Sociology* 8: 48–78.

———. 1992. *Faces in the revolution.* Cape Town: David Philip.

Summerfield, D. 1999. A critique of seven assumptions behind psychological trauma programmes in war-affected areas. *Social Science and Medicine* 48: 1449–62.

———. 2004. Cross-cultural perspectives on the medicalization of human suffering. In *Posttraumatic stress disorder,* ed. G. Rosen, 233–245. New York: Wiley.

Swartz, L. 1998. *Culture and mental health.* Cape Town: Oxford University Press.

Terr, L. 1991. Childhood traumas. *American Journal of Psychiatry* 148: 10–20.

Tolfree, D. 2003. *Community based care for separated children.* Stockholm: Save the Children Sweden.

Triandis, H. 2001. Individualism and collectivism. In *The handbook of culture and psychology,* ed. D. Matsumoto, 35–50. New York: Oxford University Press.

Tutu, D. 1999. *No future without forgiveness.* New York: Doubleday.

UNAIDS. 2004. Global estimates for adults and children end 2003. Sept. 2, 2004. Accessed at www.unaids.org/html/pub/topics/epidemiology/slides/.

U.N. Department of Peacekeeping Operations. 1999. *Disarmament, demobilization, and reintegration of ex-combatants in a peacekeeping environment.* New York.

UNICEF. 1996. *The State of the world's children 1996.* New York.

———. 1997. *Cape Town annotated principles and best practices.* Cape Town.

———. 1999. *The State of the world's children 2000.* New York.

———. 2002a. *International criminal justice and children.* Rome: UNICEF/Innocenti Research Centre.

———. 2002b. *Children affected by armed conflict.* New York.

———. 2003. *Adult wars, child soldiers.* Bangkok.

———. 2004a. *Children and DDR.* New York.

———. 2004b. *Truth and Reconciliation Commission report for the children of Sierra Leone.* Accra: Graphic Packaging.

———. 2005. *A protective environment for children.* New York.

UNICEF, USAID, and UNAIDS. 2004. *Children on the brink 2004.* Washington, DC: USAID.

Urdal, H. 2004. *The devil in the demographics.* Social Development Paper no. 14. Washington, DC: World Bank.

U.S. State Department. 2004. *Trafficking in persons report.* Washington, DC. Downloaded July 24, 2004 from www.state.gov/g/tip/rls/tiprpt/2004/.

Utas, M. 2004. Fluid research fields. In *Children and youth on the front line,* ed. J. Boyden and J. de Berry, 209–236. New York: Berghahn.

van de Put, W., and M. Eisenbruch. 2004. Internally displaced Cambodians: Healing trauma in communities. In *From clinic to community,* ed. K. Miller and L. Rasco, 133–160. Upper Saddle River, NJ: Erlbaum.

Vandergrift, K. 2004. Challenges in implementing and enforcing children's rights. *Cornell International Law Journal* 37(3): 547–553.

van der Kolk, B. 1996. The body keeps score: Approaches to the psychobiology of PTSD. In *Traumatic stress,* ed. B. van der Kolk, A. McFarlane, and L. Weisaeth, 214–241. New York: Guilford.

Veale, A. 2003. *From child soldier to ex-fighter.* Institute for Security Studies Monograph no. 85. Downloaded August 25, 2004, from www.iss.co.za/Pubs/Monographs/No85.

Verhey, B. 2001. *Child soldiers: Preventing, demobilizing and reintegrating.* Africa Region Working Paper Series no. 23. Washington, DC: World Bank. Downloaded Jan. 3, 2002, from www.worldbank.org/afr/wps/index.htm.

———. 2003. *Going home.* London: Save the Children UK.

———. 2004. *Reaching the girls.* London: Save the Children UK.

Volkan, V. 1997. *Bloodlines.* New York: Farrar, Straus and Giroux.

Waller, J. 2002. *Becoming evil.* New York: Oxford University Press.

Watchlist on Children and Armed Conflict. 2006. *Struggling to survive.* New York.

Weinstein, J., and M. Humphries. 2005. *Disentangling the determinants of successful demobilization and reintegration.* Center for Global Development, Working Paper no. 69. Washington, DC: Center for Global Development.

Werner, E. 1998. *Reluctant witnesses.* Boulder, CO: Westview.

Werner, E., and R. Smith. 1992. *Overcoming the odds.* Ithaca, NY: Cornell University Press.

Wessells, M. G. 1997. Child soldiers. *Bulletin of the Atomic Scientists* 53(6): 32–39.

———. 1998. Children, armed conflict, and peace. *Journal of Peace Research* 35(5): 635–646.

———. 1999. Culture, power, and community: Intercultural approaches to psychosocial assistance and healing. In *Honoring differences,* ed. K. Nader, N. Dubrow, and B. Stamm, 267–282. Philadelphia: Taylor and Francis.

———. 2003. *Children on dangerous streets.* Richmond, VA: Christian Children's Fund International.

———. 2006. Child soldiering: Entry, reintegration, and breaking cycles of violence. In *The psychology of resolving global conflicts: From war to peace*, vol. 3, ed. M. Fitzduff and C. Stout, 243–266. Westport, CT: Praeger Security International.

Wessells, M. G., and D. Jonah. 2006. Reintegration of former youth soldiers in Sierra Leone: Challenges of reconciliation and post-accord peacebuilding. In *Youth and post-accord peacebuilding*, ed. S. McEvoy, 27–47. South Bend, IN: University of Notre Dame Press.

Wessells, M. G., and K. Kostelny. 2002. *After the Taliban*. Richmond, VA: Christian Children's Fund International.

Wessells, M. G., and C. Monteiro. 2000. Healing wounds of war in Angola. In *Addressing childhood adversity*, ed. D. Donald, A. Dawes, and J. Louw, 176–201. Cape Town: David Philip.

———. 2001. Psychosocial interventions and post-war reconstruction in Angola. In *Peace, conflict, and violence*, ed. D. Christie, R. V. Wagner, and D. Winter, 262–275. Upper Saddle River, NJ: Prentice Hall.

———. 2004a. Healing the wounds following protracted conflict in Angola. In *Handbook of culture, therapy, and healing*, ed. U. P. Gielen, J. Fish, and J. G. Draguns, 321–341. Mahwah, NJ: Erlbaum.

———. 2004b. Psychosocial assistance to internally displaced people in Angola. In *The mental health of refugees*, ed. K. Miller and L. Rasco, 67–94. Mahwah, NJ: Erlbaum.

West, H. 2004. Girls with guns: Narrating the experience of war of FRELIMO's "female detachment." In *Children and youth on the front line*, ed. J. Boyden and J. de Berry, 105–129. New York: Berghahn.

White, R. 1984. *Fearful warriors*. New York: Free Press.

Williamson, J., and L. Cripe. 2002. *Assessment of DCOF supported child demobilization and reintegration activities in Sierra Leone*. Washington, DC: USAID.

Williamson, J., and M. Robinson. 2006. Psychosocial interventions, or integrated programming for well-being? *Intervention* 4: 4–25.

Wilson, K. 1992. Cults of violence and counter-violence in Mozambique. *Journal of Southern African Studies* 18: 527–582.

Women's Commission for Refugee Women and Children. 2000. *Untapped potential*. New York.

———. 2004. *No safe place to call home*. New York.

———. 2005. *Youth speak out*. New York.

Yule, W., R. Stuvland, F. Baingana, and P. Smith. 2003. Children in armed conflict. In *Trauma interventions in war and peace*, ed. B. Green et al., 217–242. New York.

Index